# SIMPLY PROGRAMMING
## C# AND VISUAL BASIC . . .

# SIMPLY PROGRAMMING
## C# AND VISUAL BASIC . . .

JOHN QUEEN

Copyright © 2013 by John Queen.

| Library of Congress Control Number: | | 2013907606 |
|---|---|---|
| ISBN: | Softcover | 978-1-4836-3280-3 |
| | Ebook | 978-1-4836-3281-0 |

This book was printed in the United States of America.

Rev. date: 06/13/2013

**To order additional copies of this book, contact:**
Xlibris Corporation
1-888-795-4274
www.Xlibris.com
Orders@Xlibris.com
132311

# About the author . . .

I am not the usual technocrat. I am a **"technician"** more than a philosophy or theory person. I **make things happen,** I travel the shortest route possible from idea to results.

My objective is to *help* the *"willing"* become the *"able"*, *NOT* doing the job for them.

Or, put another way by better writers;

2 Timothy 2:15 King James Version
*Study* to shew thyself approved unto God, *a workman that needeth not to be ashamed*, rightly dividing the word of truth.

1 Thessalonians 4:11 King James Version
And that ye *study* to be quiet, and to *do your own business*, and to *work with your own hands*, as we commanded you;

I realize there are those who are not pro religion (Christian to be more specific) and might be against such thinking . . . those people are important to me as well, but I cannot be swayed from my own beliefs to accommodate theirs. I am instead concerned that I motivate and enable everyone that will make the effort to become informed and self sufficient . . . The rest . . . . I leave in the hands of their almighty, by whatever name they choose and as their beliefs dictate.

34  My proudest achievement is my family of five
35  children who are busy becoming successful,
36  responsible persons, probably due to their mother's
37  ability more than mine.
38
39  My academic exprience is engineering, chemistry,
40  mathematics and psychology. I attended the
41  University of Kentucky, Washburn University of
42  Topeka, Kansas and Cumberland College of
43  Williamsburg, Kentucky.
44
45  My work world experience includes installing TV
46  antennae in the days when you needed them . . .
47  repairing radios and televisions, playing guitar in a
48  60's rock band, working in a hospital as an emergency
49  room orderly, piloting military fighters, electrician for
50  Goodyear Tire & Rubber co., engineering switching
51  offices for the AT&T system, programming IBM
52  mainframes, database programming (the 6$^{th}$ largest
53  and busiest one in the USA), IT Team Leader for a
54  major Healthcare IT system, instructing and managing
55  a major corporate training center and operating a
56  software development company of my own. I also
57  designed and built a house of my own from the
58  foundation up, nail by nail, board by board, wire by
59  wire and pipe by pipe and rebuilt several cars and
60  engines for my kids as needed . . .I even taught them a
61  few mechanic skills.
62
63  I ***RESPECT*** and ***EXPECT*** real ***EFFORT*** with real
64  ***RESULTS***.
65

66 If it doesn't work . . . FIX IT!! If it works . . . make it
67 better.
68 Once it's working right . . . SHARE IT!!
69
70 Enjoy the book . . . use it as a reference and make any
71 suggestions you have to make it better. All references
72 to C# and Visual Basic refer to the trade marked and
73 copy righted Microsof products. I acknowledge and
74 respect theirs rights.
75
76 If you **like it**, **tell others**, **don't like it tell me**, but **tell**
77 **me why**. I continue learning too and so will you!!
78
79                     John Queen . . . Erwin, Tennessee
80                            jxqueendad2@gmail.com
81
82                        Table of Contents
83

# 123 Introduction to C# and VB, Simply
# 124 Programming . . .

125

126 This book is for anyone *interested* in *working* with
127 either C# or Visual Basic or both. Honestly, if you are
128 a person with a trace of logical thinking and the desire
129 to learn, you can do everything discussed in this book.
130 When you're done, you can be confident that you are

131  able and ready to pursue and master advanced
132  programming topics with every reason to expect
133  complete success.
134
135  The vocabulary you will need is developed in a
136  methodical, thoughtful process by relating techniques
137  to results. It is not a memorization exercise. My
138  personal preference is C#, probably because I started
139  working with "C" at AT&T Computer Systems when
140  "C" was in it's infancy. For a beginner, VB is a little
141  less demanding and accomplishes the same job, just a
142  little differently in terms of syntax and a few key
143  words.
144
145  Remember the old saying "Monkey see, Monkey do"?
146  It should say "Monkey see, Monkey do, Monkey
147  learn"!!!
148
149  The text is very focused . . .Almost every sentence is
150  an instruction to *do* something . . . or explains very
151  pointedly the expected results of what you are going
152  to do. In most "Teach Yourself books" you read
153  many, many pages and get (forget) concepts confused
154  before you put them to work. Forgetting or being
155  confused by waiting will not be your experience this
156  time. Concepts are presented in bite-sized units that
157  make immediate use of the ideas. The focus is
158  "doing".
159
160  I'll say it several times before we're done . . . If
161  you're not making any mistakes, you're not trying
162  hard enough!! Experiment and learn.
163

164 I progresses rapidly through the fundaments of
165 developing and testing applications that work, with
166 minimal discussion of issues of little or no immediate
167 use. The vocabulary is kept to every possible extent,
168 to plain English.
169
170 The examples are written with the idea that they will
171 be used as reference and "copy and paste" code for
172 other application the reader will develop on their own,
173 later. Neither time nor effort is wasted filtering
174 through text that accomplishes nothing. All text is
175 related to the task at hand. Even in database tutorial,
176 where some serious explaining is done before coding.
177
178 The coding is kept to simple, straight-forward, step by
179 step processing. Commands are not nested inside
180 other commands which makes them in-decipherable
181 to most people getting started in the field and gives
182 me reason to hesitate when I see the extreme forms of
183 this style of coding. Code for both C# and VB are
184 provided for *"every"* exercise. The ***downloadable***
185 ***code*** examples are available from the publishers
186 website and they work!!!
187
188 I advise against trying to copy and paste code from
189 the book's text . . . word processors can and do
190 mangle code for formatting and cosmetic reasons that
191 the program compilers don't quite understand.
192
193 ***Download and work from the example files***. The text
194 is for studying, the code included there is for
195 understanding, not executing.
196

197 The topics cover the gamut from simple forms and
198 controls to accessing databases and making updates or
199 additions to the database tables using SQL Server
200 2012 express.
201
202 When I show you a line of code, it is used with the
203 controls (and their events) we just added to the form.
204 This is how applications work and you won't have to
205 wait to see the results in some future discussion.
206
207 When I add a control to an exercise, I add the relative
208 code *immediately*. Code is useless without controls
209 and controls are useless without the code.
210
211 The book's *organization* is built around units of code
212 and controls that work together to do something
213 useful, not individual items that stand alone in a
214 theoretical discussion.
215
216 There are several units listed in the table of contents.
217 As you read through the units you will see that *each*
218 *line is numbered*.
219
220 When you go between the text and the Microsoft
221 Visual Studio editor to implement an instruction you
222 won't waste time looking for the location of your
223 instruction in the text when needed. You can return to
224 the *exact* spot you were reading from before with no
225 lost time or distraction.
226
227 This might sound somewhat trivial . . . *it is not trivial*,
228 instructions without line numbers are a major source
229 of frustration when you are trying to concentrate. You

230 forget where the instructions were located and waste
231 time and energy searching for them.
232
233 At regular intervals you are asked to "stretch" your
234 efforts somewhat. This is a major boost to the learning
235 process. For example, I'll provide code for C# and ask
236 you to convert the code to Visual basic or vice-versa.
237 Don't worry, I'll put the answer out of immediate
238 view in an appendix until you have made your best
239 effort on your own.
240
241 Again, *I cannot, and do not try, to teach you*
242 *everything* there is to know. *I do equip you* to learn
243 advanced concepts on your own. I did that on my own
244 and so can you!!!!
245
246 With the knowledge you gain from this book you can
247 create quite sophisticated applications. You are
248 limited only by your own imagination and effort. Go
249 for it!!! I knw, it's too soon to be repeating myself
250 but, No mistakes equals not . . . etc, ect.
251
## 252 C# and Visual Basic . . . Simply
## 253 programming
254
255
256     *C# and Visual Basic . . . Simply Programming*
257       (Copy rights reserved for John Queen, Erwin
258             Tennessee as of Jan 20 2013)
259
260 *A word of caution* . . . this subject can eat you alive.
261 You can be hooked and spend days on-end sitting in
262 front of your computer.

263

264 *I advise against that very strongly for reasons of*
265 *Health and Happiness!!*
266

267 You need an escape. I play guitar, watch sports, mess
268 around with our horses and "*ALWAYS*" make sure I
269 am **paying attention** to my *wife* and *family*.
270

271 Those are the reasons for living, this is just a means of
272 "earning" my living, welllll mostly. The truth is you
273 can get a real ego trip from making a computer do
274 what you want, the way you want, when you want.
275 Enjoy what you're doing . . . don't be enslaved by it.
276 *Beware!!!*
277

278 OK, having said that, this is a "What to do, do this"
279 book . . . Not a "Why to do" or "Philosophy of doing
280 " or "History of development" book. All of that gets
281 in the way when you are first starting.
282

283 In this phase of programming, history of the evolution
284 of the technology doesn't have many benefits that you
285 can use. Later, if you're still interested that's a
286 different story.
287

288 "Experts" are a dime a dozen and, many times, worth
289 just about that much. I am not trying to impress you
290 **with what I know**, but **what I can share** with you.
291 Hopefully, you can use the knowledge to improve
292 your life and enjoy it more. Computers and computing
293 are going to be with us a long, long time in one form
294 or another.
295

296 What qualifies me to write a book? Lots of study,
297 programming experience and raising five kids.
298
299 With that qualification set I think I can do just about
300 anything. Also a degree or two unrelated to
301 programming (well, unrelated as I see it . . . math,
302 chemistry, engineering, psychology).
303
304 I started programming in 1971 with an IBM System
305 36 Mainframe, well, e thought it was back then, and
306 something called RPG . . . as a matter of survival.
307
308 My database experience goes back a long, long way
309 also . . . around 1972. I started with something called
310 Informix and have worked with many more since then
311 including IBM's DBase, SQL and Oracle. I've also
312 worked quite a lot in the UNIX operating
313 environment.
314
315 I'm on Facebook.com as John Queen, Erwin
316 Tennessee if you want to know more.
317
318 The **example** code works correctly **in the
319 environment I describe** in the list of development
320 tools . . . . **No ifs, ands or buts**. I developed then
321 tested every single example multiple times. ***Outside
322 that environment*, I make no claims** about whether
323 they work or not. I wrote more than 600 of them then
324 chose the ones that best meet the teaching/learning
325 requirements, **as I see them**.
326
327 **I *Do NOT RECOMMEND COPYING* and
328 *PASTING*** Code from this textbook straight into your

329  MVS editor (Microsoft Visual Studio Editor—see the
330  tools list).
331
332  Word processors do things to the text that your MVS
333  editor/compiler does not tolerate well for the purpose
334  of making the document more readable and
335  cosmetically appealing.
336
337  Download the example code from the website of the
338  publisher and use those files directly or copy and
339  paste that code into MVS. The code (text) in the book
340  is for studying, not for compiling and executing.
341
342  There are scads of books with code that doesn't
343  work . . . at least as advertised and written. Many
344  times when the code works, the explanations are
345  wrong and that's probably just as bad or worse.
346
347  There are also some very good ones with code that
348  does work and good,complete, understandable
349  explanations. The problem is that you don't know
350  which is which until you try them. Testimonials are
351  bountiful but not very reliable as a general rule.
352  Members of the technical community don't want to
353  offend others and there are many benefits of having
354  strong support in this career field and most others as
355  well.
356
357  I suggest that you ***keep an un-modified copy*** and a
358  ***working copy of the files.***
359
360  One thing at a time . . . ***don't skip around***. Each task
361  builds on the previous ones. My code is simple, bare-

362  boned code. There are many ways to enhance it with
363  things like error trapping and other functions. That's
364  **not** where we are right now.
365
366  Here's what you can **expect** . . . nothing more, nothing
367  less;
368
369          Instructions you can understand, in plain
370          English.
371          Examples that work, make a point and build on
372          each other.
373          Windows forms applications . . . . Not " **
374          console" applications.
375          Getting user input and using it to accomplish a
376          job . . .
377          Returning the desired results to the user when
378          the job is done.
379          Variable usage like strings, integers etc.
380          Commonly used controls, textboxes, buttons,
381          labels etc . . . nothing exotic.
382          Control processes like looping, counting,
383          ending.
384          File operations . . .reading, creating, appending
385          deleting etc . . .
386          Basic Database applications . . . reading,
387          updating, deleting.
388          E-Mail consultation as possible given volume
389          and time constraints.
390
391  ** NOTE: (Remember Microsoft DOS, Circa 1980,
392  and the Command line prompt (C:\>) where you typed
393  in your commands . . . that's a console application)
394

395 **When we're done** you will have a firm grasp of the
396 fundamentals. You will be able to write your own
397 programs that work and accomplish meaningful tasks
398 and results. *You won't know* all there is to know
399 about programming or C# or Visual Basic. You never
400 will. I won't either.
401
402 My objective is to equip you with enough knowledge
403 to go on and learn as much advanced programming as
404 you want after getting the fundamentals down. I
405 learned on my own . . . with a little help from time to
406 time. *So can you!!!!*
407
408 The art of **programming** is pretty **straight-forward**,
409 but **deceptively demanding**.
410
411 Take a task and break it down to the most minute
412 level of detail possible then make one small step at a
413 time. Check your work, revise it until you are satisfied
414 and it works correctly, every time. That's
415 programming.
416
417 **Pick a time** when you can **concentrate** on this project
418 and try to limit yourself to no more than 2 hours per
419 session. **Don't do** this **when** you are **sleepy**, very
420 **tired**, **angry** or otherwise **distracted**.
421
422 It's ok to stop mid-way through a project and come
423 back later. Your sub- conscious mind will solve many
424 issues for you when you are away from the keyboard.
425 Give it a chance.
426

427 ***Caution*** . . . A big aid to programming is the "Cut &
428 Paste" capability. Be aware that not everything cuts
429 and pastes characters exactly as the same character
430 your Microsoft Visual Studio editor compiler
431 expects . . . .
432
433 Examples that I know of include the single quotation
434 mark and the normal, "double quotation mark". Word
435 processors have the "apostrophe" . . . that is not the
436 same as the "single quotation mark" necessarily as
437 well as the difference of the double quotation marks
438 that are paired together.
439
440 Copying code from a book is a great time-saver but it
441 can also introduce errors at times.
442
443 Another example is where the Word processor spreads
444 (wraps) text over more than one visible line. The
445 Microsoft Visual Studio (MVS) editor expects a
446 special "Line Continuation" character when code is
447 spread over more than one line. These differences and
448 others can cause compiler errors!!!
449
450 In other words the program won't work.
451
452 ***Copy and Paste from the example code files.***
453
454 Now, you'll need some **tools** to work with. This is the
455 list;
456
457 The SQL **tools can wait** if you so desire. We won't
458 need them just yet. But when we get to the Database
459 examples, you'll need them.

460
461 You need these ***development tools*** for this work, some
462 are **free** from Microsoft@;
463
464        Relatively modern PC or Laptop.(Mine is an
465        HP/Compaq Presario 2010 model)
466        Any PC that uses the Windows XP operating
467        system or later is fine.
468        Enough hard drive and RAM capacity to satisfy
469        your performance expectations.
470        (I have a 500 gByte hard drive and 4 gByte of
471        RAM)
472        Microsoft Windows Operating system . . . XP
473        or Windows 7 or 8 (I use 7)
474        Microsoft Visual Studio (I am using MS Visual
475        Studio 2010)
476        Microsoft SQL Server (I use SQL Server 2012
477        Express . . . free)
478        Microsoft SQL Visual Management Studio (I
479        use SQL 2012 Express . . . free)
480        Microsoft's "Northwind" example database
481        (free from Microsoft)
482
483        Knowledge of **Notepad** . . . It is a Windows
484        accessory. It creates clean, un-formatted "text
485        files". I use those as "Target Files" for
486        applications as we go along.
487
488        ***Instructions for installing these are available***
489        ***directly from Microsoft.com.***
490
491 AS I said . . .experts are a dime a dozen (just ask one)
492 and many times worth just about that much. I am not

493 trying to impress you with what I know, but what I
494 can share with you.
495
496 My **expectation** of you is that you **want to learn**, are
497 **willing to do the work necessary** to learn and able to
498 **accept** that *errors are part of learning* . . . not the
499 Black Plague. I make plenty of them and if you don't,
500 you're not trying hard enough.
501
502 Right now you should **know** about the **basics of using**
503 **a computer**, how to **get around in Windows**, **create**
504 **or modify folders** . . . a little **word processing** is
505 good for right now and some **Spread Sheet**
506 **experience** might help when we get into the database
507 portion of the book. I also think that High School
508 **Algebra** is an **advantage** . . . but **not** a **necessity**.
509 Mathematical talent and training are great but not an
510 absolute requirement for programming. **Common**
511 **sense and persistence** with **attention** to detail ARE.
512
513 Don't rush out and buy a lot of books just yet.
514
515 I suggest that you save your money until you see just
516 how interested in programming you really are. Follow
517 my instructions, be persistent and, for Gosh sakes,
518 *make some mistakes*!! When things go wrong . . .
519 **Exhaust every effort possible before you ask for**
520 **help** . . . that is where a lot of the real learning takes
521 place. But, at the same time, **don't suffer too long** . . .
522 If you have tried your best and it's still a problem, **ask**
523 **for help**. Most mistakes are quite simple and easy to
524 resolve. **Typos are the biggie**!!
525

526 Experiment . . . I cannot and do not try to cover every
527 possible detail of using things like "all" properties of
528 the control objects we will be using in this book.
529 ***Experiment with these things!!! Learn by trying and***
530 ***doing!!!***
531
532 OK, if you have the tools installed . . . let's get going.
533
534 Create three(3) new "FOLDERS" on your hard drive.
535
536 Something like . . . VS VB Projects and VS CS (for
537 C#) Projects. "Two" project folders for the programs
538 you will create. I used "JQ VS VB Projs " and "JQ
539 VS CS Projs". The third is for Target files for your
540 programs . . . I called mine "App Target Files". We
541 will put things like test files there later as we develop
542 more complex programs/applications.
543
544 One folder is for C# projects, the other for the VB
545 projects. Be organized, it pays high dividends.
546
547 Why? Because later you will find yourself hard
548 pressed to locate examples of various things that you
549 want for reference. Organization is a major part of
550 success in that regard. Cut and paste is a large staple
551 of programming. You will do a lot of this. Make it
552 easy on yourself. As you progress you may want to
553 create sub-folders in each category i.e. Database, etc..
554 That's up to you.
555
556 I suggest that you start with Visual Basic. I'll show
557 you exactly how in a moment.

558 VB is more forgiving than C# . . . but attention to
559 detail is the key for both. If you want to do both, that
560 is fine. Both languages are 80% of the same stuff . . .
561 with some differences in syntax and a few "Key
562 Words".
563
564 **If** you **choose C#**, that's fine too. I have included
565 **examples for each** language.
566
567 Got your tools installed, ready to use and your new
568 folders created? Then we are on to the next step. Let's
569 *do* something and *learn* a little.
570

571 # Project 1—Forms, Button and
572 # Messageboxes
573
574 We are going to do a pretty simple project to get
575 started by creating a new project, adding a button and
576 a messagebox into the mix to see how all this works
577 together.
578 The screen produced by the program (code) will look
579 like this;
580

581

582                    **Screen 1a**

583

## 584 Project 1 . . . . Creating a project with Visual
## 585 Studio

586

587 *NOTE:* There is **NOT** a downloadable example for
588 this project

589

590 This is an incredibly **easy** but very **important** step. It
591 is not the usual "Hello World" exercise you see in
592 most books.

593

594 It illustrates what a project is, how it is created, saved
595 and executed. Don't minimize the importance of
596 doing this . . . you will repeat several of these steps
597 every time we create a project.

598

599 The **important thing** and focus here is **establishing a**
600 **routine**!!!

601

602 When you installed Microsoft Visual Studio an Icon
603 to start the application (yes, it is an application) was

604 probably placed on your desktop. If not . . . don't
605 worry, we'll get one there. *If* it's there, start Visual
606 Studio (MVS in the future) by double clicking the
607 Icon.
608
609 ***Otherwise, click your start button*** on the bottom left
610 of your screen and locate and click Microsoft Visual
611 Studio on the start menu. *If* you don't see it at first,
612 click "All Programs" and look again. When you find
613 it . . . "Right-Click" the item and hold down the right
614 mouse button. Drag the item to an empty spot on your
615 desktop and release the mouse button. Choose "Create
616 shortcut" from the pop-up menu and an Icon will be
617 created for future use.
618
619 Now, start start Visual Studio (MVS) by double
620 clicking the Icon. The first time you do this it will
621 take several seconds for the application to load and
622 start up . . . have patience!! Visual Studio is a large,
623 complex application. It takes some time to get going.
624
625 When Microsoft Visual Studio (***hereafter called***
626 ***MVS***) is ready to use the "Start Page" will be
627 displayed.
628
629 Take a few moments and look at the wealth of
630 information shown there . . . don't worry, we'll get to
631 the items one by one as we go along. Just familiarize
632 yourself with the general appearance for now. *If* you
633 don't see the "Start Page" . . . ***click VIEW*** on the top
634 menu strip of the screen and then choose "Start Page".
635
636 A photo of the screen is shown on the below.

637

638

639                              **Screen1**

640

641 Horizontally across the top of the page in the
642 menu/toolbar area called the . . . the **item of interest**
643 right now is the "**Tools**" item. *Click "Tools".*

644

645 A **drop down menu** will appear with a list of a dozen
646 or more choices . . . we want the one called "Options".
647 *Click Options.*
648 <Tools> + (then) <Options>

649

650 Another drop down menu appears . . . . Scan down
651 until you see "Projects and Solutions". *Click*
652 *"Projects and Solutions".*

653

654 Another menu appears . . .
655 Look to the right side and locate "Project Location".
656 There is a box where we can type in the folder's
657 complete, exact name just below project location.
658 This is where we store the name of the folder you
659 created earlier, where your project files will be stored.
660 It must include the hard drive letter, probably C,

661 followed by a colon and a back slash and the EXACT
662 name of the folder you created.
663
664 BY EXACT I mean *"EXACT"* . . . capital letters if
665 you used any, spaces etc. You can either type this
666 information in the box or click the " . . ." ellipse and
667 browse to the folder and *click open*. This will
668 automatically populate the box for you with the
669 correct information. I prefer this way because it
670 eliminates typos . . . a major pain in the rear as you
671 program.
672
673 The final entry might look like this . . .depending on
674 how you named your new folders . . . . "C:\ VS VB
675 Projs", without the quotation marks.
676
677 Notice there are two (2) boxes below the one we just
678 filled in. Repeat the same information in those two
679 boxes. You can type it in, copy and paste from the
680 first box or browse to the folder again.
681
682 To copy, pace the cursor on the first character and
683 then click and hold down the left mouse botton, the
684 information is now selected and high-lighted. Right
685 click the mouse and choose copy. Next place the
686 cursor in the second box, right click the mouse and
687 choose paste. Do the same for the third box.
688 You don't have to select and copy again, just right
689 click and paste. This is the easiest and fastest method
690 an minimizes errors.
691
692 When done, *click OK*, at the bottom of the menu.
693 Your information will be stored and ready there until

694 you change it, even if we close MVS and re-open it
695 later.
696
697 *If* we decide to start a new project and keep it in a
698 *different* folder, we will need to update this
699 information accordingly. This might happen as we
700 switch between different languages and want to stay
701 organized. Very ***highly recommended***!
702
703 When we clicked OK our information was stored, the
704 menu closed and we reverted to the start page. This is
705 supposed to happen. Now you are ready to proceed
706 with coding your project.
707
708 The next step is to tell MVS we want to create a new
709 project. There are two ways to do this. On the start
710 page there is a "new project" option . . . you can click
711 that -or- on the top of the screen . . .in the menu strip,
712 ***click File***, then ***click "New Project"***. I prefer the
713 second method. Your choice . . . . The end result is the
714 same.
715
716 As we go on I will use <Click on this> + (then)
717 <Click on this> as short hand notation for what to
718 click.
719
720 Either way, we are going to be presented with another
721 menu . . . This time we will define the type of project,
722 the programming language to be used and the name of
723 the project.
724

725 *Naming things is an important issue*. **Use names** that
726 are truly **descriptive of the job** you are doing **and the**
727 **tools** used in the project.
728
729 Develop this habit now and it will pay large dividends
730 as we go along. Re-naming items later is possible, but
731 it is a headache you don't need. Avoid being fast for
732 the sake of immediate ease . . . it's similar to packing
733 moving boxes without labeling the boxes' contents.
734 Faster, but painful later. Sometimes I even include the
735 page number where the code was discussed for
736 reference.
737
738 By now, you have noticed that we are going to click
739 on a lot of menus and options as we go along. For
740 simplicity and for less typing I will begin to use this
741 format; <Menu> + <Option> + <Menu> +
742 <Option> . . . . It means click item 1, then item2, then
743 item 3 . . . etc. etc.
744
745 When there is more than one way to do a job, I'll tell
746 you if I know. You can decide which option you want
747 to use . . . If I have a preference, I'll say so. Further
748 down the road you will learn that there is a simpler,
749 faster way to do some things I ask you to do. That's
750 fine, but, **I think** you should **know the nuts and bolts**
751 to a certain extent before you drive the car so bear
752 with me.
753
754 Back to our project . . . . We clicked "File" and are
755 ready to choose the language, project type and give it
756 a name.
757

758 New project cause another screen to appear with two
759 areas "Panes".
760 (see photo below)
761

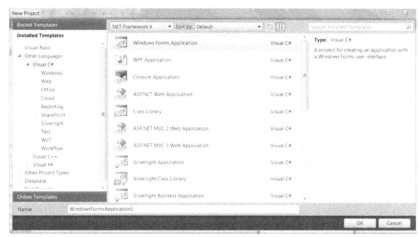

762
763                    **Screen 2**
764
765 The left Pane gives you 4 or 5 choices . . . Visual
766 Basic, Other Languages, Database, etc. etc. For Visual
767 Basic Click "Visual Basic", or, if you want to use C#,
768 Click "Other Languages", then C#.
769
770 Either way . . . A group of choices appear in the Pane
771 to the right. We are going to *click "Windows Form"*.
772 That means that a Form (also know as an Object) will
773 be created for our use.
774
775 That's where the action is. This Form will be given
776 the default name of "Form1" by MVS.
777
778 At the bottom of our menu page is a line containing a
779 default project name . . . Click in the box and re-name
780 the project as you like. Remember . . . something

781 meaningful and descriptive. I suggest something like
782 "VB Blank Form Proj" or what ever you think is
783 meaningful to yourself.
784
785 Finally . . . *click OK.*
786
787 *That's it!!!* You have a working, perfectly functional
788 application/project that can be executed. It **doesn't do**
789 **anything useful yet,** but it does function to the point
790 of **displaying a blank** form.
791
792 When you clicked OK, MVS reverted back to a screen
793 that is where future coding will commence and also
794 has the ability to execute (**Run**) your program/Project.
795
796 On the top menu strip . . . click the Green, right-
797 pointing arrow . . .wait a few seconds and your blank
798 form will appear on your screen in a finished,
799 functioning format.
800
801 *If* you **don't see a GREEN ARROW** . . . click
802 "**Debug**" on the menu strip and then click *"Start*
803 *debugging"*.
804
805 If it doesn't or sends an error message in a smaller
806 window at the bottom of your screen . . . you missed
807 something.
808
809 In that case back up, review the instruction, correct
810 the steps taken as needed and try again.
811
812 So why all the hoopla? Well, you **learned** a little
813 about **MVS** . . . menus and **option selection** and

814 hopefully, gained a little confidence in yourself and
815 the MVS ability.
816
817 ***Click the Red "X"*** at the top right corner of the form
818 to close the program.
819
820 Have a Pepsi or a cup of coffee and enjoy the
821 moment.
822
823 **Behind the scene** a lot of things happened here.
824 **Several** "Program/Project" **files** were created, the
825 necessary user code was "**Compiled**" into a format
826 the computer can understand and execute, and the
827 Blank **form** was **displayed**.
828
829 Close MVS by **clicking** the **top right corner** of your
830 screen "**X**".
831
832 When you're ready . . . return to this point and we'll
833 go on. ***Note the line number on the left edge of this***
834 ***page.***
835
836 That's how you will know exactly where you left off
837 when you return. Trivial now, but not so much as
838 things get deeper.
839
840 See, No Math, no "Engineering", No History, Simply
841 Programming.
842
843 As you know . . . The . . . When you come back, we'll
844 take a look at "some" of the details. The ones you can
845 use later.
846

847  In days gone by . . . . Programming used a Top-Down
848  model, Code was written to do certain things one at a
849  time and produce the expected results.
850
851  **Todays programming** model is different . . . It is
852  called *"Event Driven Programming"*. This means
853  that the **code** written **executes** to a certain point,
854  displays a screen or form of some sort and then **waits**
855  **for the user to do something. Usually** this means
856  **typing** in some information or **clicking** a **button** or
857  touching an **Icon** on the screen.
858
859  When the user does this . . . the **program responds**
860  by deciding what "**EVENT**" took place and
861  **executing** the block of **coded instructions** for that
862  event. That particular block of **code** is called an *event*
863  *handler*. We will soon see how that code looks and
864  write some of our own code (Event Handler).
865
866  **All** of the **events** we will deal with are **pre-defined**
867  events. Our job will be to provide the instructions to
868  be executed when the event occurs.
869  A few examples of events are . . . Click, Double
870  Click, Mouse Over, Mouse ButtonDown, Mouse
871  ButtonUP, Selection Changed and so on.
872
873  To write event handlers (Code), we need a place to
874  store our code. That place is **inside** the **files created**
875  automatically for us **by MVS** when we created our
876  project. Let's take a closer look.
877

878 Before we open MVS . . . let's use Windows Explorer
879 to examine the contents of the folder where you stored
880 your Blank form Application.
881
882 ***Right click the Start button on the bottom left of***
883 ***your desktop and choose Open Explorer***.
884
885 **Browse** to your **folder** and **open** the folder by **double**
886 **clicking** the folder Icon. You will see a sub-folder
887 with the name of your project. Double click that
888 folder to open it.
889
890 You will **see** eleven or twelve files created by **MVS**
891 that literally **define** your project in MVS generated
892 code. Those files **include Form1.cs** (for C# projects,
893 **Form1.vb for VB** projects) and some others well get
894 to later. Note that the **suffix** of the file name shows
895 **the programming language** used to create the
896 project.**VB** for Visual Basic and **CS** for C#.
897
898 *Close Windows Explorer and Open (start) MVS.*
899
900 As MVS starts it displays the start page once again. If
901 not <View> + <Start Page>. You re-open your project
902 by clicking the project name on the start page -or-
903 <File> + <Open Project> and then browse to your
904 folder and sub-folder for the project we just saw. Your
905 choice.
906
907 Within the sub-folder for the project is a file named
908 "Your Project Name" +.vbproj or.csproj suffixed to
909 the name. *Select that file and Click Open* at the
910 bottom of the screen by clicking it. *If* you clicked the

911 project name on the start page, this happens
912 automatically.
913
914 When MVS has time to load your project it shows you
915 a new screen called the IDE, Integrated Development
916 Environment. The important **part** for now is the
917 **Design** view, A picture of your form . . . The Solution
918 Explorer . . . a list of the files we saw earlier in
919 Windows Explorer and The Text Editor . . . where we
920 will type our code.
921
922 *If* the Solution Explorer is not visible,
923 <View>+<Solution Explorer>. It should appear as a
924 pop-up window on the right side of the screen. *If not*
925 and it is taking up the whole screen . . . right click the
926 Solution Explorer tab at the top edge of the screen's
927 tab and *click "Dock"*.
928
929 *Note* **the Solution Explorer box is relocatible and**
930 **re-sizeable. Put it where you like.**
931
932 Now let's make a point.
933 <Tools>+<Options>+<Projects and Solutions >
934
935 Examine the three boxes containing the folder names
936 and locations we established earlier when we created
937 the project. Having seen this, *click OK* and return to
938 the *IDE* (Integrated Development Environment)
939 screens. MVS stored our information for us and re-
940 loaded the information when we re-opened the
941 project.
942
943 Lets move on. <File> + <Close Project>.

944
## Project 2—Controls and Handling events
947
948 *If* you closed MVS . . .**re-start** MVS.
949
950 <Files> + <New Project> Select Language, Windows
951 Form, Project Name <OK>.
952
953 Suggestion . . . VS VB Proj Form Button
954 MessageBox.
955 -or- CS Proj Form Button MessageBox
956
957 Remember the <Tools> + <Options> + <Projects and
958 Solutions> location info? That **stays the same** unless
959 we decide to change it.
960
961 When our IDE screen appears . . . . *If* Solution
962 Explorer is not visible . . .
963 <View> + <Solution Explorer>.
964
965 At this time we should have a Form1 that has been
966 created for us by MVS.
967 The screen we want for now is the "Designer view", a
968 picture of the blank
969 form. *IF* this is not what you see . . . <View> +
970 <Designer>. Form1 doesn't really do anything yet,
971 but if we want we can execute (Run) the
972 project/Program and the blank form will be displayed.
973
974 Add some functionality to the Form1. On the left side
975 of the IDE you might see a **ToolBox** Item. *IF*
976 **not** . . .<View> + <ToolBox>.

977
978 In the **toolbox** are several **controls** (Objects) we can
979 use with our program. Scan down the list and **locate**
980 **"Button"**.
981
982 Either **double click** "Button" or click it, hold the
983 Mouse Button down and Drag it into the Design view
984 of the Form1. When you move the cursor out of the
985 toolbox . . . it will temporarily hide in the left margin
986 and we will see the Button control on the form.
987
988 You locate the button where you please on the form
989 by clicking and dragging the button. It is also **re-**
990 **sizeable**. You can re-size by clicking the button once
991 (Selecting it) then **click** and **hold** the cursor on one of
992 the small **rectangles** that appear on the button's edges
993 and **dragging** them to stretch the size.
994
995 The Button is a control. It is also called an Object.
996 The form itself is also an Object. Objects can contain
997 other Objects. We could add many Buttons or other
998 controls to the form the same way. Each control
999 would be an Object. Form1 has a "Collection" of
1000 Objects.
1001
1002 Two *important words* . . . **Objects** and **Collections**.
1003 Almost everything in C# and VB are Objects. Almost
1004 every "Object" has a "Collection" of the "Objects" it
1005 contains.
1006
1007 A "**Collection**" is a **list** of the **Objects** contained
1008 within the parent object.

1009 This will become much more important as we get
1010 deeper into programming.
1011 VB and C# are "Event driven-Object Orientated"
1012 Programming languages.
1013 You will hear the acronymn used as OOP -or- OOPs.
1014

1015 Each **Object** has a **name** and several other properties
1016 like size and color and we can define (Set) them to be
1017 what we want the them to be. A third **important**
1018 **word . . . "Properties"**.
1019

1020 Again, **names are important**. Choose a name that
1021 **describes** the **type** of control used and the **function**
1022 the control will be **used for**. It becomes important as
1023 we write code for the Event Handlers. The more
1024 controls (Objects) we have, the more important the
1025 name becomes.
1026

1027 For example . . . the button we added might be named
1028 btnShowMessage.
1029

1030 Right click the button added to Form1 and Select
1031 Properties on the
1032 pop-up menu. In the top of the menu are a few
1033 Icons . . .*Click A-Z*.
1034 The properties of button1, the default name, will be
1035 shown alphabetically, except for the name . . .which
1036 will be near the top of the list. Click in the space to
1037 the right of the name property and enter the name you
1038 have chosen.
1039

1040 Afterwards, click in any other property you like and
1041 the name you entered will be saved by MVS.

1042
1043  Next *scroll* down the list of properties to
1044  *"BackColor"*. Click in the space to the right of Back
1045  Color and an ellipse (. . .) will appear. Click the
1046  ellipse. Another menu comes up . . . . *Click* the
1047  *"custom"* tab and *select* (Click) the background color
1048  you want for the button. Click on any other property
1049  item and the color is saved.
1050
1051  *Scroll* further down the list of properties and click in
1052  the box by *"Text"*.
1053  Type "Show Message" in the box. Click and other
1054  property and the text will be saved by MVS.
1055
1056  To this point we have defined (SET) three properties
1057  for the button. All others are set the same way. You
1058  will see that we can also change the properties for a
1059  control as we execute our code. This is called Run-
1060  time or dynamic modification of properties.
1061
1062  *Note* the other Icons in top part of the properties
1063  window. One is a lightening bolt.
1064
1065  **Click the Lightening Bolt.**
1066
1067  This time we are given a list of the pre-defined
1068  *"Events"* possible for this particular control (Object).
1069  Scroll down and double *double click on the "Click"*
1070  event word.
1071
1072  Very quickly we are transported into the "Code file"
1073  text Editor for Form1 and placed inside a skeleton
1074  *event handler* for btnShowMessage. The battle is

1075 enjoined and the troops are mustered. Time to write
1076 some code. Note that the name for this file we are in
1077 is Form1.VB for VisualBasic -or- Form1.cs for C#.
1078
1079 Look around a little. Scroll all the way to the top of
1080 the text editor screen.
1081 You will see something that looks a little like this if
1082 you're in C#.
1083
```
1084 using System;
1085 using System.Data;
1086 using System.Text;
1087 using System.Windows.Forms;
```
1088
1089 **If you're using VB it will look somewhat**
1090 **different . . . but accomplishes the same job.**
1091
```
1092 Imports System
1093 Imports System.Windows.Forms
1094 Imports System.Data
1095 Imports System.Text
```
1096
1097 These lines are telling the compiler what Libraries of
1098 information and specifications to use in your project.
1099
1100 Remember the compiler takes our English language
1101 code and translates that into a format (binary format
1102 ultimately) the computer processor can understand
1103 and execute. These libraries tell the computer what
1104 rules to follow and what format to expect and use for
1105 compiling the code.
1106
1107 This whole library and system structure together is
1108 known as Microsoft.Network -or- Framework. It is

1109  powerful and enormous and we will barely scratch the
1110  surface in this book.
1111
1112  Your project will include only the parts of the library
1113  it needs to do the job we define. These parts become
1114  part and parcel of our project and are stored in the
1115  project files.
1116
1117  If we ask the project to do something outside the parts
1118  we have told it to include, or violate the syntax rules,
1119  we will receive a compile error. The program will not
1120  execute and we will get an error message with some
1121  clues about what went wrong. This is NOT
1122  catastrophic. We stop, find the error, correct it and try
1123  again. Such is the life of a programmer.
1124
1125  Meanwhile, a little further down the screen we see
1126  something like this . . .
1127

```
1128  For C#;
1129  namespace "Your project name" without the
1130  quotation marks.
1131  {
1132  public partial class Form1: Form
1133      {
1134      public Form1()
1135         {
1136             InitializeComponent();
1137         }
1138
1139      . . . . More code
1140      . . . . More code
1141      . . . . More code
1142      . . . . More code ad infinitum.
1143      }
1144
```

1145  For **VB**;
1146
1147  Public Class Form1
1148          Private Sub btnShowMessage_Click(sender As
1149          System.Object, e As System.EventArgs)
1150          Handles btnShowMessage.Click
1151          MessageBox.Show("A button was clicked",
1152          "Report event")
1153  End Sub
1154  . . . . More code
1155  . . . . More code
1156  . . . . More code
1157  . . . . More code ad infinitum.
1158  End Sub
1159
1160  These are very broad definitions of the file structure
1161  for the project. Everything else is included with this
1162  "namespace" or Class as it is termed for Visual Basic.
1163  It includes many references to other files as needed
1164  but this is the center of our attention.
1165
1166  You are not expected to and do not have a need to
1167  remember this verbatim. I don't and I won't. Don't be
1168  over whelmed by what you see, Just get acquainted
1169  with the general appearance and we will get into more
1170  depth as needed if and when it makes sense.
1171
1172  Programming requires that we make it clear when
1173  blocks of code *begin*,that do a particular job, and
1174  when they *end*. In *C#* this is often done by enclosing
1175  blocks of related code inside *curly braces*,
1176
1177      Class "Class Name"
1178      {
1179         code;
1180      }

1181
1182  With Visual Basic (*VB*) it is done with words like;
1183
```
1184    Class (or Sub) "Classname"
1185       Code
1186       More Code
1187    End Class
```
1188
1189  More to follow shortly.
1190
1191  For now, let's get back to the task at hand . . ., writing
1192  a handler for the btnShowMessage click event.
1193
1194  *Scroll* back down to where we started this discussion
1195  just a bit ago. *Inside* the skeleton *event handler* for
1196  the btnShowMssage_Click event.
1197
1198  In *C#* the code we are entering goes between the curly
1199  braces defining the event handler like so;
1200
```
1201  public void btnShowMessage_Click(object sender,
1202  EventArgs e)
1203     {
1204     MessageBox.Show("A button has been
1205     clicked");
1206  // Note the semicolon at the end of the
1207  command/statement
1208  // in C# . . . . this is a syntax requirement of
1209  C#.
1210     }
```
1211
1212  **Also take note of the.. //Coments . . . you can enter**
1213  **comments.**
1214  **You can enter comments directly in you C# Code**
1215  **by starting a line with "//". *I recommend a lot of***
1216  ***comments.* It documents what you are doing right**

1217 **where you need it when reviewing a program long**
1218 **after you wrote it.**
1219
1220 **In *VB* the code goes between the Sub—End sub**
1221 **phrases like this;**
1222

```
1223 Private Sub btnShowMessage_Click(sender As
1224 System.Object, e As System.EventArgs) Handles
1225 btnShowMessage.Click
1226     MessageBox.Show("a Button has been
1227     clicked")
1228 End Sub
```

1229
1230 **Entering comments in VB is similar to C# . . .**
1231 **just *start* the line with a *single quotation mark*..**
1232

```
1233 'Add your comment here.
```

1234
1235 **You're ready to run the program. Click the Green**
1236 **Arrow head at the top of the MVS screen**
1237 **-or-**
1238 **choose <Debug><Start Debugging>.**
1239
1240 **In a few seconds your screen/form will be**
1241 **displayed. Click "Show Message" and a**
1242 **messageBox will appear confirming your**
1243 **Action/Event. Click OK to close the messageBox**
1244 **then close the program.**
1245
1246 ***If* this doesn't happen review the instructions,**
1247 **correct any mistakes and try again.**
1248
1249 **Now you have a functioning program that presents**
1250 **a form containing a button control. When you**
1251 **click the button it fires off the "Click" event of the**

1252 **control/Object and your code handles the event by**
1253 **displaying a messageBox.**
1254
1255 Remember I mentioned dynamically setting or
1256 modifying properties at run time? Let's give it a shot.
1257
1258 Immediately following the last line of code you
1259 entered
1260 i.e. **MessageBox.Show("a Button has been**
1261 **clicked")**
1262 enter this command on a new line.
1263
1264 `btnShowMessage.BackColor = Color.Red;` (for *C#*)
1265
1266 `btnShowMessage.BackColor = Color.Red` (for *VB*)
1267
1268 Note the semicolon for C# . . . omitting the semi colon
1269 will cause a compiler error. VB does not use a
1270 semicolon.
1271
1272 *Run* the program again. Click the Green Arrow head
1273 or <Debug> + <Start Debugging>. Your choice.
1274
1275 The form is displayed as before and the background
1276 color of the button is as we originally defined (Set)
1277 that property to be, clicking the Show Message Button
1278 causes the MessageBox to appear and closing the
1279 MessageBox we find the color of the Button has
1280 changed.
1281
1282 We have covered a lot of ground. *Review*, make sure
1283 you are comfortable with your work so far and the

1284  instructions you have followed and what you have
1285  learned.
1286
1287  You created new folders, put a new Icon on your desk
1288  and started Microsoft Visual Studio with the Icon.
1289  You learned several of the menu items on the start
1290  page as well as the text editor (IDE). You created a
1291  new project with a blank form and then added a
1292  control/Object to the form. You learned to use the
1293  toolbox. Next you learned about setting the properties
1294  of the button control with the properties window for
1295  the button. Finally you learned about selecting the
1296  "Event" and writing a handler with your code for the
1297  "Event" including re-setting a property for the button
1298  control dynamically as your program executed.
1299
1300  You probably made an error or two . . . the world
1301  didn't end and you corrected the errors and ran your
1302  program.
1303
1304  Confusion at this point will not simply go away on it's
1305  own. If left to fester it will compound itself as we
1306  move forward. *Review*!!!
1307
1308  When you're satisfied, reward yourself with some
1309  fruit or nuts or whatever and then come on back when
1310  you're ready.
1311
1312  *Next up* . . . textbox controls/Objects, user input and
1313  variables. We're ready to get serious. We will learn to
1314  make our program do useful work and present the
1315  results to the user in an acceptable format.
1316

1317 Consider now what you think of programming. Is it
1318 your cup of tea?? I hope so . . . I find it rewarding,
1319 fun, useful and a way to be helpful to others. All in
1320 all, not a bad deal.
1321

# 1322 Project 3—TextBox Controls/Objects,
# 1323 User Input and Variables

1324
1325 Variables are software devices that act as storage for
1326 information, usually information entered by a user of
1327 an application.
1328
1329 The type of variable used is dependent on the type of
1330 information it will hold. Most common are variables
1331 holding either alphanumeric characters or symbols
1332 having no mathematical value and unusable for
1333 arithmetic operations are *strings*.
1334
1335 The second common type are called *integers* of
1336 various types that contain numbers having
1337 mathematical value and are useful for arithmetic
1338 operations.
1339
1340 Another variable type is one that can hold Time and
1341 Date information.
1342
1343 Our program must provide a mechanism for
1344 gathering, storing and manipulating this information
1345 for the users and presenting the results in a readable,
1346 understandable format.
1347
1348 Some information is held temporarily and lost when
1349 the program ends. At other times the information is

1350 gathered, manipulated and stored permanently in files
1351 on the computers hard drive.
1352
1353 We will deal with each requirement separately and in
1354 time cover them all.Let's start by learning to collect
1355 information from a user.
1356
1357 Assuming Microsoft Visual Studio is closed . . . *Start*
1358 *MVS* by either clicking the MVS Icon or by using the
1359 Windows Start Icon and selecting MVS from the
1360 menu. Your choice.
1361
1362 Using the same process as before create a new project
1363 in the language of your choice, selecting a Windows
1364 Form template and giving your project a
1365 name.REMEMBER . . . *Names* are *important*, be
1366 descriptive and include the language and major
1367 controls being used if possible in the name.
1368
1369 I suggest something like . . .
1370
1371 "VS VB Variables Textboxes User Input Proj"
1372 -or-
1373 "VS CS Variables Textboxes User Input Proj".
1374
1375 The "VS" is for Visual Studio.
1376
1377 Click OK and wait for MVS to create a project for
1378 you with a blank form.
1379
1380 When the form is displayed open the toolbox and we
1381 will add our controls to the form.*<View><ToolBox>*
1382

1383 *If* the form is not visible *<View><Solution*
1384 *Explorer>.*
1385 The Solution Explorer Window will appear and the
1386 files contained in your project will appear inside the
1387 window.
1388
1389 Select Form1 in the Solution Explorer window. Look
1390 at the top of the Solution Explorer window and note
1391 the Icons there. One Icon causes the code for the form
1392 to be displayed . . . the other of importance right now
1393 is the Design View Icon . . . which displays the form
1394 as it will appear visually to the user.
1395 ***Click the Design View Icon.***
1396
1397 When the form appears open the toolbox and let's ***add***
1398 ***two textboxes*** and two label controls/Objects, then
1399 ***add one Button Control/Object.***That's a total of five
1400 (5) controls/objects added to the form's control
1401 collection. More about this collection later.
1402
1403 Position the controls as you want them to appear by
1404 clicking them one at a time and dragging them to their
1405 final position. Position one label above each textbox.
1406 Leave a small space between the edge of each label
1407 and it's corresponding textbox. We will use the labels
1408 to give the user an explanation of what he/she is to do.
1409 You can relocate the controls later for appearance
1410 purposes later if you wish.
1411
1412 Now we will begin setting the "properties" for each
1413 control. ***Right click*** one of the textboxes and ***choose***
1414 ***properties*** from the pop-up menu. ***Click the A-Z Icon***
1415 at the top of the properties window.

1416
1417 ***Scroll down*** to the ***"Name" property*** and name this
1418 textbox ***txtBoxUserInput***. Notice the property
1419 ***"Enabled"***. This should be ***true***, allowing the user to
1420 access and type information into the box later. ***If*** it is
1421 ***false, change it to true.*** Otherwise the user cannot
1422 click in the box and type in the information we want
1423 to gather.
1424
1425 Set txtBoxUserInput's ***text property*** to ***empty*** . . . . No
1426 characters showing in the line to the right.
1427
1428 Leave the properties window open and ***click*** (select)
1429 the second textbox by clicking it. The properties
1430 window will updated to show the properties of this
1431 textbox automatically . . . . A small time saver.
1432
1433 Set the ***name property*** to txtBoxDisplayInfo . . .
1434 spaces are not allowed in the name. Set the text
1435 property to empty . . . no characters showing in the
1436 box. Set the "***Enabled***" property to ***false***. We do not
1437 want the user to be able to type in this box.
1438
1439 On to the button . . . Set the ***name*** property to
1440 ***btnReDisplay*** and ***text property*** to ***re-Display, change***
1441 the ***backcolor*** to something you like and ***experiment*** a
1442 little with the ***font*** property.
1443
1444 Do the same steps for each label control and give
1445 them names beginning with "lbl" + something
1446 meaningful to you. Remember . . . ***NO Spaces in the***
1447 ***name***. Also set the "***Autosize***" property to ***false***.
1448 Stretch the borders to the size you like that

1449 accommodates the text you entered in the text
1450 property. Set the "*Enabled*" property to *false*. We
1451 don't want anyone typing in our labels.
1452
1453 Now we're ready to write code. Remember before that
1454 we accessed the code file by opening the properties
1455 for the control and clicked the Lightening bolt ICON,
1456 then selected "Click Event".
1457
1458 This time, let's take a short cut . . . Just *Double-Click*
1459 the *button control* on the *designer view* of the
1460 form . . . Bingo, the code file opens and you're inside
1461 the skeleton for the Handler code of the default "Click
1462 event". Each control has a *default "Event"*. You go
1463 there by double clicking on the control.
1464
1465 Notice that my instructions are becoming less verbose
1466 as we go along. Yes, after two or three times I expect
1467 you to remember more of the "How To" step by step
1468 process. *If* necessary, *review*!!!
1469
1470 OK . . . . The code. Having "double-clicked" the
1471 button control on the designer view of the form . . . .
1472
1473 First we are going to create a string variable to hold
1474 the user's input.
1475
1476 For *C#* type this . . .
1477
1478 `String myStrUsersInput = "";`
1479
1480 For *VB* type this . . .
1481
1482 `Dim myStrUserInput as string = ""`

1483
1484 This statement causes the compiler to create
1485 (instantiate or construct) a string variable for us that is
1486 empty and ready to use. **Dim** means . . . reserve
1487 enough space in memory for this variable.
1488
1489 We are using a "***string***" variable because we are going
1490 to get alphanumeric characters from the user that have
1491 **no mathematical value** and cannot be used for
1492 arithmetic operations in our code unless we do
1493 something to convert the input into another type of
1494 variable.
1495
1496 Next we want to retrieve the information the user
1497 entered in the textbox and store it in our string
1498 variable.
1499
1500 For **C#** type this statement . . .
1501
1502 `myStrUserInput = txtBoxUserInput.text;`
1503
1504 ** Remember the semicolon after the statement!!
1505
1506 For **VB** type this statement . . .
1507
1508 `myStrUserInput = txtBoxUserInput.text`
1509
1510 Here's what's happening . . . our program displayed
1511 the form we created and the controls we added to it.
1512 The controls have the properties we defined for them
1513 during our coding process. This included empty
1514 textbox textual content.(AlphaNumeric characters
1515 without mathematical value).
1516

1517 We are allowing the user to change (re-Set) the text
1518 property of txtBoxUserInput . . . Then we retrieve the
1519 text property that they modified . . . programmatically.
1520
1521 `myStrUserInput = txtBoxUserInput.text;` // C# code
1522 `myStrUserInput = txtBoxUserInput.text;` // VB code
1523
1524 **Note** the use of the "***dot notation***" the controls name,
1525 followed by a "Dot or period", followed by the name
1526 of the property we want. Also **note** the **"=" operand**,
1527 known as the assignment operand. This causes the
1528 computer to go get the value we want and store it the
1529 variable. It looks for this value in the Target control
1530 we specified by name and more specifically in that
1531 control's "property" specified with "Dot notation".
1532
1533 At this point your event handler code for the
1534 btnUserInput Click event looks like this . . .
1535
1536 For *VB* Code . . .
1537

```
1538 Private Sub btnUserInput_Click(sender As
1539 System.Object, e As System.EventArgs) Handles
1540 btnUserInput.Click
1541     Dim myStrUserInput as String = ""
1542     myStrUserInput = txtBoxUserInput.text
1543 End Sub
```

1544
1545 For *C#* code
1546

```
1547 private void btnUserInput_Click(object sender,
1548 EventArgs e)
1549 {
1550     string myStrUserInput = "";
1551     myStrUserInput = textBox1.Text;
1552     textBox2.Text = myStrUserInput;
```

1553 }

1554

1555 *Run* your program.

1556

1557 Type some simple text into the textboxUserInput.
1558 Click the button and watch what happens. The text
1559 from the first control is retrieved and a copy
1560 inserted into the second textbox. The text wasn't
1561 removed and transported to another place . . . a
1562 copy was made and the copy inserted into a second
1563 location.

1564

1565 *If* you had an error . . . *review*, correct and try again.
1566 Don't try to move on without getting this step clear in
1567 your mind by solving issues that you have, if any.

1568

1569 Strings are very useful, flexible and you will use them
1570 hundreds, perhaps, thousands of times. You can a
1571 string any name you like, make it something
1572 meaningful that describes what you are going to do
1573 with the string. *Note*: String names *cannot* have
1574 spaces in them.

1575

1576 Here's a quick example . . . supposed you wanted to
1577 add some information to the string before displaying it
1578 in the second textbox. Strings can be *concatenated*
1579 (glued to gather or appended to each others).

1580

1581 Let's modify our code a little.

1582

1583 If you're still in the event handler code great. *IF* not,
1584 double click the button control on the form designer

1585 view and you will be placed into the event handler
1586 code.
1587
1588 For VB Code . . .
1589

```
1590 Private Sub btnUserInput_Click(sender As
1591 System.Object, e As System.EventArgs) Handles
1592 btnUserInput.Click
1593 "Add this new line of code. Note the comment marks
1594 "Remember you can put comments in you code too,
1595 just
1596 "like this comment.
1597
1598 "By the way . . . It's perfectly OK to "copy and
1599 then"
1600 "paste rather than typing everything over and
1601 over.
1602 "Copy and paste from the example files, not the
1603 book.
1604
1605     Dim myStrModifier as string = "You enter this
1606     text:"
1607     Dim myStrUserInput as String = ""
1608     myStrUserInput = myStrModifier &
1609     txtBoxUserInput.text
1610
1611 End Sub
```

1612
1613    For *C#*
1614

```
1615 private void btnUserInput_Click(object sender,
1616 EventArgs e)
1617 {
1618     string myStrModifier = "";
1619     myStrModifier = "You entered this text: ";
1620     string myStrUserInput = "";
1621     myStrUserInput = myStrModifier + textBox1.Text;
1622     textBox2.Text = myStrUserInput;
1623 }
```

1624
1625 **Run your program again. The text from the first**
1626 **textbox has been modified a little before putting a**
1627 **copy into the second textbox.**
1628
1629 *If* **you have an error . . . you know the story.**
1630 *Review*!!!!
1631
1632 **What we did was repeat the things we did before,**
1633 **but before copying the text into the second box we**
1634 **appended it to the end of a second string, then**
1635 **placed it into the second Box. You can also say that**
1636 **we "concatenated" the two strings.**
1637
1638 This is deceptively simple, but very powerful. You'll
1639 use it a lot. When working with strings remember that
1640 *spaces are characters* too whether they are visible or
1641 not.
1642
1643 Strings in commercial applications can be thousands
1644 of characters long. Strings are a very important part of
1645 the Microsoft.network architecture. There are many
1646 tools (*methods*) for working with strings. It is
1647 worthwhile for us to spend a little more effort and
1648 time on this and understand a few of them before
1649 going forward.
1650
1651 For example . . . . suppose for some reason we decide
1652 we want everything we do work with should be in
1653 lower case letters. There is a tool (method) for that.
1654 Strings like controls are *objects*. As you know,
1655 Objects have properties and they also have
1656 "*Methods*".

1657
1658 We going to use one now called *"ToLower"*, meaning
1659 convert this string to all lower case characters.
1660
1661 Add this line of code to your btnUserInput click event
1662 handler.
1663
1664 *C#*
1665 `myStrUserInput = myStrUserInput.ToLower();`
1666
1667 *VB*
1668 `myStrUserInput = myStrUserInput.ToLower()`
1669
1670 Now when you run your program enter some capital
1671 letters to the textbox.
1672
1673 The text when copied over will be converted into all
1674 lower case characters.
1675
1676 Conversely you can convert a string to all upper case
1677 characters by typing in *ToUpper* as the *method.*
1678
1679 *C#*
1680 `myStrUserInput = myStrUserInput.Upper();`
1681
1682 *VB*
1683 `myStrUserInput = myStrUserInput.ToUpper()`
1684
1685 Notice that we are using "dot notation" again, this
1686 time to use *"CALL"* a method.
1687
1688 By now your event handler code is much larger . . . it
1689 should look like this;
1690

1691  For VB Code . . .

1692

```
1693  Private Sub btnUserInput_Click(sender As
1694  System.Object, e As System.EventArgs) Handles
1695  btnUserInput.Click
1696  "Add this new line of code. Note the comment marks
1697  "Remember you can put comments in you code too,
1698  just "like this comment.
1699
1700  "By the way . . . It's perfectly OK to "copy and
1701  then"
1702  "paste rather than typing everything over and
1703  over.
1704  "Copy from the example files, not the book.
1705
1706      Dim myStrModifier as string = "You enter this
1707      text: "
1708      Dim myStrUserInput as String = ""
1709      myStrUserInput = myStrModifier &
1710      txtBoxUserInput.text
1711      myStrUserInput = myStrUserInput.ToLower()
1712      textBox2.Text = myStrUserInput
1713  End Sub
```

1714

1715      For C#

1716

```
1717  private void btnUserInput_Click(object sender,
1718  EventArgs e)
1719  {
1720      string myStrModifier = "";
1721      myStrModifier = "You entered this text: ";
1722      string myStrUserInput = "";
1723      myStrUserInput = myStrModifier + textBox1.Text;
1724      myStrUserInput = myStrUserInput.ToLower();
1725      textBox2.Text = myStrUserInput;
1726  }
```

1727

1728  Let's make a brief introduction of another variable
1729  type to use with our string methods . . . the integer.

1730 Actually there are several sizes or type of integers.
1731 More later on that subject. For now, just know that an
1732 integer holds information that has mathematical value.
1733
1734 Integers are defined (Declared) like this . . .
1735
1736 C#
1737 `Int myInt = 99999; // or whatever`
1738
1739 VB
1740 `Dim myInt as integer = 9999`
1741
1742 Suppose we want to know how many characters there
1743 are in a string . . . we can ask our program to tell us.
1744
1745 We will "CALL" another method of the string Object.
1746 "Length".
1747
1748 C#
1749 `myINt = myStrUserInput.Lenght();`
1750
1751 VB
1752 `myInt = myStrUserInput.Length()`
1753
1754 Now that we have the information we wanted, we can
1755 use it in different ways. We can do arithmetic with it
1756 or we can display it as text. We can also do other
1757 things like locate a particular Character's position in
1758 the string and refer to that specific character as
1759 needed.
1760
1761 If we display it as text we must first convert the
1762 integer into string format. No problem, we have
1763 another tool just for that job called "**Convert**".

1764  So lets get the information about our user's input and
1765  display it in a messageBox.
1766
1767  Define (Declare another string)
1768
1769  C#
```
1770  String myStringLength = "";
1771  myStrStringLenght = Convert.ToString(myInt);
```
1772
1773  VB
```
1774  Dim myStringLength as integer
1775  myStringLength = StringName.Length()
1776  myStrStringLength =
1777  Convert.ToString(myStringLength)
```
1778
1779  Now display the information . . .
1780
1781  C#
```
1782  MessageBox.Show(myStrStringLength);
```
1783
1784  VB
```
1785  MessageBox.Show(myStrStringLength)
```
1786
1787  Now you can add the appropriate lines of code into
1788  your event handler and run the program.
1789
1790  Got a problem or error . . . . Review!!!!
1791
1792  Your code should look like this now
1793
1794  VB
1795
```
1796  Private Sub btnUserInput_Click(sender As
1797  System.Object, e As System.EventArgs) Handles
1798  btnUserInput.Click
1799      Dim myStrUserInput As String = ""
```

```
1800     Dim myStrModifier As String = "You entered: "
1801     myStrUserInput = myStrModifier & TextBox1.Text
1802     myStrUserInput = myStrUserInput.ToLower()
1803     TextBox2.Text = myStrUserInput
1804     Dim myInfoStr As String = ""
1805     Dim myInt As Integer = 9999
1806     myInt = myStrUserInput.Length
1807     myInfoStr = Convert.ToString(myInt)
1808     MessageBox.Show("You enter a lot of
1809     characters . . ." & myInfoStr)
1810 End Sub
1811
```

1812 C#

```
1813
1814 private void button1_Click(object sender,
1815 EventArgs e)
1816 {
1817     string myStrModifier = "";
1818     myStrModifier = "You entered this text: ";
1819     string myStrUserInput = "";
1820     myStrUserInput = myStrModifier + textBox1.Text;
1821     myStrUserInput = myStrUserInput.ToLower();
1822     textBox2.Text = myStrUserInput;
1823     int myInt = 9999;
1824     myInt = myStrUserInput.Length;
1825     string myStrInformation =
1826         Convert.ToString(myInt);
1827     MessageBox.Show("You entered a lot of
1828         characters . . ." + myStrInformation);
1829 }
1830
```

1831 *A quick Note*: C# uses the "+" symbol to concatenate
1832 strings. VB uses the & symbol for that purpose. The
1833 end result is the same. Why? . . . Who knows? . . . A
1834 developer of such tools lives in another world of
1835 minutia. It is a matter of personal style and preference
1836 I think. Undoubtedly my comment would horrify and
1837 insult many developers. But for our purpose . . . it

1838 doesn't matter. We want to know "How to" . . . not
1839 "why To".
1840
1841 ***Break time??*** We've covered a lot.
1842
1843 ***All of it is important***. Take the time to review and
1844 thoroughly understand the material covered so far.
1845 Don't try to build on a weak foundation . . . resolve
1846 the questions you have and then come back.
1847
1848 Next up . . . finding and using sub-strings within a
1849 larger string.
1850

1851 # Project 4—Locating sub-strings within
1852 # a string
1853
1854 Locating a needle in a hay stack is a job requiring
1855 patience, focus and endurance . . . not to mention
1856 accuracy. This type of work is well handled by
1857 computers.
1858
1859 Given strings of hundreds of characters you might
1860 need to located a sub string of just 3 or 4 characters
1861 and change them or take some other action.
1862
1863 Here's how . . .
1864
1865 VB
1866
1867 First..does the sub string exist within the larger
1868 string? . . .
1869
1870 `Dim tstResults as integer = strMain.Contains(strSub)`

1871

1872 **This statement returns an integer indicating**
1873 **whether the substring does exist or not**

1874

1875 '0 is False

1876

1877 C#

1878

1879 First . . . does the sub string exist within the larger
1880 string?

1881

```
1882 int intTstResults =
1883 myStrUserInput.Contains(myStrModifier);
```

1884

1885 **This statement returns an integer indicating**
1886 **whether the substring does exist or not**

1887

1888 '0 is False non zero values indicate the substring is
1889 inside the larger string

1890

1891 Next . . . since the substrings exists where is it?

1892

1893 We can call another method called "IndexOf" for this
1894 task

1895

```
1896 Int mySubStrIdx =
1897 myStrUserInput.IndexOf(myStrModifier);
```

1898

1899 Now we know what position the first character of the
1900 substring is, inside the larger string we have all the
1901 information we need.

1902

1903 *Note: Computers count things starting with 0, not 1.*

1904  The first character of the substring is located at
1905  position so and so and counting from 0!!!
1906
1907  Since we know the substring exists inside the larger
1908  string and where it is . . . we can get a copy of it if we
1909  want. All that remains is to say how many characters
1910  we want a copy of.
1911  Suppose, for example, we say five(5) . . .
1912
1913  C#
1914  ```
      string myStr =
1915  myStrUserInput.Substring(myIntSubStrIdx,5);
      ```
1916
1917  VB
1918  ```
      Dim myStr as string =
1919  myStrUserInput.Substring(myIntSubStrIdx,5)
      ```
1920
1921  If we wanted we could say any number as long as we
1922  did not exceed the length of the string (starting at the
1923  position where the sub-string starts—Plus the number
1924  of characters in the sub-string). Should that happen
1925  we get an error saying our index is out of range.
1926
1927  We can avoid that issues by using an integer variable
1928  to store the length of our sub-string and using the
1929  variable name instead of specifying a number of
1930  characters..i.e "5".
1931
1932  It looks like this . . .
1933
1934  VB
1935  ```
      Int mySubStrLength = mySubStr.Length
1936  myStrUserInput.Substring(myIntSubStrIdx,mySubStrLe
1937  ngth)
      ```
1938
      ```

```
1939  C#
1940  Int mySubStrLength = mySubStr.Length;
1941  string myStr =
1942  myStrUserInput.Substring(myIntSubStrIdx,mySubStrLe
1943  ngth);
1944
```

**1945  Let's edit our BtnUserInput Click Event handler**
**1946  code one more time . . . . using the things we just**
**1947  learned about strings and string manipulation**
**1948  methods**

```
1949
1950  C#
1951
1952  private void btnUserInput_Click(object sender,
1953  EventArgs e)
1954  {
1955      int myIntIdx;
1956      int myIntLength;
1957      string myStrUserInput = "";
1958      string myStrModified = "";
1959      string myStrPrefix = "You entered: ";
1960      myStrUserInput = textBox1.Text;
1961      myStrModified = myStrPrefix + myStrUserInput;
1962      myStrModified = myStrModified.ToLower();
1963      textBox2.Text = myStrModified;
1964      string myInfoStr = "";
1965      string myInt;
1966      string mySubStr = "";
1967      myIntLength = myStrModified.Length;
1968      myIntIdx = myStrModified.IndexOf(myStrUserInput);
1969      mySubStr = myStrModified.Substring(myIntIdx,
1970      myStrUserInput.Length);
1971      MessageBox.Show("You entered a lot of
1972      characters.." + Convert.ToString(myIntLength));
1973      MessageBox.Show("The sub-string you wanted to
1974      find begins at position " +
1975      Convert.ToString(myIntIdx));
1976      MessageBox.Show("The characters of the sub
1977      string are . . ." + mySubStr);
```

```
1978    MessageBox.Show("The string modifier you added
1979       to re-display the text in textbox2 is now part
1980       of the string myStrInformation");
1981 }
1982
```

1983  VB

```
1984
1985 Private Sub btnUserInput_Click(sender As
1986 System.Object, e As System.EventArgs) Handles
1987 btnUserInput.Click
1988     Dim myStrUserInput As String = ""
1989     Dim myStrModifier As String = "You entered: "
1990     myStrUserInput = myStrModifier & TextBox1.Text
1991     myStrUserInput = myStrUserInput.ToLower()
1992     TextBox2.Text = myStrUserInput
1993     Dim myInfoStr As String = ""
1994     Dim myInt As Integer = 9999
1995     myInt = myStrUserInput.Length
1996     myInfoStr = Convert.ToString(myInt)
1997     MessageBox.Show("You enter a lot of
1998     characters.. " & myInfoStr)
1999 End Sub
2000
```

2001  Run your program and enter a few characters in the
2002  User Input textbox then click the button. The text
2003  from the user input textbox is modified to include the
2004  "You entered lot of characters" prefix string we
2005  created,the modified string is sent to the second
2006  textbox and our string methods do their work to find
2007  the starting position of the actual characters the user
2008  input as a sub-string of the modified string.
2009
2010  Next we are sent a few messages saying where the
2011  sub-string starts and gives us back a copy of the sub-
2012  string contents.
2013

2014 Two last points on strings; Comparing and "literal
2015 strings".
2016 The easy one first . . . literal strings aer a series of
2017 AlphaNUmeric characters use without storing them in
2018 a "named" string variable. Literal strings are enclosed
2019 in quotation marks and have no mathematical value.
2020 We have been using them as part of what we
2021 displayed in our messageBoxes. We needed the exact
2022 contents right then with no need for the information to
2023 be re-used later, so we used a "literal" string. i.e.
2024
2025 C#
2026 `messageBox.Show("You entered lots of characters");`
2027
2028 VB
2029 `messageBox.Show("You entered lots of characters")`
2030
2031 By doing this the CPU (Central Processor Unit) of
2032 your computer has a little less work to do and if there
2033 are thousands of users using a program, it can make a
2034 major difference.
2035
2036 ## Comparing strings.
2037
2038 At times we need to compare two or more strings.
2039 This is what happens when you enter a password to
2040 access a program or file online for example. Once we
2041 know the results of the comparison we can make
2042 decisions and take the desired actions.
2043
2044 Here's how it's done . . .
2045
2046 C#
2047 `Str myStr1 = "ABCD";`

```
2048 Str myStr2 = "DEFG";
2049 Int myIntComparisonResults;
2050
2051 int myIntStrComparisonResults =
2052 string.Compare(myStrUserInput, mySubStr);
2053
2054 // myIntStrComparisonResults will be "0" if the
2055 strings are
2056 // the same, non-zero if they are not. Knowing
2057 this value we
2058 // can decide what to do. For example, send a
2059 messageBox
2060 // message saying if the strings are equal or not.
2061
2062 VB
2063 Dim myStr1 as string = "ABCD"
2064 Dim myStr2 as string = "DEFG"
2065 Int myIntComparisonResults
2066 int myIntStrComparisonResults =
2067 string.Compare(myStrUserInput, mySubStr)
2068
```

2069 **We can use an "If" statement and a "==" operator**
2070 **to decide about making this action**

2071

2072 **"==" means . . . compare item1 to item2 for**
2073 **equality.**
2074 **"!=" means . . . compare item1 to item2 for in-**
2075 **equality.**

2076

2077 **"if" combined with "==" mean do this "if" this**
2078 **condition is true.**

2079

2080 **"if" combined with "!=" mean do this "if" this**
2081 **condition is not true.**

2082

2083 **Visual Basic uses "==" for equality and "<>" for**
2084 **in-equality.**

```
2085
2086 C#
2087 If(myStrComparisonResults == 0)
2088 {
2089     MessageBox.Show("The strings are equal");
2090 }
2091
2092 if (myIntStrComparisonResults!= 0)
2093 {
2094     MessageBox.Show("The strings are NOT equal");
2095 }
2096
2097 VB
2098 If(myStrComparisonResults == 0) then
2099     MessageBox.Show("The strings are equal")
2100 End if
2101
2102 If(myStrComparisonResults <> 0) then
2103     MessageBox.Show("The strings are NOT equal")
2104 End if
2105
```

2106 **Modify your code for the last time to include this**
2107 **string comparson of the user input string versus**
2108 **the string displayed in the second textbox.**
2109

2110 Stay with this exercise until you completely
2111 understand all that is happening. It incorporates
2112 everything we have covered up to this point and
2113 added something new at each step. We go from
2114 starting MVS to seeing a form created to creating
2115 variables of both string and integer types, to adding
2116 controls and setting their properties . . . to getting
2117 input from a user and storing the input into strings,
2118 modifying the strings and using strings methods for
2119 calculating their length and locating sub-strings of a
2120 larger string and finally using literal strings and

2121 comparing two strings. We also got into the use of a
2122 messageBox to send us messages about what our code
2123 did and the results of the code's work . . . . That's a
2124 lot!!!!
2125
2126 I cannot over state the importance of **_adding comment_**
2127 **_lines in your code_**. I promise, someday you will come
2128 back to these examples and use them as reference
2129 material on other projects. You won't remember all of
2130 the thinking that went into writing the code.
2131 Comments will be invaluable to you at that point.
2132

## 2133 **Project 5—Options, Comfort and**
## 2134 **Convenience for use of the text editor.**

2135
2136 OK, by now the code you are creating consists of
2137 quite a few lines in the MVS text editor or IDE
2138 (Integrated Development Environment).We can make
2139 things a little easier to keep up with if we make some
2140 slight changes to the IDE options. For example, the
2141 size of the characters (font) . . . the "color" of
2142 different parts of the code in the lines and "Line
2143 Numbers" so that we can easily keep track of where
2144 we are working. Again, I cannot and do not cover all
2145 of the options. Experiment with the options until you
2146 are comfortable with the appearance of the editor!!!
2147
2148 Start MVS, if you do not have it running.
2149
2150 **_Note_**: You do not have to have a project open in order
2151 to do this modification.
2152
2153 On the top menu line of the IDE (Task bar) . . .

2154 <Tools> + <Options> + <Text Editor>.

2155

2156 <All Languages> . . . Look in the right pane, be sure
2157 the line number box is checked or selected.

2158

2159 <OK>

2160

2161 <Tools> + <Options> + <Environment> + <fonts and
2162 colors>.

2163

2164 Look down thru the table with the options in the right
2165 pane . . . Here you can set the color of each
2166 component of the code shown in the MVS text Editor.

2167

2168 The important ones to me are line numbers, "Match
2169 Bracing-rectangles" . . . the Curly braces used in C#,
2170 the Comments, but the choices are for your personal
2171 preferences. Experiment!!! *Font size* is also a very
2172 important one to me . . . You decide what is best for
2173 yourself.

2174

2175 When you're done click <OK>. These choices will
2176 remain in effect for all projects until you change them.

2177

2178 *Next up* . . . some simple math using user input,
2179 textboxes, buttons, and some arithmetic operations.

2180

## 2181 Project 6—Buttons, TextBoxes and 2182 Arithmetic

2183

2184 Now it is time to get out your math thinking cap and
2185 let's do some arithmetic.

2186

2187 If MVS is not running start it now and let's make hay
2188 (math hay).<File><New Project>
2189
2190 On the blank form *add 3 textBoxes*, *4 labels* and *4*
2191 *checkboxes* plus *1 button*.
2192
2193 Name textboxes txtBoxNum1, txtBoxNum2 and
2194 txtBoxAns.
2195
2196 Name the checkboxes CkBoxAdd, CkBoxSubtract,
2197 CkBoxDivide and CkBoxMultiply.
2198
2199 Set their respective "Checked properties" to false. Set
2200 their respective text properties to Add, Subtract,
2201 Divide and Multiply.
2202
2203 Name the button btnCalculate. Set the text property to
2204 Calculate.
2205
2206 *Note:* By now you know you cannot have spaces in
2207 the names of controls. I use "Camel-Hump" style . . .
2208 Yes, that's actually the right name, for this style of
2209 naming controls. The first letter is lowercase and the
2210 first letter of each significant syllable after that is
2211 Uppercase. It makes the code more readable.
2212
2213 The other control properties can be set to whatever
2214 appearance appeals to you. This includes Border type,
2215 BackColor, Font, and Fore Color.
2216
2217 Drag the controls into a position that makes sense to
2218 you. I used the textbox for number1 on the left . . . the
2219 text box for number2 to the right and the textbox for

2220  the answer on the far right side of the form. I Placed
2221  the Checkboxes for the math operations between the
2222  first two textboxes and *a label with the "=" sign* for
2223  it's text property just before the textbox for the
2224  answer. This seems to make sense to me and follows
2225  the way you would normally state the problem orally
2226  i.e Number1 plus Number2 equals "the answer".
2227
2228  The position of the button to do the calculation
2229  doesn't make a lot of difference. Make it a short move
2230  for the user with the mouse from the textbox for
2231  number2 and very visible.
2232
2233  OK, let's write some code. Double click the button on
2234  the form and you will land in a skeletal event handler
2235  for the click (default) event where our code is going.
2236
2237  Create the variables to store the user's input
2238  (Number1 and Number2) and one for the answer.
2239
2240  Remember, the *input* will be retrieved as a *string* and
2241  we will have to *convert* it into a number to do the
2242  math operations. No problem we will once again *call*
2243  the Convert method and end up with numbers we can
2244  use in math operations.
2245
2246  When we get a number as our answer we will *Convert*
2247  the number into a string and place the string into the
2248  answer textbox's text property.
2249
2250  The only really *new things* we are going to do here
2251  are use a *Decimal variable* type and determine the
2252  "*Checked status*" of the checkbox controls.

```
2253
2254 Let's do it . . .
2255
2256 C#
2257
2258 Right now the skeletal event handler looks like
2259 this . . .
2260
2261 private void btnCalculate_Click(object sender,
2262 EventArgs e)
2263 {
2264
2265 }
2266
```

2267 Between the curly braces we age going to add these
2268 lines of code . . .
2269

2270 Note: WE USE ***DECIMAL Variables*** because our
2271 user might not give us whole numbers to work with
2272 and our answer might not be a whole number.

```
2273
2274     decimal decAns = 0;
2275     decimal dec1 = 0;
2276     decimal dec2 = 0;
2277     dec1 = Convert.ToDecimal(txtBoxNum1.Text);
2278     dec2 = Convert.ToDecimal(txtBoxNum2.Text);
2279
2280     if (checkBoxadd.Checked) // If this device is
2281     checked
2282     {
2283         decAns = dec1 + dec2;
2284         txtBoxAns.Text = Convert.ToString(decAns);
2285     }
2286
2287     if (checkBoxSubtract.Checked) // If device is
2288     checked
2289     {
2290         decAns = dec1-dec2;
```

```
2291        txtBoxAns.Text = Convert.ToString(decAns);
2292    }
2293
2294    if (checkBoxMultiply.Checked) // If device is
2295    checked
2296    {
2297        decAns = dec1 * dec2; // . . . "*" means
2298        multiplied by
2299        txtBoxAns.Text = Convert.ToString(decAns);
2300    }
2301    if (checkBoxDivide.Checked)
2302    {
2303        decAns = dec1 / dec2; // . . . "/" means
2304        Divided by
2305        txtBoxAns.Text = Convert.ToString(decAns);
2306    }
2307
```

2308 Our completed C# event handler code should look
2309 like this . . .

```
2310
2311 private void btnCalculate_Click(object sender,
2312 EventArgs e)
2313 {
2314    decimal decAns = 0;
2315    decimal dec1 = 0;
2316    decimal dec2 = 0;
2317    dec1 = Convert.ToDecimal(txtBoxNum1.Text);
2318    dec2 = Convert.ToDecimal(txtBoxNum2.Text);
2319    if (checkBoxadd.Checked)
2320    {
2321        decAns = dec1 + dec2;
2322        txtBoxAns.Text = Convert.ToString(decAns);
2323    }
2324    if (checkBoxSubtract.Checked)
2325    {
2326        decAns = dec1-dec2;
2327        txtBoxAns.Text = Convert.ToString(decAns);
2328    }
2329    if (checkBoxMultiply.Checked)
2330    {
2331        decAns = dec1 * dec2;
```

```
2332          txtBoxAns.Text = Convert.ToString(decAns);
2333      }
2334      if (checkBoxDivide.Checked)
2335      {
2336          decAns = dec1 / dec2;
2337          txtBoxAns.Text = Convert.ToString(decAns);
2338      }
2339 }
2340
```

2341 When we re-set the properties of the IDE code editor
2342 to make things a little more convenient and easy . . .
2343 code like this is the major reason why we did that.
2344

2345 Place the cursor over the first curly brace in the event
2346 handler. Note that the curly braces background color
2347 changes. Now, scroll down the screen until you get to
2348 the last curly brace and note that it has been similarly
2349 highlighted before you actually put the cursor on it.
2350

2351 Of course, this assumes that you followed the
2352 instructions and re-set the font and color option in the
2353 MVS text editor for brace matching.
2354

2355 This helps you to verify that each brace has a
2356 matching mate . . . if you don't, C#'s compiler will
2357 throw us an error message and refuse to cooperate. In
2358 large programs this can be a major headache. Be good
2359 to yourself . . . if you *didn't re-set the editor options*,
2360 do it now. *Please*!!! Then, re-check the brace
2361 matching function.
2362

2363 *Warning:* It is possible for users to check more than
2364 one checkbox. If this happens, more than one
2365 operation will be performed and only the last
2366 operation performed will be seen by the user.

2367
2368 No errors have occurred as far as the code is
2369 concerned. The error or weakness is in the design of
2370 the program.
2371 This is a programmer's responsibility. Choose the
2372 "best" method, given the user's needs.
2373
2374 Run the program a few times and observe that this
2375 happens (or can happen).
2376
2377 To avoid the problem, we can chose another type of
2378 control called the radio button and place the radio
2379 buttons inside a group control. This makes the radio
2380 buttons "exclusive" i.e. only one can be checked.
2381 When one is checked, the others are automatically
2382 "un-checked".
2383
2384 This is by design. There are times when a user will
2385 need to indicate more than one operation is to be
2386 done, legitimately. For example, square the number I
2387 want used and then multiply by some other value . . .
2388 such as the value for "Pi", 3.14. Or, tell Sam to drive
2389 home then mow the lawn.
2390
2391 All methods have advantages and dis-advantages. The
2392 programmer must pick the right one.
2393
2394 ***OK, let's do it again, this time, for Visual Basic.***
2395
2396 VB
2397
2398 Start MVS.
2399

2400  <File><New Project>
2401
2402  ***NOTE***: Remember to do <Tools> + <Options> and
2403  change the locations to reflect the folder for Visual
2404  Basic.
2405
2406  On the blank form add 3 textBoxes, 4 labels and 4
2407  checkboxes plus 1 button.
2408
2409  Name textboxes txtBoxNum1, txtBoxNum2 and
2410  txtBoxAns.
2411
2412  Name the checkboxes CkBoxAdd, CkBoxSubtract,
2413  CkBoxDivide and CkBoxMultiply.
2414
2415  Set their respective "Checked properties" to false. Set
2416  their respective text properties to Add, Subtract,
2417  Divide and Multiply.
2418
2419  Name the button btnCalculate. Set the text property to
2420  Calculate.
2421
2422  ***Note:*** By now you know you cannot have spaces in
2423  the names of controls. I use "Camel-Hump" style . . .
2424  Yes, that's actually the right name, for this style of
2425  naming controls. The first letter is lowercase and the
2426  first letter of each significant syllable after that is
2427  Uppercase. It makes the code more readable.
2428
2429  The other control properties can be set to whatever
2430  appearance appeals to you. This includes Border type,
2431  BackColor, Font, and ForeColor.
2432

2433 Drag the controls into a position that makes sense to
2434 you. I used the textbox for number1 on the left . . . the
2435 text box for number2 to the right and the textbox for
2436 the answer on the far right side of the form. I Placed
2437 the Checkboxes for the math operations between the
2438 first two textboxes and a **_label with the "=" sign_** for
2439 it's text property just before the textbox for the
2440 answer. This seems to make sense to me and follows
2441 the way you would normally state the problem orally
2442 i.e Number1 "plus", or what ever, Number2 equals
2443 "the answer".
2444 Right now the skeletal event handler looks like
2445 this . . .
2446
```
2447 Private Sub btnCalculate_Click(sender As
2448 System.Object, e As System.EventArgs) Handles
2449 btnCalculate.Click
2450
2451 End Sub
```
2452
2453 **_Between_** the **_Private Sub and End Sub_** phrases we are
2454 going to **_add_** these lines of **_code_** . . .
2455
2456 Note: WE USE **_DECIMAL Variables_** because our
2457 user might not give us whole numbers to work with
2458 and our answer might not be a whole number.
2459
```
2460     Dim decAns as Decimal = 0
2461     Dim dec1 as Decimal = 0
2462     Dim dec2 as Decimal= 0
2463     dec1 = Convert.ToDecimal(txtBoxNum1.Text)
2464     dec2 = Convert.ToDecimal(txtBoxNum2.Text)
2465
2466     if (ckBoxadd.Checked) 'If this device is checked
2467     {
2468         decAns = dec1 + dec2
```

```
2469        txtBoxAns.Text = Convert.ToString(decAns)
2470     }
2471
2472     if (ckBoxSubtract.Checked) 'If device is checked
2473     {
2474        decAns = dec1–dec2
2475        txtBoxAns.Text = Convert.ToString(decAns)
2476     }
2477
2478     if (ckBoxMultiply.Checked) 'If device is checked
2479     {
2480        decAns = dec1 * dec2 '. . . "*" means
2481        multiplied by
2482        txtBoxAns.Text = Convert.ToString(decAns)
2483     }
2484     if (checkBoxDivide.Checked)
2485     {
2486        decAns = dec1 / dec2 '. . . "/" means
2487        Divided by
2488        txtBoxAns.Text = Convert.ToString(decAns)
2489     }
2490
```

2491 Our completed VB event handler code should look
2492 like this . . .

```
2493
2494 private void btnCalculate_Click(object sender,
2495 EventArgs e)
2496 {
2497     Dim decAns as Decimal = 0
2498     Dim dec1 as Decimal = 0
2499     Dim dec2 as Decimal = 0
2500     dec1 = Convert.ToDecimal(txtBoxNum1.Text)
2501     dec2 = Convert.ToDecimal(txtBoxNum2.Text)
2502     if (checkBoxadd.Checked)
2503     {
2504        decAns = dec1 + dec2
2505        txtBoxAns.Text = Convert.ToString(decAns)
2506     }
2507     if (checkBoxSubtract.Checked)
2508     {
2509        decAns = dec1–dec2
```

```
2510        txtBoxAns.Text = Convert.ToString(decAns)
2511    }
2512    if (checkBoxMultiply.Checked)
2513    {
2514        decAns = dec1 * dec2
2515        txtBoxAns.Text = Convert.ToString(decAns)
2516    }
2517    if (checkBoxDivide.Checked)
2518    {
2519        decAns = dec1 / dec2
2520        txtBoxAns.Text = Convert.ToString(decAns);
2521    }
2522 }
2523
```

2524 When we re-set the properties of the IDE code editor
2525 to make things a little more convenient and easy . . .
2526 code like this is the major reason why we did that.
2527

2528 Place the cursor over the first curly brace in the event
2529 handler. Note that the curly braces background color
2530 changes. Now, scroll down the screen until you get to
2531 the last curly brace and note that it has been similarly
2532 highlighted before you actually put the cursor on it.
2533

2534 Of course, this assumes that you followed the
2535 instructions and re-set the font and color option in the
2536 MVS text editor for brace matching.
2537

2538 This helps you to verify that each brace has a
2539 matching mate . . . if you don't, VB's compiler will
2540 throw us an error message and refuse to cooperate. In
2541 large programs this can be a major headache. Be good
2542 to yourself . . . if you *didn't re-set the editor options*,
2543 do it now. *Please*!!! Then, re-check the brace
2544 matching function.
2545

2546 Here's what's supposed to be happening . . .
2547
2548 The user enters two numbers. Next the user checks the
2549 checkbox for the operation that they want. Finally,
2550 they click the calculate button. The users see an
2551 answer appear in the answer textbox.
2552
2553 Behind the scene . . . the click event is fired for the
2554 btnCalculate_Click event. The numbers entered as
2555 strings are retrieved from the textboxes and converted
2556 into "Decimal" values. The checked status of the
2557 checkboxes is retrieved by the "if" statements.
2558 When "if" sees one checkbox with the CheckBox
2559 checked, it performs the appropriate arithmetic
2560 operation and stores the result in the answer variable.
2561 The answer variable is converted into a string and the
2562 string placed in the answer textboxes "text property"
2563 and displayed.
2564
2565 ***Warning:*** It is possible for users to check more than
2566 one checkbox. If this happens, more than one
2567 operation will be performed and only the last
2568 operation performed will be seen by the user.
2569
2570 No errors have occurred as far as the code is
2571 concerned. The error or weakness is in the design of
2572 the program.
2573 This is a programmer's responsibility. Choose the
2574 "best" method, given the user's needs.
2575
2576 Run the program a few times and observe that this
2577 happens (or can happen).
2578

2579 To avoid the problem, we can chose another type of
2580 control called the radio button and place the radio
2581 buttons inside a group control. This makes the radio
2582 buttons "exclusive" i.e. only one can be checked.
2583 When one is checked, the others are automatically
2584 "un-checked".
2585
2586 This is by design. There are times when a user will
2587 need to indicate more than one operation is to be
2588 done, legitimately. For example, square the number I
2589 want used and then multiply by some other value . . .
2590 such as the value for "Pi", 3.14. Or, tell Sam to drive
2591 home then mow the lawn.
2592
2593 All methods have advantages and dis-advantages. The
2594 programmer must pick the right one.
2595

## 2596 Project 7—Using Radio Buttons and
## 2597 Group Boxes

2598
2599 So, let's revise our program and use radio buttons
2600 inside a groupBox control.
2601
2602 Back to MVS . . . this time choose the "Design view"
2603 of the form. You can either click the design view Icon
2604 in the solution explorer's menu box or expand the
2605 Form file in the "files" list of the Solution explorer by
2606 clicking the arrow next to the Form1 item. This will
2607 display two separate versions of the Form1 file; one
2608 containing the word "design ". Double clicking that
2609 line will also take you to the "Design View" screen.
2610 Your choice.
2611

2612  C#
2613
2614  Here is the revised C# version using Radio buttons.
2615
```
2616  private void btnCalculate_Click(object sender,
2617  EventArgs e)
2618  {
2619      decimal decAns = 0;
2620      decimal dec1 = 0;
2621      decimal dec2 = 0;
2622      dec1 = Convert.ToDecimal(txtBoxNum1.Text);
2623      dec2 = Convert.ToDecimal(txtBoxNum2.Text);
2624      if (radBtnAdd.Checked)
2625      {
2626          decAns = dec1 + dec2;
2627          txtBoxAns.Text = Convert.ToString(decAns);
2628      }
2629      if (radBtnSubtract.Checked)
2630      {
2631          decAns = dec1–dec2;
2632          txtBoxAns.Text = Convert.ToString(decAns);
2633      }
2634      if (radBtnMultiply.Checked)
2635      {
2636          decAns = dec1 * dec2;
2637          txtBoxAns.Text = Convert.ToString(decAns);
2638      }
2639      if (radBtnDivide.Checked)
2640      {
2641          decAns = dec1 / dec2;
2642          txtBoxAns.Text = Convert.ToString(decAns);
2643      }
2644  }
```
2645
2646  **Run the program:** *note that the user cannot choose*
2647  *more than one radio button simoultaneously.*
2648
2649  *Now* . . . Even if you are normally operating in Visual
2650  Basic only . . . by now, I think you can peruse the C#

2651  code and infer what is needed to revise the Visual
2652  Basic application on your own.
2653
2654  So go for it!!! Make some mistakes and don't panic.
2655  In general this is the process;
2656
2657  Start MVS
2658  Open the Project.
2659  Choose the language
2660  Set the Options for the project location.
2661  Look at the form in Designer View.
2662  Delete/Add the controls (Radio Buttons vs Check
2663  Boxes).
2664  Add the groupBox and get the radio button inside the
2665  groupBox.
2666  Set the properties.
2667  Revise the Event handler code.
2668      Don't use semicolons after statements.
2669      Use VB format for declaring variables.
2670      Revise the "if" statements to check "RadioButton"
2671  status.
2672
2673  Run the program.
2674
2675  If you succeeded, Congratulations!!! *IF* you got some
2676  errors that's fine too, you're going to learn even more.
2677  Review!!! Try again.
2678
2679  Just in case you're really stuck, peek into Appendix
2680  A . . . You'll find the VB Code there.
2681
2682  *What's up next . . .*
2683

2684 Now, after a break that is much deserved, we are
2685 going into the issue and process of doing things like
2686 "Looping", "Decision Making" and exiting a process
2687 when it is appropriate. Grab a bite, get a drink, hit
2688 the . . . welll, you know, then come on back!!!
2689

## 2690 **Project 8—Looping, Making decisions**
## 2691 **and exiting**

2692
2693 Often you need to do something over and over until a
2694 certain condition is met, then stop. You've gotten a
2695 little flavor for that using the "if" statement. That does
2696 the job, but you could write literally hundreds of
2697 "if's" in certain circumstances. Why, when there is an
2698 easier way?
2699
2700 An example might be searching a directory file for my
2701 name and telephone number. Another might be to
2702 simply compute a list of numbers and display them.
2703 One key point is knowing when to stop and do
2704 something about certain values.
2705
2706 We are going to start out slow and build. The first
2707 thing is knowing how to get a loop going and how to
2708 exit from the loop at the desired time. Here we go . . .
2709
2710 C#
2711
2712 Start MVS if you closed it earlier.
2713
2714 <Tools> + <Options> + <Projects and Solutions>
2715

2716 Get the location set for the folder you are using for the
2717 project. I will begin skipping this step shortly as you
2718 have seen it several times now. Yeah, I want you to
2719 take the responsibility . . . I'll teach, you . . ., You
2720 learn.
2721
2722 <File> + <New Project>
2723
2724 You know the drill. Make the name meaningful.
2725
2726 Here's the code, you decide the rest meaning controls
2727 and properties.
2728

```
2729 private void btnLoopAndDecide_Click(object sender,
2730 EventArgs e)
2731 {
2732    string myStr = "";
2733    for (int X = 0; X <= 9; X++)
2734    {
2735       myStr = Convert.ToString(X);
2736       textBox1.Text = myStr;
2737       if (X == 8) // if X is equal to 8
2738       {
2739          textBox1.Text = "Loop ended"+" " + "X's
2740          Value was "+ Convert.ToString(X);
2741          break;
2742       }
2743    }
2744 }
```

2745
2746 Again, pay attention to the curly braces. They must
2747 exist in matching sets, and be in the right place.
2748
2749 I am in the habit of adding comments after curly
2750 braces . . . like // End of btnLoopAndDecide event
2751 handler

2752
2753  It helps me avoid errors and find errors when they are
2754  made. Man Oh Man . . . does every little edge add
2755  up!!!
2756
2757  You have seen most of this before. Looping is a
2758  matter of asking a computer to do something
2759  repeatedly, test for a condition that we specify and
2760  stop when the condition is satisfied.
2761
2762  X is a control variable. It's value increases by 1
2763  (X++), in this case, each time the loop executes.
2764  On every loop we check to see if X has reached a
2765  certain limit we specify (if(X==8){do something}.
2766  When X reaches our specification we ask the program
2767  to "Break;" or end the loop and this event handler
2768  returns the last value of X reached during the loop. X
2769  is an integer, we convert it to a string, add
2770  (concatenate) it with a liter string specified with
2771  quotation marks and send the
2772  entire string to the textBox's text property.
2773
2774  If you want to experiment a little, which I encourage,
2775  You can make the Loop increment X by more than 1
2776  each time through the loop. This is done by putting
2777  this in the place of "X++" in the "for statement" . . .
2778  "X += 5", for example. This increments X by 5 on
2779  each pass, instead of 1. Of course you'll need to
2780  increase your Looping maximum value of X to
2781  something larger, say 150, to give the program a little
2782  space to count.ie,
2783

2784  for(X=0;X <= 150;X += 5) . . . will do the job. X <=
2785  150 means that X is "less than or equal to 150".
2786
2787  Your test also needs a little tune up for some room to
2788  run . . .
2789
2790  If (X == 25){do something; Break;}
2791
2792  Do something, in our example, means to convert X to
2793  a string, concatenate it with a literal string and send
2794  the whole resulting string to our textBox's text
2795  property.
2796
2797  Last, we leave the event handler and the user see the
2798  last value of X in the textbox.
2799
2800  That's it . . . a working "for loop".
2801
2802  Now, can you take this example and make a transition
2803  to VB?
2804
2805  Here's a little "Heads up " Visual Basic syntax is a
2806  little different in the use of the "for" statement.
2807
2808  It goes like this . . .
2809
2810  For X = 0 to 20
2811  Do this 'No semicolon
2812  Do this too 'No semicolon
2813      If X >= 20
2814          Do this 'No semicolon
2815          Do this too 'No semicolon
2816      End if

2817 Next X 'No semicolon
2818
2819 Try it and if you get stuck, Check Appendix "B" for
2820 the code.
2821

## 2822 Project 9—Next up . . . "While Loops"
## 2823 and Decision Making

2824
2825 This is a Loop I use over and over when I am working
2826 with files from my hard drive.
2827
2828 You start by "*stating a condition*" and continue
2829 working as long as that condition remains true (2
2830 steps).
2831
2832 The code automatically evaluates the condition every
2833 time it passes through the loop, so you don't have to
2834 worry about testing for it.
2835
2836 The general structure is something like this.
2837
2838 C#

```
2839 Int x = 10;
2840 While (X <= 100)
2841 {
2842     Do this;
2843     X += 10;
2844     // the trade off, your code increments X
2845     // X+=10 increments X by 10 on each pass
2846 }
```

2847
2848 *Note*: Null means without any AlphaNumeric or
2849 Punctuation characters of any kind present.
2850 A "space" is actually a white-space character.

2851
2852  C#
2853
2854  Stretch . . . (Your thinking) a little.
2855
2856  This code excerpt reads strings from a file . . .
2857  "While" it gets a string from the file on it's pass
2858  through the loop, it is happy and keeps going.
2859  At the end of the file, it will get a "null".
2860
2861  Until that point is reached, it reads a string (line)
2862  and displays the string (line) in a messageBox.
2863
2864  At that "null" point we "break" the loop and stop
2865  trying to read more strings.
2866

```csharp
2867  string myStr = " ";
2868      while (myStr!= null)
2869      {
2870          myStr = myRdr.ReadLine();
2871          if (myStr == null)
2872          {
2873              break;
2874          }
2875          MessageBox.Show(myStr);
2876      }
```

2877
2878  For the moment, just grasp the general idea, don't get
2879  hung up on the details of reading a file. At the right
2880  time, we'll get to that.
2881
2882  *"While"* **we have this new idea in mind, let's use it.**
2883
2884  *<Code View Icon>* in Solution explorer or double
2885  click the button in form view. Remember?

```
2886
2887 private void btnLoopWhile_Click(object sender,
2888 EventArgs e)
2889 {
2890     int X;
2891     X = 0;
2892     while (X!= -1)
2893     {
2894         X++;
2895         if (X <= 2) // X is less than or equal to 2
2896         {
2897             MessageBox.Show("X is Not -1 X is " +
2898             Convert.ToString(X));
2899         }
2900         if (X >= 3) // X is Greater than or equal to 3
2901         {
2902             X = -1;
2903             this.Text = "Bye Bye Birdie . . . while
2904             looping is over with.";
2905             this.BackColor = Color.Yellow;
2906             label1.Visible = true;
2907             label1.Text = " I'm outta here!!! ";
2908             MessageBox.Show("X equals -1 I'm breaking
2909             up. " + Convert.ToString(X));
2910         }
2911     }
2912 }
2913
```

**2914 This is quite straight forward with a couple of new**
**2915 twists thrown in for learning new ideas.**

2916

2917 An integer X is declared and assigned a value of "0",
2918 then we start the while loop. On passing through the
2919 loop we increment X until we reach the value of 3.
2920 At that point we re-set X to -1. This causes a violation
2921 of our "while X criteria".

2922

2923 When the code realizes X is now -1, it sends a
2924 different message, Sets the "Form1 text property" to
2925 "Bye, Bye Birdie . . . while looping is over.", changes
2926 the label1 "Visible property" to "true" and it's text
2927 property to "I'm outta here!!!" and we get a
2928 messageBox message saying "Things are breaking up
2929 " etc.
2930
2931 Finally we exit the event handler code and we can
2932 close the program. That's it.
2933
2934 The new part was hiding a label for dramatic effect
2935 until we reached the end of the "While" loop and we
2936 changed the text property of the form itself.
2937 Remember Forms are objects/controls of a sort
2938 themselves and they can be treated as such.
2939
2940 Now for the same exercise in VB.
2941
2942 *VB*
```
2943 Private Sub btnWhileLooping_Click(sender As
2944 System.Object, e As System.EventArgs) Handles
2945 btnWhileLooping.Click
2946    Dim X As Integer = 0
2947    While (X <> -1)
2948    X = X + 1
2949      If (X <= 2) Then ' X is less thanor equal to 2
2950          MessageBox.Show("X is Not -1 X is " +
2951          Convert.ToString(X))
2952      End If
2953      If (X >= 3) Then ' X is Greater than or
2954      equal to 3
2955          X = -1
2956          Me.Text = "Bye Bye Birdie . . . while is
2957          over with."
2958          Me.BackColor = Color.Aqua
2959          Me.Label1.Visible = True
```

```
2960          Me.Label1.Text = " I'm outta here!!! "
2961          MessageBox.Show("X equals -1 I'm breaking
2962          up. " + Convert.ToString(X))
2963     End If
2964   End While
2965 End Sub
```

2966

2967 The explanation is essentially the same with a couple
2968 of syntax adjustments for visual basic and the lack of
2969 the curly braces and semicolons.

2970

2971 An integer X is declared and assigned a value of "0",
2972 then we start the while loop. On passing through the
2973 loop we increment X until we reach the value of 3.
2974 At that point we re-set X to -1. This causes a violation
2975 of our "while X criteria".

2976

2977 When the code realizes X is now -1, it sends a
2978 different message, Sets the "Form1 text property" to
2979 "Bye, Bye Birdie . . . while looping is over.", changes
2980 the label1 "Visible property" to "true" and it's text
2981 property to "I'm outta here!!!" and we get a
2982 messageBox message saying "Things are breaking up
2983 " etc.

2984

2985 Finally we exit the event handler code and we can
2986 close the program. That's it.

2987

2988 The new part was hiding a label for dramatic effect
2989 until we reached the end of the "While" loop and we
2990 changed the text property of the form itself.
2991 Remember Forms are objects/controls of a sort
2992 themselves and they can be treated as such. They have
2993 properties and methods and you can manipulate them.

2994
## 2995 Project 10—Next up . . . "DO Loops"
2996
2997 The do "Do Loop" is very similar to the "While
2998 Loop". The big difference is that the exit condition id
2999 tested for, last, not stated and tested for first.
3000
3001 The general idea id like this . . .
3002
3003 Do this
3004 {
3005     do something
3006     do something else
3007 } check for results to exit on
3008 -or-
3009
3010 Do this
3011 (
3012     do something
3013     do something else
3014 )while the results are this (i.e X is not -1)
3015
3016 Got the idea?? Let's dance!
3017
3018 C#

```
3019 private void btnDoLoop_Click(object sender,
3020 EventArgs e)
3021 {
3022     int X = 0;
3023     string myStr = "";
3024     textBox1.Text = "Here is the looping info . . .";
3025
3026     do
3027     {
3028         X++;
```

```
3029        myStr = myStr + ", " + Convert.ToString(X);
3030     }while (X <= 9);
3031     //
3032     textBox1.Text = textBox1.Text + myStr;
3033     MessageBox.Show("I'm done. Notice that we have
3034     a 10 in the textBox . . . that's because DO
3035     Loops test for the exit condition last. A 10
3036     gets in before the decision to exit is
3037     made.","Do Looping");
3038 }
3039
```

3040 *Note:* The final comma in the messageBox "Show
3041 Method" is followed by a literal string that will
3042 become the title shown inside the messageBox., A
3043 small but, nice thing to do.
3044 *If* I include the *line number* from the *code Editor* in
3045 the title, it becomes a strong aid for *de-bugging*
3046 (trouble shooting) my code. Just a thought!!!
3047

3048 VB
```
3049 Private Sub btnDoLoop_Click(sender As
3050 System.Object, e As System.EventArgs) Handles
3051 btnDoLoop.Click
3052     Dim X As Integer = 0
3053     Dim myStr As String = ""
3054     Do While (X <= 9)
3055        myStr = myStr + Convert.ToString(X) + ", "
3056        X = X + 1
3057     Loop
3058     TextBox1.Text = TextBox1.Text + "Done Looping,
3059     this is what I did . . . " + myStr
3060     MessageBox.Show("My Do loop completed ", "Do
3061     Looping")
3062 End Sub
3063
```

3064 *Note:* The final comma in the messageBox "Show
3065 Method" is followed by a literal string that will

3066 become the title shown inside the messageBox., A
3067 small but, nice thing to do.
3068 *If* I include the *line number* from the *code Editor* in
3069 the title, it becomes a strong aid for *de-bugging*
3070 (trouble shooting) my code.
3071 Just a thought!!!
3072
3073 *Next Up "Switch Case" Decision Making and*
3074 *ListBoxes*
3075
3076 This one takes a little more time and effort.When
3077 you're ready and refreshed let's do it!!!! Tired?
3078 Wait . . . Distracted? Wait!!
3079

# 3080 Project 11—"Switch Case" Decision
# 3081 Making and ListBoxes

3082
3083 OK, Start your engines (Actually MVS will be fine)
3084
3085 You know the routine . . . This is a new project and
3086 we'll start with C# then do VB. Make sure the name
3087 includes "Switch Case" and ListBox.
3088
3089 Some new concepts are going to be applied here, so
3090 take your time, get idea down then get the next one
3091 and we'll reach the target before you know it.
3092
3093 *Add a listBox, Button and textbox* to your form.
3094 Arrange them as you like, set their properties and then
3095 we'll write the code. Remember, NAMES, NAMES,
3096 NAMES!!! Make them meaningful.
3097

3098 Here's a couple of new words for you . . . "Item" &
3099 "Index".
3100
3101 A listBox is a control/Object but it is also like a
3102 variable in some ways. We can store information in a
3103 listBox and it retains the information. In fact, we can
3104 store several "Items" of information in the control and
3105 each one will have an index (Number) that it can be
3106 identified by and referenced by.
3107
3108 The indexes are created automatically and start with
3109 "0" and counted from there by "1's" as you go
3110 through the "Collection" of items for the
3111 Control/Object.
3112
3113 Some "Items" are normally added at design Time and
3114 can be modified at run-Time if we want to do that.
3115 Let's Check this out.
3116
3117 Right Click the listBox and go to the property
3118 window.
3119 Scroll to the "Items" property and notice that it says
3120 "Collection" in the box on the right with an ellipse
3121 ". . ." showing.
3122
3123 <Ellipse ". . .">
3124
3125 Now an editing window appears and ask you to type
3126 in you items, one per line. **Enter** "One","Two",
3127 "Three", "Four" . . . each being followed by <Enter
3128 Key>.
3129

3130 When you click any other property *note* that your
3131 entries now show in the listBox on the design view of
3132 the form. *If* they don't do it again.
3133
3134 Recall that I said we can modify the "Items" with
3135 code. We are going to do that right now.
3136
3137 Double Click a blank spot on your form in the
3138 designer view.
3139
3140 We are immediately taken into a skeletal event
3141 handler for the form . . .in the Form _Load event
3142 handler. Code we place here will execute as soon as
3143 your form starts "Loading" when your program is
3144 executed ("Run").
3145

```
3146 private void Form1_Load(object sender, EventArgs
3147 e) // Skeletal
3148 {// Skeletal
3149    listBox1.Items.Add("A");// We added this code
3150    listBox1.Items.Add("B");// We added this code
3151    listBox1.Items.Add("C");// We added this code
3152    listBox1.Items.Add("D");// We added this code
3153 }// Skeletal
```

3154
3155 **Now we move down into the btnSwitch_click event**
3156 **handler**
3157

```
3158 private void btnSwitch_Click(object sender,
3159 EventArgs e)
3160 {
3161    string myStr1 = "";
3162    string myStr2 = "";
3163    myStr1 = Convert.ToString(listBox1.SelectedIndex);
3164    myStr2 = Convert.ToString(listBox1.SelectedItem);
3165    int intSwitch = Convert.ToInt32(myStr1);
3166       // Space for the Switch-Case Code
```

```
3167            //
3168  }
3169
```

3170  **The listBox we added has some very useful**
3171  **abilities, one being the ability to give us an index**
3172  **telling that selected Item 0, 1,2 3, etc..**
3173
3174  **It can also give us the contents of that item as it**
3175  **appears in the visible list of items. So we declare an**
3176  **integer variable to hold the index and a string**
3177  **variable to hold the item visible contents.**
3178
3179  **Like usual, if we want to display the index as text,**
3180  **we convert it into a string. We declared a second**
3181  **string for that purpose.**
3182
3183  Having captured that information we are ready to use
3184  it to do our Switch-Case function. "Switch-Case" is a
3185  way to make a variety of actions possible for the value
3186  of a given variable i.e. intSwitch in this instance,
3187  without writing a large number of if statements.
3188  Each expected or possible for the value of intSwitch is
3189  a "Case"
3190  And some associated actions to take for that particular
3191  value (Case), should it occur.
3192
3193  We structure the Switch-Case code as follows;
3194

```
3195  switch(intSwitch)
3196  {
3197      case 0:
3198      intSwitch = 0;
3199      textBox1.Text = "From Switch-Case; The number
3200          entered is " + Convert.ToString(intSwitch);
3201      textBox1.Text = textBox1.Text + ". The Item's
```

```
3202          Content is " + myStr2;
3203      break;
3204
3205      case 1:
3206      intSwitch = 1;
3207      textBox1.Text = "From Switch-Case; The number
3208          entered is " + Convert.ToString(intSwitch);
3209      textBox1.Text = textBox1.Text + ". The Item's
3210          Content is " + myStr2;
3211      break;
3212
3213      case 2:
3214      intSwitch = 2;
3215      textBox1.Text = "From Switch-Case; The number
3216          entered is " + Convert.ToString(intSwitch);
3217      textBox1.Text = textBox1.Text + ". The Item's
3218          Content is " + myStr2;
3219      break;
3220
3221      case 3:
3222      intSwitch = 3;
3223      textBox1.Text = "From Switch-Case; The number
3224          entered is " + Convert.ToString(intSwitch);
3225      textBox1.Text = textBox1.Text + ". The Item's
3226          Content is " + myStr2;
3227      break;
3228
3229      case 4:
3230      intSwitch = 4;
3231      textBox1.Text = "From Switch-Case; The number
3232          entered is " + Convert.ToString(intSwitch);
3233      textBox1.Text = textBox1.Text + ". The Item's
3234          Content is " + myStr2;
3235      break;
3236
3237      case 5:
3238      intSwitch = 5;
3239      textBox1.Text = "From Switch-Case; The number
3240          entered is " + Convert.ToString(intSwitch);
3241      textBox1.Text = textBox1.Text + ". The Item's
3242          Content is " + myStr2;
3243      break;
```

```
3244
3245    case 6:
3246    intSwitch = 6;
3247    textBox1.Text = "From Switch-Case; The number
3248        entered is " + Convert.ToString(intSwitch);
3249    textBox1.Text = textBox1.Text + ". The Item's
3250        Content is " + myStr2;
3251    break;
3252
3253    case 7:
3254    intSwitch = 7;
3255    textBox1.Text = "From Switch-Case; The number
3256        entered is " + Convert.ToString(intSwitch);
3257    textBox1.Text = textBox1.Text + ". The Item's
3258        Content is " + myStr2;
3259    break;
3260
3261    case 8:
3262    intSwitch = 8;
3263    textBox1.Text = "From Switch-Case; The number
3264        entered is " + Convert.ToString(intSwitch);
3265    textBox1.Text = textBox1.Text + ". The Item's
3266        Content is " + myStr2;
3267    break;
3268 }
3269
```

3270 **Note: We are still inside the btnSwitch_Click**
3271 **Event handler code and the attending curly braces**
3272 **for that event. But, the Switch-Case routine brings**
3273 **with it it's own set of curly braces.**
3274

3275 **This new block of code "inside" the braces of the**
3276 **btnSwitch_Code event handler block. This is very,**
3277 **very important. The added in block functions as a**
3278 **part of the btnSwitch event handler. You will see**
3279 **this many, many times as you get into more**
3280 **complex programs.**
3281

3282 **One last but important point. If the user clicks the**
3283 **"Switch button" before selecting an item in the**
3284 **listBox, nothing happens . . . The values we need to**
3285 **"Switch" are not available until an item is**
3286 **"Selected" by the user.**
3287
3288 **This can be avoided by placing a label containing**
3289 **user instructions on the form . . . I recommend that**
3290 **you do that.**
3291 *Add* **a label and set the text property to**
3292 **instructions for the user.**
3293
3294 ## VB Select-Case
3295
3296 Instead of "Switch-Case" Visual Basic uses Select-
3297 Case. It does essentially the same job with different
3298 terminology (of course no semicolons)
3299
3300 OK, Start your engines (Actually MVS will be fine)
3301
3302 You know the routine . . . This is a new project and
3303 we'll start with C# then do VB. Make sure the name
3304 includes "Select Case" and ListBox.
3305
3306 Some new concepts are going to be applied here, so
3307 take your time, get idea down then get the next one
3308 and we'll reach the target before you know it.
3309
3310 ***Add a listBox, Button and textbox*** to your form.
3311 Arrange them as you like, set their properties and then
3312 we'll write the code. Remember, NAMES, NAMES,
3313 NAMES!!! Make them meaningful.
3314

3315 Here's a couple of new words for you . . . "Item" &
3316 "Index".
3317
3318 A listBox is a control/Object but it is also like a
3319 variable in some ways. We can store information in a
3320 listBox and it retains the information. In fact, we can
3321 store several "Items" of information in the control and
3322 each one will have an index (Number) that it can be
3323 identified by and referenced by.
3324
3325 The indexes are created automatically and start with
3326 "0" and counted from there by "1's" as you go
3327 through the "Collection" of items for the
3328 Control/Object.
3329
3330 Some "Items" are normally added at design Time and
3331 can be modified at run-Time if we want to do that.
3332 Let's Check this out.
3333
3334 Right Click the listBox and go to the property
3335 window.
3336 Scroll to the "Items" property and notice that it says
3337 "Collection" in the box on the right with an ellipse
3338 ". . ." showing.
3339
3340 <Ellipse ". . .">
3341
3342 Now an editing window appears and ask you to type
3343 in you items, one per line. **Enter** "One","Two",
3344 "Three","Four" . . . each being followed by <Enter
3345 Key>.
3346

3347 When you click any other property **note** that your
3348 entries now show in the listBox on the design view of
3349 the form. **If** they don't do it again.
3350
3351 Recall that I said we can modify the "Items" with
3352 code. We are going to do that right now.
3353
3354 Double Click a blank spot on your form in the
3355 designer view.
3356
3357 We are immediately taken into a skeletal event
3358 handler for the form . . .in the Form _Load event
3359 handler. Code we place here will execute as soon as
3360 your form starts "Loading" when your program is
3361 executed ("Run").
3362
```
3363 private void Form1_Load(object sender, EventArgs
3364 e) // Skeletal
3365     ' Skeletal
3366     listBox1.Items.Add("A")' We added this code
3367     listBox1.Items.Add("B")' We added this code
3368     listBox1.Items.Add("C")' We added this code
3369     listBox1.Items.Add("D")' We added this code
3370     ' Skeletal
```
3371
**3372 Now we move down into the btnSelect_click event**
**3373 handler**
3374
```
3375 private void btnSelect_Click(object sender,
3376 EventArgs e)
3377     string myStr1 = ""
3378     string myStr2 = ""
3379     myStr1 = Convert.ToString(listBox1.SelectedIndex)
3380     myStr2 = Convert.ToString(listBox1.SelectedItem)
3381     int intSelect = Convert.ToInt32(myStr1)
3382         ' Space for the Select-Case Code
3383         '
```

3384
3385 **The listBox we added has some very useful**
3386 **abilities, one being the ability to give us an index**
3387 **telling that selected Item 0, 1,2 3, etc..**
3388
3389 **It can also give us the contents of that item as it**
3390 **appears in the visible list of items. So we declare an**
3391 **integer variable to hold the index and a string**
3392 **variable to hold the item visible contents.**
3393
3394 **Like usual, if we want to display the index as text,**
3395 **we convert it into a string. We declared a second**
3396 **string for that purpose.**
3397
3398 Having captured that information we are ready to use
3399 it to do our Select-Case function. "Select-Case" is a
3400 way to make a variety of actions possible for the value
3401 of a given variable i.e. intSelect in this instance,
3402 without writing a large number of if statements.
3403 Each expected or possible for the value of intSelect is
3404 a "Case"
3405 And some associated actions to take for that particular
3406 value (Case), should it occur.
3407
3408 We structure the Select-Case code as follows;
3409
3410 OK, Start your engines (Actually MVS will be fine)
3411
3412 You know the routine . . . This is a new project and
3413 we'll start with C# then do VB. Make sure the name
3414 includes "Select Case" and ListBox.
3415

3416 Some new concepts are going to be applied here, so
3417 take your time, get idea down then get the next one
3418 and we'll reach the target before you know it.
3419
3420 ***Add a listBox, Button and textbox*** to your form.
3421 Arrange them as you like, set their properties and then
3422 we'll write the code. Remember, NAMES, NAMES,
3423 NAMES!!! Make them meaningful.
3424
3425 Here's a couple of new words for you . . . "Item" &
3426 "Index".
3427
3428 A listBox is a control/Object but it is also like a
3429 variable in some ways. We can store information in a
3430 listBox and it retains the information. In fact, we can
3431 store several "Items" of information in the control and
3432 each one will have an index (Number) that it can be
3433 identified by and referenced by.
3434
3435 The indexes are created automatically and start with
3436 "0" and counted from there by "1's" as you go
3437 through the "Collection" of items for the
3438 Control/Object.
3439
3440 Some "Items" are normally added at design Time and
3441 can be modified at run-Time if we want to do that.
3442 Let's Check this out.
3443
3444 Right Click the listBox and go to the property
3445 window.
3446 Scroll to the "Items" property and notice that it says
3447 "Collection" in the box on the right with an ellipse
3448 ". . ." showing.

3449
3450  <Ellipse ". . .">
3451
3452  Now an editing window appears and ask you to type
3453  in you items, one per line. ***Enter*** "1", "2", "3", "4" . . .
3454  each being followed by <Enter Key>.
3455
3456  When you click any other property ***note*** that your
3457  entries now show in the listBox on the design view of
3458  the form. ***If*** they don't do it again.
3459
3460  Recall that I said we can modify the "Items" with
3461  code. We are going to do that right now.
3462
3463  Double Click a blank spot on your form in the
3464  designer view.
3465
3466  We are immediately taken into a skeletal event
3467  handler for the form . . .in the Form _Load event
3468  handler. Code we place here will execute as soon as
3469  your form starts "Loading" when your program is
3470  executed ("Run").
3471

```
3472  private void Form1_Load(object sender, EventArgs
3473  e) // Skeletal
3474     ' Skeletal
3475     listBox1.Items.Add("A");// We added this code
3476     listBox1.Items.Add("B");// We added this code
3477     listBox1.Items.Add("C");// We added this code
3478     listBox1.Items.Add("D");// We added this code
3479     ' Skeletal
```

3480
3481  **Now we move down into the btnSelect_click event**
3482  **handler**
3483

```
3484 private void btnSelect_Click(object sender,
3485 EventArgs e)
3486    Dim myStr1 as string = ""
3487    Dim myStr2 as string = ""
3488    myStr1 = Convert.ToString(listBox1.SelectedIndex)
3489    myStr2 = Convert.ToString(listBox1.SelectedItem)
3490    Dim intSelect as integer = Convert.ToInt32(myStr1)
3491       // Space for the Select-Case Code
3492       //
3493
```

3494 **The listBox we added has some very useful**
3495 **abilities, one being the ability to give us an index**
3496 **telling that selected Item 0, 1,2 3, etc.**
3497

3498 **It can also give us the contents of that item as it**
3499 **appears in the visible list of items. So we declare an**
3500 **integer variable to hold the index and a string**
3501 **variable to hold the item visible contents.**
3502

3503 **Like usual, if we want to display the index as text,**
3504 **we convert it into a string. We declared a second**
3505 **string for that purpose.**
3506

3507 Having captured that information we are ready to use
3508 it to do our Select-Case function. "Select-Case" is a
3509 way to make a variety of actions possible for the value
3510 of a given variable i.e. intSelect in this instance,
3511 without writing a large number of if statements.
3512 Each expected or possible for the value of intSelect is
3513 a "Case"
3514 And some associated actions to take for that particular
3515 value (Case), should it occur.
3516

3517 We structure the Select-Case code as follows;
3518

```
3519 Private Sub btnSelect_Click(sender As
3520 System.Object, e As System.EventArgs) Handles
3521 btnSelect.Click
3522    Dim intSelect As Integer
3523    Dim myStr1 As String = ""
3524    Dim myStr2 As String = ""
3525    intSelect = ListBox1.SelectedIndex
3526    myStr1 = Convert.ToString(intSelect)
3527    myStr2 = ListBox1.SelectedItem
3528    ''
3529    intSelect = Convert.ToInt32(myStr1)
3530    Select Case intSelect
3531       Case 0
3532          intSelect = 0
3533          TextBox1.Text = "From Select-Case; The
3534 number entered is " + Convert.ToString(intSelect)
3535          TextBox1.Text = TextBox1.Text + ". The
3536 Item's Content is " + myStr2
3537       Case 1
3538          TextBox1.Text = "From Select-Case; The
3539 number entered is " + Convert.ToString(intSelect)
3540          TextBox1.Text = TextBox1.Text + ". The
3541 Item's Content is " + myStr2
3542       Case 2
3543          TextBox1.Text = "From Select-Case; The
3544 number entered is " + Convert.ToString(intSelect)
3545          TextBox1.Text = TextBox1.Text + ". The
3546 Item's Content is " + myStr2
3547       Case 3
3548          TextBox1.Text = "From Select-Case; The
3549 number entered is " + Convert.ToString(intSelect)
3550          TextBox1.Text = TextBox1.Text + ". The
3551 Item's Content is " + myStr2
3552          ''
3553       Case 4
3554          TextBox1.Text = "From Select-Case; The
3555 number entered is " + Convert.ToString(intSelect)
3556          TextBox1.Text = TextBox1.Text + ". The
3557 Item's Content is " + myStr2
3558       Case 5
3559          TextBox1.Text = "From Select-Case; The
3560 number entered is " + Convert.ToString(intSelect)
```

```
3561            TextBox1.Text = TextBox1.Text + ". The
3562 Item's Content is " + myStr2
3563      Case 6
3564            TextBox1.Text = "From Select-Case; The
3565 number entered is " + Convert.ToString(intSelect)
3566            TextBox1.Text = TextBox1.Text + ". The
3567 Item's Content is " + myStr2
3568      Case 7
3569            TextBox1.Text = "From Select-Case; The
3570 number entered is " + Convert.ToString(intSelect)
3571            TextBox1.Text = TextBox1.Text + ". The
3572 Item's Content is " + myStr2
3573    End Select
3574
```

3575 **Note: We are still inside the btnSelect_Click Event**
3576 **handler code and the attending Sub-End Sub**
3577 **phrases for that event. But, the Select-Case routine**
3578 **consists of it's own block of code.**
3579
3580 **This new block of code is "inside" the Sub-End**
3581 **Sub phrases of the btnSelect_Code event handler**
3582 **block. This is very, very important. The added in**
3583 **block functions as a part of the btnSelect event**
3584 **handler. You will see this many, many times as you**
3585 **get into more complex programs.**
3586
3587 **One last but important point. If the user clicks the**
3588 **"Select button" before selecting an item in the**
3589 **listBox, nothing happens . . . The values we need to**
3590 **"Select" are not available until an item is**
3591 **"Selected" by the user.**
3592
3593 **This can be avoided by placing a label containing**
3594 **user instructions on the form . . . I recommend that**
3595 **you do that.**

3596 *Add* a label and set the text property to
3597 instructions for the user.
3598
3599 On the property window for a labels text property
3600 *note* the arrow or ellipse to the far right. The Item
3601 will pop-up a small editing window. Enter your
3602 comments in the editing window. It's much easier
3603 that way.
3604
3605 *Next Up . . .Methods and Functions & arithmetic . . .*
3606 *creating, calling and passing "parameters"*
3607
3608 **Take a break** . . . get refreshed and come on back
3609 when you're ready.
3610

# 3611 Project 12—Methods and Functions &
# 3612 arithmetic . . . creating, calling and
# 3613 passing "parameters"

3614
3615 *DoAddition() Method*
3616
3617 Oh boy!! How may ways can you skin a cat? Well, it
3618 depends . . . only one if you have just one cat. Why
3619 limit yourself?
3620
3621 A method is a way to maximize the use of code that
3622 does something that needs to be done more than once.
3623 For example . . . adding a couple of numbers
3624 perchance even three numbers.
3625
3626 I can write . . . Add number one and number two and
3627 tell me the results as many times as I want -or-

3628

3629 I can write "Do Addition . . .here are two numbers"

3630 "Do Addition" . . . would be called a "method".

3631 Number one and Number two would be called

3632 "Parameters". I pass the "Method" my "Parameters"

3633 and wait for the results.

3634

3635 This is said to be "Calling a Method". In essence . . . I

3636 have created my own C# or Visual Basic command.

3637

3638 Got the idea? Let's check it out. We'll need a new

3639 project and some controls . . . ***Add three textboxes, a***

3640 ***button*** and as many labels as you like to explain to the

3641 user what to do.(Yeah, I expect "you" to be able to do

3642 that now.) ***IF*** you can't remember how.. ***Review!!!***

3643 ***Names are important!!!! Name the button***

3644 ***"btnDoAddition".***

3645

3646 Get into the btnDoAddition's click_event handler

3647 code.

3648

3649 Create some variables . . . Integer Number1, Integer

3650 Number2, Integer Number3 and integer IntAnswer.

3651 This time put the integer declarations way up on the

3652 screen . . . Just after the "initialize component"

3653 closing curly brace.

3654 Also ***prefix*** the declaration for each integer with the

3655 word "***public***". This makes the variables available for

3656 use within any events or methods, anywhere in the

3657 program.

3658

3659 If we used "***private***" and placed them inside the event

3660 handler . . .

3661 They would be "Local in Scope" . . .i.e. available only
3662 inside that specific event handler block of code.
3663
3664 That would become tedious if we created another
3665 method for doing Subtraction or Division or whatever.
3666 Public variables are also called universal or global
3667 variables sometimes.
3668
3669 Now let's create our Method "DoAddition".
3670
3671 We are going to put it outside the btnDoAddition's
3672 event handler's just after closing curly brace for the
3673 click event handler.
3674
3675 In fact, we are going to make a slightly different
3676 version also called DoAddition also and put them
3677 together (Close by each other).
3678
3679 Here's why.
3680
3681 Suppose the user wants to add three numbers instead
3682 of just two.
3683 We need a method that meets that need. Not a
3684 problem we just "Overload" our method i.e. use the
3685 same name but make a version able to add three
3686 numbers.
3687
3688 I mentioned "Parameters" earlier. When we call a
3689 method, we "pass" some information to the method to
3690 accomplish it's task with. In this case, numbers
3691 (integers).
3692

3693  We "Call" the method by typing it's name followed
3694  by Parentheses containing the Parameters i.e.
3695
3696  DoAddition(intNumber1, intnumber 2)
3697  -or-
3698  DoAddition(intNumber1, intnumber 2, intNumber3)
3699
3700  Our program looks for a version of the DoAddition
3701  method that has the same number of Parameters
3702  ("*Signature*") as the Number of Parameters we pass
3703  during our "Call" command.
3704
3705  In case the user wants the possibility of adding three
3706  numbers we need to accommodate them. If the user
3707  wants to add more than two numbers? we'll we add a
3708  third textbox and we add another integer, no problem.
3709  But if the use leaves the $3^{rd}$ box blank . . . we have a
3710  situation our code doesn't understand,
3711
3712  There are several ways to address this . . . you have to
3713  decide which is best for the situation. One way is to
3714  declare default values for every integer. Another is to
3715  check to see if the third textbox has anything entered
3716  in it.
3717
3718  For the purpose of learning, I chose the second. Our
3719  code will determine if the user wants two or three
3720  numbers added and send the work to the right version
3721  of our DoAddition method.
3722
3723  C#
```
3724  using System;
3725  using System.Collections.Generic;
3726  using System.ComponentModel;
```

```
3727 using System.Data;
3728 using System.Drawing;
3729 using System.Linq;
3730 using System.Text;
3731 using System.Windows.Forms;
3732
3733 namespace CS_Do_Addition_Method
3734 {
3735    public partial class Form1: Form
3736    {
3737       public Form1()
3738       {
3739          InitializeComponent();
3740       }
3741       public int intNumber1 = 0;
3742       public int intNumber2 = 0;
3743       public int intNumber3 = 0; // for the 3rd box
3744       public int intAnswer = 0;
3745       //
3746       public void btnDoAddition_Click(object
3747       sender, EventArgs e)
3748       {
3749          intNumber1 =
3750 Convert.ToInt32(txtBoxNum1.Text);
3751          intNumber2 =
3752 Convert.ToInt32(txtBoxNum2.Text);
3753          //
3754          if (txtBoxNum3.Text == "") // not a 3rd
3755 number
3756          {
3757             DoAddition(intNumber1, intNumber2);
3758          }
3759          if (txtBoxNum3.Text!= "") // Is a 3rd
3760 number
3761          {
3762             intNumber3 =
3763 Convert.ToInt32(txtBoxNum3.Text);
3764             DoAddition(intNumber1, intNumber2,
3765 intNumber3);
3766          }
3767       }
3768       // DoAddition Method & Overload//
```

```
3769        //
3770        // Our method must be prepared to accept
3771           parameters
3772        //
3773        // When we typed
3774           DoAddition(intNumber1,intNumber2),
3775        // our code transferred the value of those
3776           integer variables
3777        // to the variables declared in the first
3778           line of our method
3779        // intNum1, intNum2.
3780        //
3781        // Now, the method has the information
3782           needed to do the
3783        // work expected of it.
3784        // The same explanation applies to our
3785           "overloaded"
3786        // method which handles 3 numbers.
3787        //
3788        // The word "void" means that everything
3789           that needs doing
3790        // is going to be done right here. We don't
3791           get an answer
3792        // and send it someplace else in the
3793           program.
3794        // It stays here and shows in the
3795           textBoxAnswer!!
3796        //
3797        public void DoAddition(int intNum1, int
3798 intNum2)
3799        {
3800            intAnswer = intNumber1 + intNumber2;
3801            txtBoxAnswer.Text =
3802 Convert.ToString(intAnswer);
3803        }//end DoAddition with 2 numbers
3804        //
3805        public void DoAddition(int intNum1, int
3806        intNum2, int intNum3)
3807        {
3808            intAnswer = intNumber1 + intNumber2 +
3809 intNum3;
```

```
3810            txtBoxAnswer.Text =
3811 Convert.ToString(intAnswer);
3812       }//end DoAddition with 3 numbers
3813    }// End doAddition & Overload
3814 }// End Code
3815
```

3816 Run your program and keep up with what's going on
3817 in your mind.
3818 Have a problem?? Review!!!
3819

## 3820 Project 13—Next up . . . .Functions
## 3821 "DoSubtraction"
3822

3823 A "Function" is similar to a method, but it returns a
3824 value to the command that called it. It doesn't keep
3825 the information and do anything with it, it sends back
3826 the answer.
3827

3828 A call for a function must include a variable to receive
3829 the value the function sends back as well as
3830 Parameters to do the work we want done.
3831

3832 A function call looks like this . . .
3833

3834 myIntVarAns = doSubtraction (Num1,Num2);
3835

3836 Now, IntVarAns contains a number calculated by the
3837 function.
3838 I can do whatever I want with the answer.
3839

3840 Let's build a function.
3841

3842 *The doSubtraction function*
3843

3844  This is very much like Method doAddition.

3845

3846  Variables are declared up-top in the code file and
3847  given a "public" prefix. We protect ourselves again
3848  the user leaving blank textboxes using "if" to test for
3849  contents. If we find blanks we assign default values to
3850  the variables.

3851

3852  The doSubtraction function is declared as a public
3853  integer function with two anticipated parameters
3854  i.e.Outside the event handler for the
3855  btnDoSubtraction_click event.

3856

3857  The two significant differences are that we declare an
3858  integer function because it "returns" an integer as the
3859  answer. We use the return statement to cause it to
3860  send our answer back to our call. Nothing else is done
3861  with the answer inside the function.

3862

3863  Here is the complete code . . . by now you are able to
3864  decipher it for yourself with very little help. *If* not,
3865  *Review*!!!

3866

3867  C#
3868  using System;
3869  using System.Collections.Generic;
3870  using System.ComponentModel;
3871  using System.Data;
3872  using System.Drawing;
3873  using System.Linq;
3874  using System.Text;
3875  using System.Windows.Forms;
3876
3877  namespace CS_Function_doSubtraction
3878  {
3879      public partial class Form1: Form

```
3880     {
3881         public Form1()
3882         {
3883             InitializeComponent();
3884         }
3885         public int intNum1 = 0;
3886         public int intNum2 = 0;
3887         public int intAnswer = 0;
3888
3889         private void btndoSubtraction_Click(object
3890 sender, EventArgs e)
3891         {
3892             if (textBox1.Text!= "")
3893             {intNum1 =
3894 Convert.ToInt32(textBox1.Text);}
3895             if (textBox1.Text == "") {intNum1 =
3896 1000;}
3897             //
3898             if (textBox2.Text!= "") {intNum2 =
3899 Convert.ToInt32(textBox2.Text);}
3900             if (textBox2.Text == "") {intNum2 = 1;}
3901             //
3902             intAnswer =
3903 doSubtraction(intNum1,intNum2);
3904             textBox3.Text =
3905 Convert.ToString(intAnswer);
3906         }
3907         public int doSubtraction(int int1, int int2)
3908         {
3909             intAnswer = int1-int2;
3910             return intAnswer;
3911         }
3912     }
3913 }
3914
3915 VB
3916
```

3917 *Note:* With Visual Basic we do *not* have to *declare*
3918 the function as *integer* it is inferred by the type
3919 variables in the first line of the declaration and the

3920 **type of value it is asked to return Since it is**
3921 **"public" it can be called from any place in the**
3922 **class's (form's) code.**
3923
3924 **You have seen all of this code before, but take your**
3925 **time and fully understand what is happening.**
3926
3927 **If you don't, review!!!**

```
3928 Public Class Form1
3929     Dim intNumber1 As Integer = 0
3930     Dim intNumber2 As Integer = 0
3931     Dim intAnswer As Integer = 0
3932
3933     Private Sub Button1_Click(sender As
3934 System.Object, e As System.EventArgs) Handles
3935 Button1.Click
3936
3937         If (TextBox1.Text <> "") Then
3938           ' <>means does NOT equal
3939           intNumber1 =
3940           Convert.ToString(TextBox1.Text)
3941         End If
3942         '
3943         If (TextBox1.Text = "") Then
3944             intNumber1 = 1000
3945         End If
3946         '---
3947         If (TextBox2.Text <> "") Then
3948         intNumber2 = Convert.ToString(TextBox2.Text)
3949         End If
3950         '--
3951         If (TextBox2.Text = "") Then
3952             intNumber2 = 1
3953         End If
3954         '- Call the function
3955         intAnswer = doSubtraction(intNumber1,
3956 intNumber2)
3957         '-Convert the answer to a string and display
3958         Dim myStr As String =
3959 Convert.ToString(intAnswer)
```

```
3960            TextBox3.Text = myStr
3961      End Sub
3962      '--
3963      Public Function doSubtraction(intNum1 As
3964 Integer, Intnum2 As Integer)
3965          intAnswer = intNum1–intNum2
3966          Return intAnswer
3967      End Function
3968 End Class
3969
```

**Other math functions are done the same way with different operands (\* for multiple, / for divide etc.)**

One operation you might not be familiar with is *"**Modulus Division** ".* The type of division you usually see is Eucleadian division i.e. 4 / 2 = 2. The symbol for this Modulus division is "%" for c# and "Mod" for VB. This is where you divide some number by another and get the remainder for an answer, i.e. 10 % 4 = 2 plus a remainder of 2, which is the answer you see. Yes, there is a need for this.Suppose you were give the year s a date of 2049 . . . and asked whether it is a leap year or not. 2049 % 4 = 512 plus a remainder of 1. Therefore it is not a leap year. By contrast if give 2048 and I do modulus divesion 2048 % 4= 512 no remainder so it is a leap year.

*Next Up* . . . **File Operations**

# Project 14—File Operations; Reading, Writing, Appending.

3993 This is much easier than you might expect. Pay
3994 attention to details, that's where the Devil lives.
3995
3996 Files are information storage arrangements on
3997 your computer's hard drive.The information is
3998 stored there permanently or at least until we
3999 decide to modify it or erase it or the hard drive
4000 crashes and destroys it.
4001 Yep, it happens.
4002
4003 There are two basic types of files. Text and Binary.
4004 In this book we will deal only with text files, files
4005 that contain alphanumeric characters. Binary files
4006 are more complex and are used in applications like
4007 spread sheets and such.
4008
4009 Think of files as containers for row after row (or
4010 line after line) of characters (or strings). Our job is
4011 to put information in (write), take information out
4012 (read) or modify information.
4013
4014 Of course, we could also delete the entire file or
4015 create a new one if we needed to do that.
4016
4017 A file is kept in a folder on the hard rive, perhaps
4018 in a sub-folder of a folder . . .or sub-folder of a
4019 sub-folder . . .etc etc.
4020 Finally arriving at the correct folder-subfolder . . .
4021 we see the file.
4022
4023 It has a name and a suffix that designates the type
4024 of file it is . . . i.e. txt for text, like this,
4025 "myFile.txt".

4026
4027 **The complete name (path) of a file consists of the**
4028 **drive letter, the folder in a sequence separated by a**
4029 **backslash "\" the folders and sub-folders separated**
4030 **by backslashes and the file name, a dot "." and**
4031 **finally the suffix (txt).**
4032
4033 *i.e. "C:\myfolder\my sub-folder\sub-sub folder\file*
4034 *name.txt"*
4035
4036 *You must know this "EXACT" information to access*
4037 *the folder for any reason, in your code.*
4038
4039 Special objects are used to access a file. They are not
4040 visible to a user, only to the code. They are called
4041 "*StreamReader*" and "*StreamWriter*" objects (others
4042 exist, we are using these two).
4043
4044 *C# Declaration . . .* looks like this
4045
```
4046 strPath = "C:\\App Target Files\\ToDo.txt"
4047 //
4048 StreamReader mySR = new StreamReader(strPath);
4049 // for reading a file
```
4050
4051 **The declaration goes inside, for example, the**
4052 **btnReadFile_ Click event handler code.**
4053
4054 **Of course, this requires that there be a file to read.**
4055 **You can create a file using Windows notepad.**
4056
4057 **<start><all progams><notepad>**
4058 **Type in a few items, one per line and save the file**
4059 **as "ToDo"**

4060 **in the App Target Files Folder you created.**
4061 **Be sure there are no blank lines in the file, either at**
4062 **the top of the list or, between items.**
4063
4064 **Hit <Enter> after each item,** *including the last one.*
4065
4066 *For example "Acceptable";*
4067 **Pay bills**
4068 **Food shopping**
4069 **Drop off dry cleaning**
4070 **(Etc, etc)**
4071
4072 *For example "un-Acceptable";*
4073 **Pay bills**
4074 **Food shopping**
4075
4076 **Drop off dry cleaning**
4077 **(Etc, etc)**
4078
4079 **we read a line (string) by this command . . .**
4080
4081 `str myLine = myReader.ReadLine();`
4082
4083 **As each line is read we need to decide what to do**
4084 **with it and where to keep it or display it, like any**
4085 **other string.**
4086
4087 **When the file has been read (a null string is**
4088 **found) . . . we need to "close" the StreamReader**
4089 **and "dispose" of it for several reasons.**
4090
4091 One is to free up the computer's resources another is
4092 to release the StreamReader's ownership of the file. It

4093 cannot be opened by other Objects while we are
4094 "Reading" the file. There are exceptions, but this is
4095 the preferred rule.
4096
4097 We declared and the initialized the StreamReader
4098 using two steps. Note the use of the "*New*" word
4099 when we initialize.
4100 We are creating "instantiating" a copy of an object
4101 that is defined in the Mircosoft.net frame work
4102 library, a "*New*" one.
4103 We are setting one of it's properties by telling it the
4104 "*Path*" to the file we want to read.
4105
4106 File content's are being put into a comboBox
4107 control/Object. Think of it as a cross between a
4108 textbox and listBox.
4109
4110 Here's the completed code.
4111
4112 C#

```
4113 public void btnShow_Click(object sender, EventArgs e)
4114 {
4115     str myStr = " "; // Note the spaces in myStr
4116     // This prevents the code from seeing myStr as
4117     // empty (null) at the beginning of the while
4118         loop.
4119     //
4120     str myPath = "C:\\App Target Files\\ToDo.txt""
4121     // Declare a StreamReader
4122     StreamReader mySR;
4123     //
4124     // Initialze the StreamReader
4125     mySR = new StreamReader(myPath);
4126     // Clear the comboBox
4127     comboBoxToDo.Items.Clear();
4128     //
4129     // Read lines for the file the file, stop
```

```
4130     // when the end is reached.
4131     while ((myStr = mySR.ReadLine())!= null)
4132     {
4133        // Add the line to the comboBox
4134        comboBoxToDo.Items.Add(myStr);
4135     }
4136     // Release the file and resources
4137     mySR.Close();
4138     mySR.Dispose();
4139 } //end btnShow_click
4140
```

4141 That's it. We read a file and displayed it's contents.
4142 Error's??? Yeah, *REVIEW*!!!

4143

4144 *Lions, Tiger and Bears, Oh My!!!*
4145 **I know, but remember, I raised five kids.**

4146

4147 **Convert the file reading code to a Visual Basic**
4148 **version. You're up to it. Stretch, Do it!!!!! Get**
4149 **stuck, See appendix "C".**

4150

4151 *Next up . . . Writing to a file.*

4152

4153 **Files aren't much good unless you can put things**
4154 **into them.**
4155 **That's called, "Writing" to a file.**

4156

4157 **Here we go.**

4158

4159 **New project? Up to you. You can either do a new**
4160 **project or incorporate writ a file into the project**
4161 **where you read files. Your choice. Of course, you**
4162 **could do both.**

4163

4164 **Either way, you need some controls for getting**
4165 **user input (things to write to the file) a button to**
4166 **call the File writing routine . . . and some way to**
4167 **tell the user that the job was completed.** *Decide*
4168 **how you want to do that.**
4169
4170 **Hmmm . . . .,**
4171 **This guy is asking more and more from you.**
4172 **Surprised??**
4173 **Well, that's programming. Deciding "What to do",**
4174 **then "How to do", then "Doing it", testing it and**
4175 **making it work.**
4176 **I'll teach, but you gotta do the learning and it's not**
4177 **a passive process. Get started . . . time's a wasting,**
4178 **users (and clients) are waiting.**
4179
4180 *C# Writing to Files*
4181
4182 **Files aren't much good unless you can put things**
4183 **into them.**
4184 **That's called, "Writing" to a file.**
4185
4186 **Here we go.**
4187
4188 **New project? Up to you. You can either do a new**
4189 **project or incorporate writ a file into the project**
4190 **where you read files. Your choice. Of course, you**
4191 **could do both.**
4192
4193 **Either way, you need some controls for getting**
4194 **user input (things to write to the file) a button to**
4195 **call the File writing routine . . . and some way to**

4196 tell the user that the job was completed. *Decide*
4197 how you want to do that.
4198
4199 Hmmm . . . .,
4200 This guy is asking more and more from you.
4201 Surprised??
4202 Well, that's programming. Deciding "What to do",
4203 then "How to do", then "Doing it", testing it and
4204 making it work.
4205 I'll teach, but you gotta do the learning and it's not
4206 a passive process. Get started . . . time's a wasting,
4207 users (and clients) are waiting.
4208
4209 First . . . The user needs a way to tell us they want
4210 to save "something" to a file.
4211
4212 Second . . . the user need's some place to enter the
4213 information to be save in a file.
4214
4215 Third . . . we need to collect the information, then
4216
4217 Fourth, Save it in the file, then,
4218
4219 Fifth . . . tell them it was saved and
4220
4221 Sixth . . . show them it was saved.
4222
4223 This means four controls/objects at least, two
4224 "events" and two code blocks (event handlers).
4225 Make some decisions! Then, write some code.
4226
```
4227 public void btnAddItem_Click(object sender,
4228 EventArgs e)
4229 {
```

```
4230      txtBoxToDo.Text = "";
4231      txtBoxToDo.Visible = true;
4232      // No need to be visible, until needed for input
4233      txtBoxToDo.Focus();
4234      // Focus puts the cursor in that control
4235      // ready to type input
4236      btnSaveItem.Visible = true;
4237      // not needed until the user
4238      // is ready to type input
4239      myStr = txtBoxToDo.Text;
4240 }// end BtnAddItem_Click
4241
```

## 4242 Now that we have the user's input, we save it.

```
4243
4244 private void btnSaveInfo_Click(object sender,
4245 EventArgs e)
4246 {
4247      SetMyCustomFormat();
4248      // date selected variables declared
4249      mySeekDay = " ";
4250      mySeekMo = " ";
4251      mySeekYr = " ";
4252      mySeekDateFinal = " ";
4253      //Get the Date from the DatePicker
4254      DateTime mySaveDate =
4255 Convert.ToDateTime(dateTimePicker1.Text);
4256      intIdxItemFound = 0;
4257      //populate selected date variables
4258      mySeekDay = Convert.ToString(mySaveDate.Day);
4259      mySeekMo = Convert.ToString(mySaveDate.Month);
4260      mySeekYr = Convert.ToString(mySaveDate.Year);
4261      // prefix "0" to single digit days and month
4262 strings
4263      int intLenMo = mySeekMo.Length;
4264      if (intLenMo == 1)
4265      {
4266          mySeekMo = "0" + mySeekMo;
4267      }
4268      int intLenDay = mySeekDay.Length;
4269      if (intLenDay == 1)
4270      {
```

```
4271          mySeekDay = "0" + mySeekDay;
4272      }
4273      //Define the date to save string
4274      string myDateToSave = mySeekMo + "/" +
4275  mySeekDay + "/" + mySeekYr;
4276      //define the string to save
4277      string myStringToSave = myStrDate + " " +
4278  txtBoxAddInfo.Text;
4279      // define the streamReader
4280      StreamReader mySr = new StreamReader("C:\\App
4281  Target Files\\BlockedDates.txt");
4282      // Read list of blocked dates
4283      string myStrBlockedDate = "XX";//avoid an empty
4284  string to start with
4285      while (myStrBlockedDate!= "" &&
4286  myStrBlockedDate!=null)
4287      {
4288          myStrBlockedDate = mySr.ReadLine();
4289          // End when string read is empty
4290          if (myDateToSave == "" || myStrBlockedDate
4291  == null)
4292          {
4293              //release streamReader and File
4294              mySr.Close();
4295              mySr.Dispose();
4296              break;
4297          }
4298      }
4299      //
4300      // if Date selected is not matched to a blocked
4301  date save
4302      // the item
4303      if (myDateToSave!= myStrBlockedDate)
4304      {
4305          StreamWriter myWrt = new
4306  StreamWriter("C:\\App
4307          Target Files\\ToDo.txt", true);
4308          // MessageBox.Show(myStrToSave);
4309          myWrt.WriteLine(myStringToSave);
4310          // release streamwriter & File
4311          myWrt.Close();
4312          myWrt.Dispose();
```

```
4313    }
4314    if (myDateToSave == myStrBlockedDate)
4315    {
4316        MessageBox.Show("This is a blocked date. ","
4317 Blocked
4318        Date vs Save");
4319        txtBoxAddInfo.Text = "";
4320        // cannot save to blocked date, return to
4321 user screen
4322        return;
4323    }
4324    // re-set add info textbox to empty
4325    txtBoxAddInfo.Text = "";
4326    listBox1.Sorted = true;
4327    listBox1.Visible = true;
4328    //re-load ToDo Items file
4329    btnLoadToDoItems.PerformClick();
4330 }// End SaveInfo
4331
```

4332 ***Next Up:*** Files . . . Read, Write, Append, Delete

4333

4334 OK, that's writing/Saving items to a file. But what if
4335 you want to "delete " something that's already in the
4336 file? Any ideas??

4337

4338 There are times when you tear down what's "there"
4339 and build what you want to be "there". So you pick
4340 out what you want to keep, store it temporarily, tear
4341 down the old and build the new.

4342

4343 Here's what's needed . . .

4344

4345 Hint: "Items", "listBoxes" have "Items"!!!

4346

4347 Knowing which "items" to delete, which to keep.
4348 Where to put the Keepers" temporarily.
4349 Re-storing the file, the way you want it.

4350  Showing your results.
4351
4352  Here's what we are going to do.
4353
4354  Create a new project, add controls to our form, let the
4355  user see what's in the file, then, use control to tell us
4356  what to delete, do the deletion and show our results.
4357
4358  We will "ListBox"controls as the focus of the user
4359  interface.
4360  First we'll open the current file, read it and display the
4361  contents in one listbox, ask the user to highlight
4362  (select) the item to delete, store the "Keeper items" in
4363  a second list box and delete the old file. Of course, the
4364  listBox with the old list of "Items" has to be
4365  "Cleared" of the old "Item".
4366
4367  Next, we will read each "Keeper" item from the
4368  second listBox and write a new file with the "Keeper"
4369  items in the file.
4370
4371  Last, we will show the user the results.
4372
4373  ListBoxes are ideal for this application because the
4374  user simply Clicks the item to delete and we can get
4375  the information easily from the Index of the Item as
4376  well as the Item's contents. Remember that indexes
4377  are number "0" to . . .whatever.
4378
4379  So . . . Create a new project, choose the language and
4380  location options and give the project a meaningful
4381  name.
4382

4383  Something like . . .
4384
4385  "VB ListBox File Read Write Append Delete Proj"
4386  -or-
4387  "CS ListBox File Read Write Append Delete Proj"
4388
4389  Add two (2) ListBoxes, One (1) textbox and three (3)
4390  buttons to the form . . . Labels as you like, set
4391  properties and *Let's write Code*. One label should
4392  instruct the user as to "What to do".
4393
4394  As implied the suggested project names imply, the
4395  user can see, Add and Delete file information.
4396
4397  Once again . . . ***Make Decisions*** and live with them.
4398
4399  We will again declare and use StreamReaders and
4400  StreamWriters to manipulate the file behind the scene.
4401
4402  Files, SteamReaders, StreamWriters, Read,
4403  Write,Append Delete
4404
4405  ***VB* The Complete Code**
4406

```
4407  Imports System
4408  Imports System.IO
4409  Imports System.IO.Stream
4410  Imports System.IO.StreamReader
4411  Imports System.IO.StreamWriter
4412  Imports System.Text
4413  Public Class Form1
4414      Private Sub btnReadFile_Click(sender As
4415  System.Object, e As System.EventArgs) Handles
4416  btnReadFile.Click
4417          ' Empty keepers list
4418          lstBoxKeep.Items.Clear()
```

```
4419        ' Prepare for file reading
4420        Dim Rdr As New
4421  System.IO.StreamReader("C:\App Target Files\File
4422  IO With Visual Basic.txt")
4423        Dim intNameCount As Integer = 0
4424        Dim myStrReadFromFile As String = " " ' Note
4425  the spaces inside quotations, string is not null
4426        Dim intKeeperCount As Integer
4427        'Do Until myStr = Nothing/null
4428        While (myStrReadFromFile <> "")
4429        myStrReadFromFile = Rdr.ReadLine()
4430          If myStrReadFromFile <> "" Then
4431              lstBoxNames.Items.Add(myStrReadFromFile)
4432              intNameCount += 1 ' Count the lines
4433  read
4434          End If
4435        End While
4436        ' Release the resources and file
4437        Rdr.Close()
4438        Rdr.Dispose()
4439        lblKeepersCount.Text = "There are " +
4440  Convert.ToString(intKeeperCount) + " Keepers"
4441        lblNamesReadCount.Text =
4442  intNameCount.ToString & " Names were loaded. "
4443    End Sub
4444    Private Sub btnExit_Click(sender As
4445  System.Object, e As System.EventArgs) Handles
4446  btnExit.Click
4447        Application.Exit()
4448    End Sub
4449    '
4450    ' Get User iput for name to add to file
4451    Private Sub btnAddNewName_Click(sender As
4452  System.Object, e As System.EventArgs) Handles
4453  btnAddNewName.Click
4454        Dim myStrName As String
4455        myStrName = txtBoxNewName.Text
4456        Dim intStrLength = myStrName.Length
4457        If intStrLength = 0 Then
4458          MessageBox.Show("No name was entered for
4459  addition to file.", "Check name to add")
4460          Return
```

```
4461          End If
4462          '
4463          ' Prepare to write new name to file
4464          Dim myFileWtr As New StreamWriter("C:\App
4465 Target Files\File IO With Visual Basic.txt", True)
4466          myFileWtr.WriteLine(myStrName)
4467          myFileWtr.Close()
4468          myFileWtr.Dispose()
4469          lstBoxNames.Items.Add(myStrName)
4470          Dim intNamesShown As Integer =
4471 lstBoxNames.Items.Count
4472          lblNamesReadCount.Text = "The are " +
4473 Convert.ToString(intNamesShown) + " names in the
4474 file now."
4475          txtBoxNewName.Text = ""
4476      End Sub
4477      '
4478      'Clear listBoxes
4479      Private Sub btnClearList_Click(sender As
4480 System.Object, e As System.EventArgs) Handles
4481 btnClearList.Click
4482          lstBoxNames.Items.Clear()
4483          lstBoxKeep.Items.Clear()
4484      End Sub
4485      '
4486      ' Delete a Name
4487      Private Sub btnDeleteName_Click(sender As
4488 System.Object, e As System.EventArgs) Handles
4489 btnDeleteName.Click
4490          ' Clear Keepers ListBox
4491          lstBoxKeep.Items.Clear()
4492          ' Select Name to delete
4493          Dim strToDelete As String =
4494 lstBoxNames.SelectedItem.ToString
4495          ' Get index of selected Name
4496          Dim IntDelIdx As Integer =
4497 lstBoxNames.SelectedIndex
4498          Dim intCmp As Integer
4499          Dim intkeepersCount As Integer
4500          Dim strTarget As String = " "
4501          ' Read and compare lines with name to delete
```

```
4502        Dim myFileRdr2 As New
4503 System.IO.StreamReader("C:\App Target Files\File
4504 IO With Visual Basic.txt")
4505        ' Variable to count names kept
4506        Dim intKeepersCount2 As Integer
4507        '--## Begin reading and comparing strings
4508 from file
4509        While strTarget <> ""
4510        strTarget = myFileRdr2.ReadLine()
4511        intCmp = StrComp(strTarget, strToDelete,
4512 CompareMethod.Text)
4513        ' Compare
4514          If intCmp <> 0 And strTarget <> "" Then
4515              intKeepersCount2 += 1 ' Count the
4516 keeper lines read
4517              'Add to Keeper list if StrToDelete is
4518 not equal to line read from file
4519              lstBoxKeep.Items.Add(strTarget)
4520          End If
4521        End While
4522        ' Dipsplay number of Keepers
4523        lblKeepersCount.Text = " There were " +
4524 Convert.ToString(intKeepersCount2) + " Keeper
4525 names."
4526        '-- Release the reader resources and file
4527        myFileRdr2.Close()
4528        myFileRdr2.Dispose()
4529        '
4530        ' If it exists, delete the old file of names
4531        Dim myboolean As Boolean =
4532 My.Computer.FileSystem.FileExists("C:\App Target
4533 Files\File IO With Visual Basic.txt")
4534        If myboolean = True Then
4535            My.Computer.FileSystem.DeleteFile("C:\App
4536 Target Files\File IO With Visual Basic.txt")
4537        End If
4538        '
4539        '-- Write the names to be kept into a new
4540 file
4541        Dim myFileWrt2 As StreamWriter
```

```
4542          myFileWrt2 = New
4543  System.IO.StreamWriter("C:\App Target Files\File
4544  IO With Visual Basic.txt", True)
4545          ' Loop throught the list of keeper names and
4546  write to the file
4547          Dim intStart As Integer = 0
4548          Dim intStop As Integer =
4549  lstBoxKeep.Items.Count-1
4550          Dim strToWrite As String
4551          intkeepersCount = 0
4552          For intStart = 0 To intStop
4553          lstBoxKeep.SelectedIndex = intStart
4554          strToWrite = lstBoxKeep.SelectedItem
4555          'test code MessageBox.Show(strToWrite)
4556          myFileWrt2.WriteLine(strToWrite)
4557          intkeepersCount += 1
4558          Next
4559          ' Release the resources and file
4560          myFileWrt2.Close()
4561          myFileRdr2.Dispose()
4562          ' Update the keepers count label
4563          lblKeepersCount.Text = "There are " +
4564  Convert.ToString(intkeepersCount) + " keeper
4565  Names"
4566          ' Update the Names Count label
4567          lblNamesReadCount.Text = "There are " +
4568  Convert.ToString(intkeepersCount) + " Names in the
4569  file."
4570          ' Remove the deleted name for the listBOx of
4571  names
4572          lstBoxNames.Items.RemoveAt(IntDelIdx)
4573      End Sub
4574  End Class
4575
```

4576 That's it a complete, working VB file IO application.
4577 Take this code, change a file name and a few control
4578 properties and you have another completely new
4579 application for another user and situation.
4580 Organization . . . that's a major part of re-using code.
4581

4582 *Appendix D* shows an application of this same type,
4583 using another file name and of course C#.
4584

## 4585 Project 15—Advanced Controls . . .
## 4586 Calendar and DateTimePicker

4587
4588 <Tools>+<Options>+<Projects and
4589 Solutions>+<Location>
4590
4591 <Language C#><Windows Form> *"Names are*
4592 *important"* <OK>
4593
4594 So far we have used relatively simple controls to
4595 gather user input and display information. Now we
4596 come to a more complex project using a more avanced
4597 control, the Calendar.
4598
4599 This is a dynamic, visual presentation of a month.
4600 You can scroll to either past, present or future months.
4601 Properties are set in the design view from the property
4602 window. The control can display multiple months
4603 either in a vertical or horizontal arrangement.
4604
4605 Ironically the control provides you with very little
4606 information (directly from the control) when you
4607 select certain days by clicking them. However you can
4608 write code for whatever you want to happen using
4609 other controls like textboxes or list boxes in
4610 conjunction with the "Date changed" event.
4611
4612 The most useful event is the Date_changed event. A
4613 range of dates can be set/selected programmatically
4614 although the process is rather awkward. Using this

4615 capability is even more tedious and in my opinion, not
4616 worth the effort.
4617
4618 A ***better choice*** in my opinion, is it's cousin, the
4619 DateTimePicker control.
4620
4621 You can scroll to either past or present months.
4622 Properties are set in the design view from the property
4623 window. The control cannot display multiple months
4624 simultaneously but has the ability to scroll into past or
4625 future months, which works just as well.
4626 Also it shows the calendar days by clicking the scroll-
4627 down arrow. This saves space on the user's screen for
4628 other items if needed.
4629
4630 The most useful event is the Value_changed event. A
4631 range of dates ***cannot*** be set/selected. **Not** major loss
4632 as I see it.
4633
4634 It has properties and events we can use to write
4635 support code around.For example, click on a date and
4636 use the "Value Changed" event to save a ToDo item,
4637 OR, click a date and see a list of scheduled activities
4638 for that date..
4639
4640 When combined with the usual controls we can use
4641 the DateTimerPicker to time-stamp items before
4642 saving them. Later we can use that information to ***sort***
4643 the items according to dates in a listBox control.
4644
4645 Also, we can format the Dates shown and used as we
4646 want them to be . . . we are not constrained to the

4647 ideas of a developer who has probably never sold or
4648 implemented an application in his or her life.
4649
4650 *<View> -or- <Tool Box> + <DatePicker>*
4651
4652 *<View> -or- <Tool Box> + <Button>*
4653
4654 I have learned the hard and frustrating way that the
4655 DatePicker control has an irritating behavior of
4656 immediately on program start-up selecting the date in
4657 the control as today's date. So far so good . . . but
4658 then, *by default*, fires the Value_changed event. If you
4659 have code written in that event handler, the code is
4660 executed whether desired or not. Point is be careful
4661 that the code does what you want..nothing more or
4662 less.
4663
4664 OK, let's code!!!
4665
4666 C#
4667
4668 On the form in design view "*double click*" an empty
4669 spot and get into the "Form_Load" event handler
4670 code. Alternatively, click the "Code Icon" in the
4671 solution explorer window. *PS* . . . I always keep the
4672 solution explorer visible.
4673
4674 When we're finished you will have developed 16
4675 event handlers, plus 2 stand-alone methods, for 18
4676 total code blocks. This is not a trivial project. It puts
4677 to work everything covered so far in the book.
4678

4679 I cannot over emphasize the importance of
4680 commenting the code and using all of the capabilities
4681 of the MVS IDE for your benefit. If you cannot find
4682 the example code you're looking for it might as well
4683 not exist.
4684
4685 You will come back over and over to use this example
4686 for reference . . . make sure it is usable for that
4687 purpose with comments and curly brace-matching.
4688
4689 *Controls Needed . . .*
4690
4691 3 labels, 13 buttons, 6 radio buttons, 2 textBoxes, 3
4692 listBoxes, 1 datePicker.
4693
4694 Your names do not have to be the ones I used, but
4695 remember your event handler will have the names
4696 "YOU" use.
4697
4698 *Name properties*;

| 4699 *buttons;* | *ListBoxes* | *Labels* |
|---|---|---|
| 4700 | | |
| 4701 1)btnLoadToDoItems | ListBox1 | lblWordSeek |
| 4702 2)btnLoadToDayItems | ListBox2 | lblAddInfo |
| 4703 3)btnLoadSelDayItems | ListBoxBlocked | label1 |
| 4704 4)btnClearTodayItems | | |
| 4705 5)ClearToDoItems | | |
| 4706 6)btnSaveInfo | | |
| 4707 7)btnDeleteItem | | |
| 4708 8)btmWordSearch | | |
| 4709 9)btnBlockDate | | |
| 4710 10)btnHideBlockedDates | | |
| 4711 11)btnDeleteItem | | |
| 4712 12)SelectedDayItems | | |
| 4713 13)bntNextMonth | | |

4714  14)btnThisMonth
4715  15)btnSaveAndRepeat
4716  16)radRepeat3Times
4717  17)radRepeat6Times
4718  18)radRepeat9Times
4719  19)radRepeat12Times
4720  20)radRepeat24Times
4721  21)radRepeat36Times
4722
4723  *Hint:* On the toolbox . . . Double_Click the control
4724  you are adding. Each Double_click
4725  Adds one of that control. I "Double_click" 13 times,
4726  i.e., to add 13 buttons, then drag them around to
4727  where I want them. It is less tedious and saves some
4728  time.
4729
4730  As you Double_click the controls are added to the
4731  form in a stack . . . drag the top one, then the others.
4732  Last one added is the visible one. As you move them,
4733  name them. One more comment . . . We will be using
4734  lots of "StreamReaders", "StreamWriters","if" and
4735  "while" statements in this project to read files and
4736  iterate the items in our list boxes. When we do it will
4737  be to evaluate the contents of strings and make
4738  decisions what action should be taken. Be sure to *take*
4739  *your time* and *understand the structure* of the loops
4740  thoroughly. There are several "if" statements "inside"
4741  the while loops. This is because we need to act on the
4742  information we are processing one item at a time.i.e.
4743  read a line from file and decide what to do with it.
4744
4745  It is *VERY IMPORTANT* to declare, *use and then*
4746  *close/dispose* the "Stream" objects *within the loops*
4747  we are using at the moment. Two reasons . . . one,

4748 free the system resources and two . . . to release the
4749 file we are working with for use with the next event
4750 we are handling. *A file cannot be opened for reading*
4751 *and then written to without closing it first and visa*
4752 *versa.* This *error* can be very *hard to find* later when
4753 you're working with new event handler code blocks.
4754
4755 We will discuss de-bugging and error
4756 detection/trapping late in the text.
4757
4758 First, let's get the libraries needed for this project
4759 defined.
4760
```
4761 using System;
4762 using System.Collections.Generic;
4763 using System.ComponentModel;
4764 using System.IO;
4765 using System.Data;
4766 using System.Drawing;
4767 using System.Linq;
4768 using System.Text;
4769 using System.Windows.Forms;
```
4770
4771 **These are probably automatically added for you.**
4772 **But check to be sure these are there.**
4773
4774 Scroll all the way to the top line of the MVS code
4775 editor and *after* the "*initialize*" curly braces enter this
4776 code . . .we will need these variables in several event
4777 handlers as we go along. Putting them here and using
4778 "*public*" in the declaration makes them available
4779 throughout the application.
4780
```
4781 public int intLastLoaded;
4782 public int intIdxItemFound;
4783 public int intItemFound = 0;
```

```
4784 public string myStrDate = " ";
4785 public string myStrNowYear = " ";
4786 public string myStrNowMonth = " ";
4787 public string myStrNowDay = " ";
4788 public string myStrFinalNow = " ";
4789 public string myStrFinalPicked = " ";
4790 public string mySeekDateFinal = " ";
4791 public string mySeekMo = " ";
4792 public string mySeekDay = " ";
4793 public string mySeekYr = " ";
4794 public string myStr = " ";
4795 public string myStrRead = " ";
4796 public string myStringToSave = " ";
4797 public string strToDelete = " ";
4798
```

4799 *Inside* the *Form1_Load* event handler Enter
4800 (Double_Click an empty spot on the form);
4801

4802 `intLastLoaded = 0;`// *This is setting a flag we will use*
4803 *later.*
4804 `btnLoadToDoItems.PerformClick();`//*Loads the*
4805 *ToDoItems*
4806 //
4807 //The flag is used to know when the ToDoItems were
4808 loaded by this event when we are
4809 //inside other event handlers. All we have to do is
4810 check for the value '0" of the flag.
4811

4812 //The datePicker shows today's date as it's text, but no
4813 //"Value_changed" event fires. *The ToDo Items are*
4814 *loaded be cause we //did a btnLoadToDoItems* in our
4815 *code..with the*
4816 *"tnLoadToDoItems.performClick"command.*
4817

4818 *Another Hint:*

4819 Remember the editor options we set up for matching
4820 curly braces??
4821 For this project and other even larger ones this can be
4822 a real headache saver!!!
4823 I also add short comments like //***End of Namespace***
4824 after the curly braces, i.e., this helps me make sense of
4825 the code blocks and aids with trouble shooting.
4826
4827 That is no trivial issue and is well worth the time and
4828 effort.
4829
4830 Back to work. Enter the following code outside an
4831 event handler, it is a stand-alone method. It has it's
4832 own curly braces and should not mixed in with
4833 another event handler.
4834

```
4835 public void SetMyCustomFormat()
4836 {
4837     // Set the Format type and the CustomFormat
4838 string.
4839     dateTimePicker1.Format =
4840 DateTimePickerFormat.Custom;
4841     dateTimePicker1.CustomFormat = "MM/ dd/ yyyy";
4842 }
```

4843 **This line causes the date to be shown as i.e. 03/**
4844 **29/2015.**
4845
4846 This is much easier to work with when you time-
4847 stamp items in a file and need to do searches and sorts
4848 while reading the files later. If, for some reason
4849 beyond me, you want the month and Day spelled out
4850 you can use this format instead.
4851

```
4852 dateTimePicker1.CustomFormat = "MMMM/ dd/ yyyy -
4853 dddd";
```

4854

4855 *This line causes the date to be shown as i.e.*

4856

4857 March/ 29/2015 Friday

4858

4859 **To eliminate the slashes just type it as follows;**

4860

```
4861 dateTimePicker1.CustomFormat = "MMMM dd yyyy -
4862 dddd";
```

4863

4864 We "call" this formatting method whenever we want
4865 it by simply typing it's name i.e

4866

```
4867 SetMyCustomFormat()
```

4868

4869 **Dates used after this call will be in the shortened**
4870 **format.**

4871

4872 Another characteristic of the DatePicker is that it fires
4873 the value_changed event when code re-sets the date
4874 format as if a used chose a different date. The first
4875 time this command is used you "may" see two events
4876 happen i.e . . . a messageBox saying there are no
4877 "ToDo items". After the first instance this does not
4878 happen again . . . Just a heads-up.

4879

4880 I mentioned the Value_Changed event of the
4881 dataPicker control. We are going to use this event
4882 now to retrieve items in a file of ToDo items and
4883 show only those bearing the time stamp of the
4884 selected date.

4885

4886 When the datePicker appears the date shown as text is
4887 not usable to select Items from file for today's date.

4888 Click the scrolldown/dropdown arrow head and click
4889 today's date in the visual calendar month. The text
4890 will change to the format we used to save items i.e.
4891 01/26/2013.
4892
4893 After that, the ***Select Today's items button event***
4894 ***handler*** is ready to operate correctly. To this point our
4895 code looks like this;
4896

```
4897 using System;
4898 using System.Collections.Generic;
4899 using System.ComponentModel;
4900 using System.IO;
4901 using System.Data;
4902 using System.Drawing;
4903 using System.Linq;
4904 using System.Text;
4905 using System.Windows.Forms;
```

4906
4907 Realistically, it doesn't matter which event handler we
4908 code first. I think it is best to think and write code in
4909 the order in which users might use the program.
4910 The very first thing a person might want to do is
4911 establish some dates that are "blocked".i.e. ToDo
4912 Items cannot be entered for those dates.
4913
4914 This is another stand-alone method. It goes ***outside*** all
4915 event handler code blocks. This is simple writing
4916 information to a file that will be retrieved and use
4917 later in some of the event handlers. It has a partner
4918 called un-blocking dates. First things first.
4919 Set the dates to block. Using the datePicker, the user
4920 will first select the date to block, then click Block
4921 Date.
4922

```
4923 private void btnBlockDate_Click(object sender,
4924 EventArgs e)
4925 {
4926    mySeekDay = " ";
4927    mySeekMo = " ";
4928    mySeekYr = " ";
4929    mySeekDateFinal = " ";
4930    DateTime myTestDate =
4931 Convert.ToDateTime(dateTimePicker1.Text);
4932    //test code
4933 MessageBox.Show(Convert.ToString(myTestDate),
4934    "datePicker.Text");
4935    mySeekDay = " ";
4936    mySeekMo = " ";
4937    mySeekYr = " ";
4938    mySeekDateFinal = " ";
4939    intIdxItemFound = 0;
4940    mySeekDay = Convert.ToString(myTestDate.Day);
4941    mySeekMo = Convert.ToString(myTestDate.Month);
4942    mySeekYr = Convert.ToString(myTestDate.Year);
4943    int intLenMo = mySeekMo.Length;
4944    if (intLenMo == 1)
4945    {
4946       mySeekMo = "0" + mySeekMo;
4947    }
4948    int intLenDay = mySeekDay.Length;
4949    if (intLenDay == 1)
4950    {
4951       mySeekDay = "0" + mySeekDay;
4952    }
4953    listBoxBlocked.Visible = true;
4954    mySeekDateFinal = mySeekMo + "/" + mySeekDay +
4955 "/" + mySeekYr;
4956    StreamWriter myWrtBlock = new
4957 StreamWriter("C:\\App Target
4958 Files\\BlockedDates.txt", true);
4959    listBoxBlocked.Items.Add(mySeekDateFinal);
4960    myWrtBlock.WriteLine(mySeekDateFinal);
4961    myWrtBlock.Close();
4962    myWrtBlock.Dispose();
4963    listBoxBlocked.Visible = false;
4964 }
```

4965

## Un-blocking a date.

4967

Again this is simply getting the date to unblock and deleting that string from a file.

4970

```
private void btnUnBlockDate_Click(object sender,
EventArgs e)
{
    if(File.Exists("C:\\App Target
Files\\BlockedDates.txt"))
    {
        File.Delete("C:\\App Target
Files\\BlockedDates.txt");
    }
    //Get item from listBox
    int intUnBlock = listBoxBlocked.SelectedIndex;
    string strItemToUnblock =
Convert.ToString(listBoxBlocked.SelectedItem);
    listBoxBlocked.Items.RemoveAt(intUnBlock);
    int intBlockedKeeperItems =
listBoxBlocked.Items.Count;
    int ZZ =0;
    StreamWriter myWrt = new StreamWriter("C:\\App
Target Files\\BlockedDates.txt", true);
    while (ZZ <= intUnBlock)
    {
        listBoxBlocked.SelectedIndex=ZZ;
        strItemToUnblock =
Convert.ToString(listBoxBlocked.SelectedItem);
        myWrt.WriteLine(strItemToUnblock);
        ZZ++;
    }// End while
    myWrt.Close();
    myWrt.Dispose();
}//End un-block date
```

5001

Having set some limits on dates that are open for ToDo's we can proceed.

```
5004
5005 Typically, as I see it, this means pick a date, enter
5006 some items to save, save them, retrieve them and edit
5007 them.
5008
5009 namespace VS_CS_DateTime_Picker
5010 {
5011     public partial class Form1: Form
5012     {
5013         public Form1()
5014         {
5015             InitializeComponent();
5016         }
5017         public int intIdxItemFound;
5018         public int intItemFound = 0;
5019         public string myStrDate = " ";
5020         public string myStrNowYear = " ";
5021         public string myStrNowMonth = " ";
5022         public string myStrNowDay = " ";
5023         public string myStrFinalNow = " ";
5024         public string myStrFinalPicked = " ";
5025         public string myStr = " ";
5026         public string myPath = "C:\\App Target
5027 Files\\ToDo.txt";
5028
```

**5029 The first order of business is to write an event**
**5030 handler for the "Value_Changed event" fired by**
**5031 clicking the datePicker.**

```
5032
5033 private void dateTimePicker1_ValueChanged(object
5034 sender, EventArgs e)
5035 {
5036     SetMyCustomFormat();
5037     myStrDate = dateTimePicker1.Text;
5038     txtBoxAddInfo.Visible = true;
5039     btnSaveInfo.Visible = true;
5040 }//End DateTimePicker value changed
5041
```

5042 First, after picking a date, *save* some ToDo Items. We
5043 will use two (2) different buttons and event handlers
5044 for saving ToDo Items. The first is for saving a single
5045 item once. A bit later we will give the user the ability
5046 to save items multiple times for a range of 3 to 36
5047 months. One thing at a time, let's do save once first.
5048
5049 Double_Click <btn*Save*Info>
5050
5051 Enter your code to *save* an item.
5052

```
5053 private void btnSaveInfo_Click(object sender,
5054 EventArgs e)
5055 {
5056     SetMyCustomFormat();
5057     // date selected variables declared
5058     mySeekDay = " ";
5059     mySeekMo = " ";
5060     mySeekYr = " ";
5061     mySeekDateFinal = " ";
5062     //Get the Date from the DatePicker
5063     DateTime mySaveDate =
5064 Convert.ToDateTime(dateTimePicker1.Text);
5065     intIdxItemFound = 0;
5066     //populate selected date variables
5067     mySeekDay = Convert.ToString(mySaveDate.Day);
5068     mySeekMo = Convert.ToString(mySaveDate.Month);
5069     mySeekYr = Convert.ToString(mySaveDate.Year);
5070     // prefix "0" to single digit days and month
5071 strings
5072     int intLenMo = mySeekMo.Length;
5073     if (intLenMo == 1)
5074     {
5075         mySeekMo = "0" + mySeekMo;
5076     }
5077     int intLenDay = mySeekDay.Length;
5078     if (intLenDay == 1)
5079     {
5080         mySeekDay = "0" + mySeekDay;
```

```
5081    }
5082    //Define the date to save string
5083    string myDateToSave = mySeekMo + "/" +
5084 mySeekDay + "/" + mySeekYr;
5085    //define the string to save
5086    string myStringToSave = myStrDate + " " +
5087 txtBoxAddInfo.Text;
5088    // define the streamReader
5089    StreamReader mySr = new StreamReader("C:\\App
5090 Target Files\\BlockedDates.txt");
5091    // Read list of blocked dates
5092    string myStrBlockedDate = "XX";//avoid an empty
5093 string to start with
5094    while (myStrBlockedDate!= "" &&
5095 myStrBlockedDate!=null)
5096    {
5097        myStrBlockedDate = mySr.ReadLine();
5098        // End when string read is empty
5099        if (myDateToSave == "" || myStrBlockedDate
5100 == null)
5101        {
5102            //release streamReader and File
5103            mySr.Close();
5104            mySr.Dispose();
5105            break;
5106        }
5107    }
5108    //
5109    // if Date selected is not matched to a blocked
5110 date save the item
5111    if (myDateToSave!= myStrBlockedDate)
5112    {
5113        StreamWriter myWrt = new
5114 StreamWriter("C:\\App Target Files\\ToDo.txt",
5115 true);
5116        // MessageBox.Show(myStrToSave);
5117        myWrt.WriteLine(myStringToSave);
5118        // release streamwriter & File
5119        myWrt.Close();
5120        myWrt.Dispose();
5121    }
5122    if (myDateToSave == myStrBlockedDate)
```

```
5123     {
5124         MessageBox.Show("This is a blocked date. ","
5125 Blocked Date vs Save");
5126         txtBoxAddInfo.Text = "";
5127         // cannot save to blocked date, return to
5128 user screen
5129         return;
5130     }
5131     // re-set add info textbox to empty
5132     txtBoxAddInfo.Text = "";
5133     listBox1.Sorted = true;
5134     listBox1.Visible = true;
5135     //re-load ToDo Items file
5136     btnLoadToDoItems.PerformClick();
5137 }// End SaveInfo
5138
```

## 5139 Save and Repeat

5140
5141 This event handler makes use of the radio buttons we
5142 added and the "AddMonths" method of the
5143 datePicker.
5144

```
5145 private void bntSaveRepeat_Click(object sender,
5146 EventArgs e)
5147 {
5148     // Get the information to save
5149     string myStrToSave = txtBoxAddInfo.Text;
5150     // determine how many times to repeat the item
5151     // this number is saved in our variable for
5152     // counting the number of loops to execute
5153     // declare and initialize variable
5154     int intCheckedRepeat = 1;
5155     if (radRepeat3Times.Checked) {intCheckedRepeat
5156 = 3;}
5157     if (radRepeat6Times.Checked) {intCheckedRepeat
5158 = 6;}
5159     if (radRepeat9Times.Checked) {intCheckedRepeat
5160 = 9;}
5161     if (radRepeat12Times.Checked)
5162     {intCheckedRepeat = 12;}
```

```
5163      if (radRepeat24Times.Checked)
5164      {intCheckedRepeat = 24;}
5165      if (radRepeat36Times.Checked)
5166      {intCheckedRepeat = 36;}
5167      //####
5168      dateTimePicker1.CustomFormat = "MM/dd/yyyy";
5169      DateTime myDateToSave = dateTimePicker1.Value;
5170      //test code . . .
5171      // MessageBox.Show(Convert.ToString(myBaseDate));
5172      //
5173      // Save to file
5174      //
5175      int XX = 1;
5176      // Start of Repeated Save ToDo Items
5177      for (XX = 1; XX <= intCheckedRepeat; XX++)
5178      {
5179          StreamWriter mySW = new StreamWriter
5180          ("C:\\App Target Files\\ToDo.txt", true);
5181          //test code . . .
5182          // MessageBox.Show(Convert.ToString(myBaseDate));
5183          mySeekDay = " ";
5184          mySeekMo = " ";
5185          mySeekYr = " ";
5186          //Get the Date from the DatePicker
5187          intIdxItemFound = 0;
5188          //populate selected date variables
5189          mySeekDay =
5190  Convert.ToString(myDateToSave.Day);
5191          mySeekMo =
5192  Convert.ToString(myDateToSave.Month);
5193          mySeekYr =
5194  Convert.ToString(myDateToSave.Year);
5195          // prefix "0" to single digit days and month
5196  strings
5197          int intLenMo = mySeekMo.Length;
5198          if (intLenMo == 1)
5199          {
5200              mySeekMo = "0" + mySeekMo;
5201          }
5202          int intLenDay = mySeekDay.Length;
5203          if (intLenDay == 1)
5204          {
```

```
5205          mySeekDay = "0" + mySeekDay;
5206        }
5207      //Define the date to save string
5208      string myStringDateToSave = mySeekMo + "/" +
5209 mySeekDay + "/" + mySeekYr;
5210      //define the string to save
5211      myStringToSave = myStringDateToSave + " " +
5212 txtBoxAddInfo.Text;
5213
5214      mySW.WriteLine(myStringToSave);
5215      mySW.Close();
5216      mySW.Dispose();
5217      myDateToSave = myDateToSave.AddMonths(1);
5218      // test code . . .
5219      //
5220 MessageBox.Show(Convert.ToString(myDateToSave));
5221      //
5222      //reset radio buttons
5223      radRepeat3Times.Checked = false;
5224      radRepeat6Times.Checked = false;
5225      radRepeat9Times.Checked = false;
5226      radRepeat12Times.Checked = false;
5227      radRepeat24Times.Checked = false;
5228      radRepeat36Times.Checked = false;
5229    }// End of Repeated Months ToDo Item Save
5230
```

5231 For the **VB Code** of this exercise see **Appendix G**

5232

5233 Next . . . the **btnLoadToDoItems click_event.**

5234 (*Pay Attention* . . . this is different form

5235 Load**Today**ToDoItems)

5236

```
5237 private void btnLoadToDoItems_Click(object sender,
5238 EventArgs e)
5239 {
5240    listBox2.Visible = false; // I'll explain why
5241 in a bit
5242    //SetMyCustomFormat();
5243    listBox1.Items.Clear();//Be sure the box is
5244 empty
```

```
5245       listBox1.Visible = true;// be sure you can see
5246 it
5247       int intNumItems = listBox1.Items.Count;
5248       btnClearToDoItems.Visible = true;
5249       //
5250       // Declare and initialize StreamReader
5251       // Read lines for the file the file, stop when
5252 the end
5253       //is reached.
5254       myStr = "xx";
5255
5256       // Note: "xx" in myStr prevents the code
5257       // from seeing myStr as empty (null) at the
5258 beginning of the
5259       // while loop.
5260       StreamReader mySR;
5261       string myToDoFileStatus;
5262       mySR = new StreamReader("C:\\App Target
5263       Files\\ToDo.txt");
5264       while (myStr!= null)
5265       {
5266          // Read the lines from the file.
5267          //one at a time
5268          myStr = mySR.ReadLine();
5269          //Check for the end of the file
5270          //stop when we find it.
5271          if (myStr == null || myStr == "")
5272          {
5273             // Getting null or "" means we hit the
5274 end of the file
5275             mySR.Close();
5276             //Release the file and resources
5277             mySR.Dispose();
5278             break;
5279          }
5280          // Add the populated strings to the
5281          // listBox
5282          if (myStr!= null && myStr!= "")
5283          {
5284             listBox1.Items.Add(myStr);
5285             // Sort by date
5286             listBox1.Sorted = true;
```

```
5287        }
5288     }//End while
5289 }//End Load ToDo items
5290
```

5291 At this point, when the program runs and
5292 LoadToDoItems is clicked . . . all items from files
5293 have been loaded into the listbox and sorted by date.
5294 That was possible because as we "save" items to file
5295 we "pre-fix" each items with the date we selected in
5296 the datePicker, in the short date format i.e.
5297 mm/dd/yyy.
5298
5299 Suppose we want to see the items for only Today's
5300 actual date, not the date we selected on the datePicker.
5301
5302 *Now We can Delete /Edit Items, as desired.*
5303
5304 The new thing in this event handler is the idea of
5305 setting flags
5306 -or- marking the trail that we have traveled.
5307

5308 // **IF the Load Items ToDo are not currently the**
5309 **last**
5310 **// operation we did . . .**
5311 **// advise the user that to delete an item, the items in**
5312 **file**
5313 **// must be loaded first and an item selected. Check**
5314 **the flag**
5315 **// we set during the "btnLoadToDoItems" event**
5316 **handler.**
5317 **// Check to see that an item is selected.**
5318

```
5319 private void btnDeleteItem_Click(object sender,
5320 EventArgs e)
```

```
5321 {
5322     int intToDoIdx;
5323     intToDoIdx = listBox1.SelectedIndex;
5324     if (intLastLoaded!= 99 || intToDoIdx==-1)
5325     {MessageBox.Show("To delete an item, click Load
5326         ToDo Items, the click the item to delete,
5327 the click
5328         delete", "Delete Attempt"); return;}
5329         intToDoIdx = listBox1.SelectedIndex;
5330         strToDelete =
5331 Convert.ToString(listBox1.SelectedItem);
5332         // test code MessageBox.Show(strToDelete +"
5333 is at item " + Convert.ToString(intToDoIdx)," To
5334 be deleted;");
5335         listBox1.Items.RemoveAt(intToDoIdx);
5336         // Delete the file if it exists.
5337         string path1 = "C:\\App Target
5338 Files\\ToDo.txt";
5339         if (System.IO.File.Exists(path1))
5340         {
5341             System.IO.File.Delete(path1);
5342             //test code MessageBox.Show(path1 + " was
5343 deleted",
5344             "TempToDoFile deleted ");
5345         }
5346         //
5347         int ItemCount = listBox1.Items.Count;
5348         //
5349         int Y=0;
5350         // Read keeper items from listBox2 and write
5351 to file.
5352         while(Y<=ItemCount-1)
5353         {
5354             listBox1.SelectedIndex = Y;
5355             myStr
5356 =Convert.ToString(listBox1.SelectedItem);
5357             // test code MessageBox.Show(myStr,
5358 "Inside write
5359             listBox Items kept to file");
5360             if (myStr!= strToDelete)
5361             {
5362                 listBox2.Height += 24;
```

```
5363                    listBox2.Items.Add(myStr);
5364                    //myWrtTemp.WriteLine(myStr);
5365                    Y++;
5366                }
5367            if (myStr == strToDelete)
5368            {
5369                //test code MessageBox.Show("Found
5370 string to delete! ","");
5371                    Y++;
5372            }
5373        }// End while
5374        myCopyFile();
5375    }// ############### End Delete
5376
```

5377 The last command in delete event handler was
5378 myCopyFile.
5379 This is a stand-alone method that we write outside all
5380 event handler code blocks.
5381

5382 myCopyFile . . . . This is very straight forward. Read
5383 the Keeper ToDo Items from listBox2 and write them
5384 to file, after deleting the old file.
5385

5386 Note:
5387 Before reading an items from a listBox it must be
5388 selected. Our code does this as follows;
5389

5390 listBox2.SelectedIndex = XX;
5391

5392 We know the number of "Items" by getting the
5393 "Items.Count" method results.
5394

5395 **int intItemListBox2 = listBox2.Items.Count;**
5396

5397 Next, we read the "Item" and store it in a string for
5398 writing to file i.e.

```
5399  myStrToCopy =
5400      Convert.ToString(listBox2.SelectedItem);
5401
```

5402  Here's the method's code.

```
5403
5404  public void myCopyFile()
5405  {
5406      listBox1.Items.Clear();
5407      int intItemListBox2 = listBox2.Items.Count;
5408      if (File.Exists("C:\\App Target
5409  Files\\ToDo.txt"))
5410      {
5411          File.Delete("C:\\App Target
5412  Files\\ToDo.txt");
5413      }
5414      string myStrToCopy = "xxx";
5415      //
5416      int XX = 0;
5417      StreamWriter mySW = new StreamWriter("C:\\App
5418      Target Files\\ToDo.txt", true);
5419      while (XX <= intItemListBox2-1)
5420      {
5421          listBox2.SelectedIndex = XX;
5422          myStrToCopy =
5423          Convert.ToString(listBox2.SelectedItem);
5424          if (myStrToCopy == "" || myStrToCopy ==null)
5425          {
5426              mySW.Close();
5427              mySW.Dispose();
5428              return;
5429          }
5430          if (myStrToCopy!= "" && myStrToCopy!= null)
5431          {
5432              listBox1.Items.Add(myStrToCopy);
5433              mySW.WriteLine(myStrToCopy);
5434          }
5435          XX++;
5436          if (XX == intItemListBox2)
5437          {
5438              mySW.Close();
```

```
5439            mySW.Dispose();
5440            listBox2.Items.Clear();
5441        }
5442    }//End While
5443 }// End Copy File
5444
```

5445 Users want options. They want "*what*" they want,
5446 "*only* what they want", "*when*" they want it.
5447
5448 *Load Today's Items ("Actual" today's date)*
5449
5450 This does NOT require selecting a date first with the
5451 dataPicker.
5452 We will use the system (your computer's) dateTime.
5453

```
5454 private void btnLoadTodayItems_Click(object
5455 sender, EventArgs e)
5456 {
5457    SetMyCustomFormat();
5458    // DateTime is a special type of
5459 variable/object method.
5460    //Get today "actual" date & Time
5461    DateTime myTestDate = DateTime.Now;
5462    //
5463    // Select the parts/properties we want and
5464    // put them in a shortened format.
5465    //
5466    // This has nothing to do with the datepicker.
5467    //
5468    mySeekDay = " ";
5469    mySeekMo = " ";
5470    mySeekYr = " ";
5471    mySeekDateFinal = " ";
5472    intIdxItemFound = 0;
5473    mySeekDay = Convert.ToString(myTestDate.Day);
5474    mySeekMo = Convert.ToString(myTestDate.Month);
5475    mySeekYr = Convert.ToString(myTestDate.Year);
5476    // The Day, Month, Year properties are not in
5477 strings
```

```
5478     // yet. So we convert them to strings.
5479     // Day, Month and Year are properties of the
5480 DateTime
5481     // We can retrieve the and use them in our
5482 code.
5483     // If the Month and day are single digits
5484     // prefix them with a "0". This keeps our
5485 prefix
5486     // to saved items the same length and in the
5487     // same string positions. We know where to
5488 retrieve
5489     // them and how to compare then when we need
5490 to.
5491     //
5492     int intLenMo = mySeekMo.Length;
5493     if (intLenMo == 1)
5494     {
5495         mySeekMo = "0" + mySeekMo;
5496     }
5497     int intLenDay = mySeekDay.Length;
5498     if (intLenDay == 1)
5499     {
5500         mySeekDay = "0" + mySeekDay;
5501     }
5502     //
5503     // Concatenate a complete shortened date
5504 format.
5505     // using strings and concatenation.
5506     mySeekDateFinal = mySeekMo + "/" + mySeekDay +
5507 "/" + mySeekYr;
5508     // test code
5509 MessageBox.Show(mySeekDateFinal,"Seek Date
5510 Final");
5511     // I use MessageBox as testing tool while
5512 developing.
5513     // After things work, I comment the line out.
5514
5515     // Make sure the "Clear" button and listBox1
5516 are visible
5517     btnClearToDoItems.Visible = true;
5518     listBox1.Visible = true;
```

```
5519     // Test Code MessageBox.Show
5520 (myStrFinalPicked,"Date // Picked.");
5521     //listBox1.Items.Clear();
5522     string myStr = " "; // Note the spaces in myStr
5523     // This prevents the code from seeing myStr as
5524     // empty (null) at the beginning of the while
5525 loop.
5526     //
5527     // Declare and initialize a StreamReader
5528     StreamReader mySR;
5529     int intStrIdx = 0;
5530     int intStrIdx2 = 0;
5531     intIdxItemFound = 0;
5532     // Read lines from the file, stop at end of
5533 file.
5534     myStrRead = "xx";
5535     mySR = new StreamReader("C:\\App Target
5536 Files\\ToDo.txt");
5537     listBox1.Items.Clear();
5538     while (myStrRead!= null && myStrRead!= "")
5539     {
5540         myStrRead = "xx";
5541         myStrRead = mySR.ReadLine();
5542         if (myStrRead == null || myStrRead == "")
5543         {
5544             mySR.Close();
5545             mySR.Dispose();
5546             return;
5547             // return exits this event handler and
5548 "returns" us to the first // screen when we hit
5549 the end-of-file.
5550         }
5551         intIdxItemFound =
5552 myStrRead.IndexOf(mySeekDateFinal);
5553         //
5554         // IndexOf returns non-zero if the date we
5555 are looking
5556         // i.e. mySeekDateFinal for is inside the
5557 string we read from
5558         // file.(myStrRead).
5559         //
5560         if (myStrRead!= null && myStrRead!= "")
```

```
5561        // Big IF lOOP
5562        {
5563            intIdxItemFound =
5564 myStrRead.IndexOf(mySeekDateFinal);
5565            listBox1.Visible = true;
5566            intItemFound = intItemFound + 1;
5567            // count the number of times we find the
5568 date
5569            // we are looking for.
5570            if (intIdxItemFound >= 0)
5571            {
5572                listBox1.Items.Add(myStrRead);
5573                // Because we found the date we are
5574 looking for add the
5575                // string we read from file to the
5576 listBox then sort the listBox.
5577                listBox1.Sorted = true;
5578            }
5579            if (intIdxItemFound == -1)
5580            {
5581                continue;
5582                // Because we did not find the date we
5583 are looking for do not
5584                // add the string we read from file to
5585 the listBox. "Continue"
5586                // and "read" another string from
5587 file.
5588            }
5589        } // End Big If Loop
5590    }//End while
5591 }//End Load actual TodayToDo items
5592
```

5593 *Load Selected Date Items-datePicker date*

5594 **// Assumes first we (user)chose a date with the**

5595 **datePicker**

5596 **// then Clicked "Show selected date".**

5597

5598 *Note:* **The only real difference here is taking the**
5599 **date from the "Selected" date of the datePicker**
5600 **and matching that date with items from file.**

```
5601 private void btnLoadSelDayItems_Click(object
5602 sender, EventArgs e)
5603 {
5604     SetMyCustomFormat();
5605     DateTime myTestDate =
5606 Convert.ToDateTime(dateTimePicker1.Text);
5607     //test code
5608 MessageBox.Show(Convert.ToString(myTestDate),
5609     "datePicker.Text");
5610     mySeekDay = " ";
5611     mySeekMo = " ";
5612     mySeekYr = " ";
5613     mySeekDateFinal = " ";
5614     intIdxItemFound = 0;
5615     mySeekDay = Convert.ToString(myTestDate.Day);
5616     mySeekMo = Convert.ToString(myTestDate.Month);
5617     mySeekYr = Convert.ToString(myTestDate.Year);
5618     //
5619     int intLenMo = mySeekMo.Length;
5620     if (intLenMo == 1)
5621     {
5622         mySeekMo = "0" + mySeekMo;
5623     }
5624     int intLenDay = mySeekDay.Length;
5625     if (intLenDay == 1)
5626     {
5627         mySeekDay = "0" + mySeekDay;
5628     }
5629     //
5630     mySeekDateFinal = mySeekMo+"/"+mySeekDay+"/" +
5631 mySeekYr;
5632     //MessageBox.Show(mySeekDateFinal,"Seek Date
5633     // Final");
5634     btnClearToDoItems.Visible = true;
5635     listBox1.Visible = true;
5636     myStrFinalPicked = dateTimePicker1.Text;
5637     // Test Code
5638 MessageBox.Show(myStrFinalPicked,"Date Picked.");
```

```
5639      string myStr = " "; // Note the spaces in myStr
5640      // This prevents the code from seeing myStr as
5641      // empty (null) at the beginning of the while
5642  loop.
5643      //
5644      // Declare a StreamReader
5645      StreamReader mySR;
5646      // Initialze the StreamReader
5647      int intStrIdx = 0;
5648      int intStrIdx2 = 0;
5649      intIdxItemFound = 0;
5650      // Read lines for the file the file, stop when
5651  the end is reached.
5652      myStrRead = "xx";
5653      mySR = new StreamReader("C:\\App Target
5654  Files\\ToDo.txt");
5655      listBox1.Items.Clear();
5656      intItemFound = 0;
5657      while (myStrRead!= null && myStrRead!= "")
5658      {
5659         myStrRead = "xx";
5660         myStrRead = mySR.ReadLine();
5661         if (myStrRead == null || myStrRead == "")
5662         {
5663            mySR.Close();
5664            mySR.Dispose();
5665            string myMsgStr =
5666  Convert.ToString(intItemFound);
5667            if (intItemFound >= 1)
5668            {
5669               MessageBox.Show("Completed Selected
5670  Date search." + " I found " + myMsgStr + " Items
5671  for that date.", "Selected Day Items");
5672            }
5673            if (intItemFound == 0)
5674            {
5675               MessageBox.Show("Completed
5676               Selected Date search." + "I found no
5677  Items for that date.", "Selected Day Items");
5678            }
5679            return;
5680         }
```

```
5681          intIdxItemFound =
5682 myStrRead.IndexOf(mySeekDateFinal);
5683      //
5684      if (myStrRead!= null && myStrRead!= "")
5685      // Big IF lOOP
5686      {
5687          intIdxItemFound =
5688 myStrRead.IndexOf(mySeekDateFinal);
5689          listBox1.Visible = true;
5690          if(intIdxItemFound >=0)
5691          {
5692              intItemFound++;
5693              listBox1.Items.Add(myStrRead);
5694              listBox1.Sorted = true;
5695          }
5696          if (intIdxItemFound == -1)
5697          {
5698              continue;
5699          }
5700      } // End Big If Loop
5701    }//End while
5702 }//End SelectedDate Load event
5703
```

5704 The code for viewing this month's items is very, very
5705 similar.
5706 "btnThisMonth"_click event handler.
5707

### Stretch . . . .

5709 Try writing that code on your own. *Take a break*
5710 *first* . . . think through the process that needs to occur,
5711 then write some code.
5712 I suggest making a copy of "btnLoadToDayItem"
5713 event code, then go through it making changes as
5714 needed.
5715 Really need help . . . see *Appendix E*.
5716
5717 btnNextMonth . . . This is a little different. It uses the
5718 DateTime variable/object 's "AddDay" method. Here

```
5719  is the part that is different . . . you complete the
5720  remainder of the code.
5721
5722  private void btnNextMonth_Click(object sender,
5723  EventArgs e)
5724  {
5725      intLastLoaded = 0;
5726      listBox1.Height = 24;
5727      SetMyCustomFormat();
5728      DateTime myDateNextMo;
5729      DateTime myTestDate = DateTime.Now;
5730      myDateNextMo = myTestDate.AddMonths(1);
5731      //test code
5732  MessageBox.Show(Convert.ToString(myTestDate),"date
5733  Picker.Text");
5734      mySeekDay = " ";
5735      mySeekMo = " ";
5736      mySeekYr = " ";
5737      mySeekDateFinal = " ";
5738      intIdxItemFound = 0;
5739      mySeekDay = Convert.ToString(myTestDate.Day);
5740      mySeekMo =
5741  Convert.ToString(myDateNextMo.Month);
5742      //myTestDate.Month);
5743      mySeekYr = Convert.ToString(myTestDate.Year);
5744      //
5745      int intLenMo = mySeekMo.Length;
5746      if (intLenMo == 1)
5747      {
5748          mySeekMo = "0" + mySeekMo;
5749      }
5750      // Determine if next month is also next Year
5751      //
5752      if (mySeekMo == "12")
5753      {
5754          mySeekMo = "01";
5755          myTestDate = DateTime.Now.AddYears(1);
5756          mySeekYr =
5757  Convert.ToString(myTestDate.Year);
5758          //mySeekYr =
5759  Convert.ToString(DateTime.Now.AddYears(1));
```

```
5760        mySeekDay = "01";
5761    }
5762    int intLenDay = mySeekDay.Length;
5763    if (intLenDay == 1)
5764    {
5765        mySeekDay = "0" + mySeekDay;
5766    }
```

5767 **Stop and think . . .imagine the steps to be taken**
5768 **and give it a shot. Stuck??**
5769 *See Appendix E.*
5770

5771 Now, there will be times when a user wants to find a
5772 specific item and cannot remember the date involved.
5773 To resolve this matter we need to be able to search for
5774 certain words they do remember.
5775

5776 It is a very similar code block to finding a specific
5777 date ToDo Items. The difference is that we take our
5778 input from a textbox.
5779 From there it is just reading a file and comparing
5780 strings until we find the right ones.
5781

5782 *btnWordSearch*
5783

```
5784 private void btnWordSearch_Click(object sender,
5785 EventArgs e)
5786 {
5787     intIdxItemFound = 0;
5788     btnWordSearch.Visible = true;
5789     //
5790     btnClearToDoItems.Visible = false;
5791     listBox1.Items.Clear();
5792     //btnLoadToDoItems.PerformClick();
5793     listBox1.Visible = false;
5794     listBox2.Visible = true;
5795     listBox2.Height = 48;
5796     listBox2.Items.Clear();
```

```
5797      listBox2.Height = 24;
5798      //
5799      intItemFound=0;
5800      intIdxItemFound = 0;
5801      intIdxItemFound = listBox1.Items.Count;
5802      // Read lines for the file the file, stop when
5803 the end is reached.
5804      string strWordToFind = txtBoxWordSearch.Text;
5805      strWordToFind = strWordToFind.ToLower();
5806      myStrRead = "XX";
5807      // Note the spaces in myStrRead
5808      // This prevents the code from seeing myStr as
5809      // empty (null) at the beginning of the while
5810 loop.
5811      int Z = listBox1.Items.Count-1;
5812      int A = 0;
5813      while (A <= Z -1)
5814      {
5815          if (A == Z)
5816          {
5817              return;
5818          }
5819          listBox1.SelectedIndex = A;
5820          myStrRead =
5821 Convert.ToString(listBox1.SelectedItem);
5822          myStrRead= myStrRead.ToLower();
5823          int intCompareIdx =
5824 myStrRead.IndexOf(strWordToFind);
5825          if (intCompareIdx== -1)
5826          {
5827              A++;
5828              continue;
5829          }
5830          //
5831          if (intCompareIdx >=0)
5832          {
5833              intItemFound += 1;
5834              listBox1.Visible = false;
5835              listBox2.Visible = true;
5836              listBox2.Height += 48;
5837              listBox2.Items.Add(myStrRead);
5838              listBox2.Sorted = true;
```

```
5839              A++;
5840          } // End Big If Loop
5841      }//End while
5842      if (intItemFound == 0) {MessageBox.Show("That
5843 word was not found.", "Word Search Results");}
5844      txtBoxWordSearch.Text = "";
5845 }//End Word search
5846
```

5847 We have completed all of the major even handlers at
5848 this point.

5849

5850 A few smaller ones remain. They are simply a matter
5851 of hiding the appropriate listBoxes.i.e.
5852 ListBoxBlockedDates, ClearWordSearch, Hide
5853 BlockedDates. In each case, change the listBox's
5854 "Visible" property to false and/or clearing the text
5855 property of a textbox in the code;

5856

5857 i.e
5858 ListBox(Name).Visible = false;

5859

5860 Appendix F has the complete code.

5861

5862 By now you're beginning to see that a seemingly
5863 simple idea can take some serious work to implement.
5864 Most of the hard work is in thinking through the tasks
5865 to be done, in small, step by step increments. You do,
5866 and I do, make mistakes. If not, you're not trying hard
5867 enough.

5868

5869 Also by now you're seeing that forms can get rather
5870 crowded with controls on relatively small projects.
5871 That means we need to use more than one form to
5872 make the program user friendly and usable.

5873

5874 Spend the time necessary to fully understand the
5875 DatePicker project we just coded. It isn't perfect but it
5876 is usable and incorporates all of the concepts and
5877 methods we have covered so far. It can be a very
5878 strong reference for project ideas of your own.
5879

5880 # Project 16—Next Up; Using multiple
5881 **forms**

5882
5883 ***VB* Simple Two Form Show Exercise**
5884
5885 Start MVS
5886 <Tools><Options>
5887
5888 Set Location to VS VB Projs (Or whatever you named
5889 your folder for VB Projects)
5890 <OK>
5891 <File>+<New Project>+<Windows Form>
5892 Enter Project name
5893 <OK>
5894 Wait for empty Form1
5895 <ToolBox>+<Button>
5896
5897 Name your button btnShowForm2
5898 Set text property to "Show Form2" other properties as
5899 you like . . .
5900
5901 Double_Click btnShowForm2
5902 Enter the following code in the event handler
5903
5904 Dim myForm as Form
5905 myForm = new Form2()
5906 me.Hide()

5907  myForm.Show()
5908
5909  It will appear that you have an error, and you do . . .
5910  Form2 doesn't exist yet. Ignore this indication for the
5911  moment.
5912
5913  In the solution explorer **Right_Click the Project**
5914  **name . . .**
5915  Choose "***Add***" from the pop-up menu.
5916  Choose "***New Item***" from the next menu.
5917  Choose "Windows Form" from the templates menu
5918  Name the form
5919  -or-
5920  I suggest that you use the default name of Form2.
5921  <Add>
5922
5923  Note the solution explorer and the new form is listed
5924  as Form2.
5925  If not, back-track and find the error.
5926
5927  <ToolBox>+<Button>
5928
5929  Name the button btnShowForm1. Set "text" as Show
5930  Form1.
5931
5932  Double_click btnShowForm1and enter this code in
5933  the event handler;
5934
5935  Me.Hide()
5936  Form1.Show()
5937

5938 Our application instantiated Form1 when we created
5939 the new project so we do not have to enter the code to
5940 do that. We simply **hide** Form2 and **Show** Form1.
5941
5942 Switch back to the code view of Form1 and verify that
5943 the error indication in the *btnShowForm2 event*
5944 *handler* has been removedfrom the editor code. If this
5945 is not the case, retrace your steps and correct the error.
5946
5947 Run the program and switch back and forth between
5948 forms a few times. As long as we are "Showing" the
5949 forms by the "Show"method, we can switch back and
5950 forth as much as we like.
5951
5952 If we eliminate the "Hide" method from our code we
5953 can see the forms "Cascaded" on the screen. In that
5954 case we can switch forms by simply clicking inside
5955 the form we want on top at any moment. There are
5956 times when that is an advantage and other times when
5957 it is not. The top form is the "Active form".
5958
5959 Forms shown by using the "Show" method as said to
5960 be "modeless". You do **NOT** have to close the top
5961 form or showing form in order to switch to another
5962 form and continue with the application.
5963
5964 Conversely, a "Modal" *must be closed or Hidden*
5965 *before proceeding with the application.* The
5966 messageBox is an example of a "Modal"
5967 form.control. To display a form in a "Modal" status,
5968 use the ShowDialog method instead of the "Show"
5969 method.
5970

5971 Take some time and experiment *"**Stretch**"* your ability
5972 and knowledge with the *Show, ShowDialog, Hide*
5973 methods. No matter how many times you read this
5974 material, you will not have a real grasp of the
5975 differences until you try them.
5976
5977 Next up . . . ***Forms and Properties***.
5978
5979 I have said many times . . . forms are objects. They
5980 have properties and we can use those properties.
5981 Forms/Objects can be defined in classes. A class is
5982 just a container for code. The Forms/Object/Classes in
5983 this example revolve around items that are visible to
5984 the user.
5985
5986 ***IMPORTANT:***
5987 ***Not all classes are visible objects to the user.***
5988 ***We can define a class that has nothing-to-do with a***
5989 ***form and define properties for that class and use***
5990 ***them from other places in the application.***
5991
5992 **More on this later, for now we are using visible**
5993 **Forms/Objects/Classes.**
5994
5995 The idea of properties is not new to you by now.
5996 Forms are objects and objects have properties and
5997 methods. These properties are a little different. We
5998 define/create them in code.
5999
6000 So we are going to start MVS and create a *new*
6001 *project* with *two forms* and create and use some
6002 properties which we will create with our code.
6003

6004  Have you wondered how the program decides which
6005  form to show first when you run the program? By
6006  default it is the first form created when you define a
6007  project. However, this is a "property" of the "project"
6008  and you can change the start up form if you want to
6009  do so.
6010
6011  In Solution Explorer Right_Click the project's name
6012  and choose properties. A menu screen will appear and
6013  one item midway down the screen is the Start-up
6014  object.
6015  Click the Drop-Down-Arrow and you will see the
6016  available options. Leave the setting as Form1 and
6017  close the menu.
6018
6019  On form1 add 3 buttons and 1 textBox.
6020
6021  Name one button "btnShowForm2", the second
6022  "btnGetForm2Property" and the third "btnExit". The
6023  textbox default name of "textBox1" is fine for now.
6024
6025  Code the btnShowForm2 event handler as follows;
6026

```
6027 Private Sub btnShowForm2_Click(sender As
6028 System.Object, e As System.EventArgs) Handles
6029 btnShowForm2.Click
6030     Dim myForm As Form2 = New Form2
6031     Me.Hide()
6032     myForm.Show()
6033 End Sub
```

6034
6035  Remember that to use a class "actively" (display and
6036  use it's visible controls) it must be "instantiated" . . . a
6037  working model built according to the blue print
6038  created when Form2 was added to the project.

6039
6040 This can be accomplished in two ways . . . .
6041
6042 Use Form2 directly i.e Form2.Show() -or-
6043 "instantiate" a working model . . .i.e
6044
6045 Dim myForm as Form2 = new Form2
6046 myForm.Show()
6047
6048 In this exercise, it wouldn't matter very much which
6049 way we chose . . . in other situations, it would matter a
6050 great deal. We will get into that when we discuss
6051 classes and objects in more detail.
6052 Enter the code for the event handler for
6053 btnGetForm2Property. Double_Click
6054 btnGetForm2Property and add this code . . .
6055

```
6056 Private Sub btnGetForm2Property_Click(sender As
6057 System.Object, e As System.EventArgs) Handles
6058 btnGetForm2Property.Click
6059 '// instantiate Form2 as myForm
6060    Dim myForm As Form2 = New Form2()
6061    Dim intMyNum As Integer
6062    '// Evalute the user input, if not provided set
6063 a default value.
6064    if(textBox1.text<> "") then
6065        intMyNum = Convert.ToInt32(TextBox1.Text)
6066    End if
6067    '//
6068    if(textBox1.text = "") then
6069        intMyNum = 1
6070    End if
6071    // Set the value of the intNumber property for
6072 Form2,
6073    // "instantiated" as "myForm", ignore the error
6074 indication
6075    // for now.
```

```
6076         myForm.intNumber = 22
6077     // Define a variable to receive the property
6078 value from
6079     // myForm.
6080         Dim intMultiplied As Integer
6081     // Call for the Property value intNumber in
6082 myForm.
6083     intMultiplied= myForm.intNumber()
6084     // Display the received property value.
6085     MessageBox.Show(Convert.ToString(intMultiplied))
6086 End Sub
6087
```

6088 Again, you will get an indications of an errors because
6089 we have not yet defined Form2 fully. Ignore the
6090 indication momentarily, that's next.
6091
6092 Switch to Form2 design view using the Solution
6093 Explorer.
6094 Add three (3) buttons to Form2. Name one
6095 "btnShowMyProperty", the second "btnShowForm1"
6096 and the third "bntExit".
6097
6098 Now the real nitty-gritty, creating a "Property" of
6099 Form2.
6100
6101 Form2 is an object and it is also a "class". A class is a
6102 container for Code . . . All Forms are "objects" and
6103 "classes". As objects, forms have properties like the
6104 ones we set using the property window. They can also
6105 have properties we define with code. If a property is
6106 "Public", that property can be retrieved and used by
6107 other classes in the project,i.e. Form1 in our example.
6108 If the form with a property we defined is
6109 "instantiated" like "myForm" in our Form1 event

6110 handlers, the instantiated form has the same properties
6111 as the original form, i.e Form2.
6112
6113 Re-read this paragraph a few times . . . it's a ***very,***
6114 ***very important*** concept!
6115
6116 OK, let's define a property for Form2. Name the
6117 property "intMyNumber" and declare the property as
6118 "Public". There are three essentail steps involved . . .
6119
6120 Declaring a "Private" variable that can only be
6121 changed by code inside this class, providing the "Set"
6122 method which allows code in this class to assign
6123 values to the private variable and the "Get" method
6124 which allows code outside the class to retrieve the
6125 value of the private variable. Below the Public Class
6126 Form2 line enter;

```
6127 '// Form property definition
6128 Private intToReturn as integer
6129 ''---------------------------------
6130 '// Public means accessible from other
6131 classes/forms
6132 '// within the project. "Property" means
6133 characteristic of
6134 '// this class. Private means accessible only from
6135 within this
6136 '// class
6137 '//
6138    Public Property intMyNumber() as integer '//
6139 Parentheses
6140    '// indicates can receive values to "Set" or
6141 assign value
6142    '// -or- return a value on request "Call".
6143      Get
6144        Return intToReturn * 2
6145      End Get
6146      '//---------------------------------
```

```
6147        '// value is a special variable created by
6148 MVS which receives
6149        '// assignments from calls from this class
6150 or other classes. We
6151        '// do not have to type in "value". MVS does
6152 it for us. WE do however, need to speify the type
6153 of data value will be receiving . . . an integer
6154 in this case.
6155        Set(value as integer)
6156           intToReturn = value
6157        End Set
6158     End Property
6159     '//----------------------------------
6160     '// Add Event handler for btnShowForm1_Click
6161     Private Sub btnShowForm1_Click(sender As
6162 System.Object, e
6163        As System.EventArgs) Handles
6164 btnShowForm1.Click
6165        Dim myForm As Form1 = New Form1()
6166        Me.Hide()
6167        myForm.Show()
6168     End Sub
6169     '//----------------------------------
6170     '// Add event handler for btnMyProperty_Click
6171     Private Sub btnMyProperty_Click(sender As
6172 System.Object, e As System.EventArgs) Handles
6173 btnMyProperty.Click
6174        intMyNumber = 88 '// Fixed value for demo
6175 purpose
6176        Dim myIntTemp As Integer = intMyNumber
6177        '// This event handler will set the private
6178 variable to 88
6179        '// "Get" will return 88*2, no user input is
6180 provided for,
6181        '// from this form (instantiated as myForm)
6182 although we could if '// we wanted to, right? **
6183 Room to stretch if you like!! **
6184        MessageBox.Show(Convert.ToString(myIntTemp))
6185     End Sub
6186 End Class
6187
```

6188 Note: Because we are switching between forms, after
6189 showing Form2 and returning to Form1 . . . Closing
6190 Form1 by the usual Top-right X on the screen doesn't
6191 work completely. Even though you can't see Form2, it
6192 is still there, just hidden. So we provide the btnExit
6193 for completely closing the program.
6194
6195 Double_Click "btnExit" on Form1 and enter this
6196 code;
6197 Application.Exit()
6198 This completely closes the entire program.
6199
6200 You may be thinking . . .
6201 "How is this class concept usable in a practical way"?
6202
6203 Remember a class is a blue print. It is a plan for
6204 building something as needed for different situations.
6205 Consider a real estate agency . . . they have hundreds
6206 of houses, all have many similar properties . . . "w"
6207 number of full bath rooms, "x" number of half-baths,
6208 "y" number of stories, "z" number of square feet etc
6209 etc.
6210
6211 A programmer could build a separate
6212 class/object/form for each house, or just one class that
6213 can be instantiated (created) as many times as needed,
6214 each instantiation given a different name such as
6215 House 190 Wolfpen Branch Road . . . and just "Set"
6216 the properties for each house. The same is true for
6217 manufacturers of Automobiles . . . and many others.
6218 Create one blueprint and "Set" the values for each
6219 instantiation then retrieve them as needed. For each
6220 new item added to an inventory, this is a mechanism

6221  for capturing information initially. Permanent
6222  retention of the data is another matter.
6223
6224  Obviously, a database is the place to keep this
6225  information permanently, but we aren't there yet . . .
6226  have patience, one step at a time. Later, we'll learn
6227  how to put the information into a database.
6228
6229  Complete VB Code is shown in Appendix H
6230
# 6231 Project 17—Class properties . . . "Set "
# 6232 and "Get" properties
6233
6234  Since we are working with classes and user defined
6235  properties, this is a good time/place to see how a class
6236  that has nothing-to-do with a form (directly) can be
6237  defined and used. I mentioned this briefly, earlier in
6238  this unit.
6239
6240  <File> + <Close Project>
6241
6242  Check for the Projects and Solutions location
6243  information.
6244
6245  <Tools><Options><Project and Solutions>
6246
6247  Be sure that the location is set for the Visual basic
6248  folder you created.
6249
6250  Again, I *caution* against copying code directly from
6251  the textbook. If you want to cut (copy) and paste code,
6252  copy directly from the example files downloaded
6253  from the website.

6254 Word processors are great but they do not always use
6255 the same characters used by the compiler.
6256
6257 ***When you're refreshed and can really concentrate***,
6258 start a new project. This is NOT a terribly difficult
6259 project, but it is longer than previous ones and
6260 requires great attention to detail.
6261 Do part of the project, take a break and come back
6262 later and finish. Take *note* of the *line numbers* of the
6263 textbook where you stop . . . *jot them down* for later.
6264
6265 <File>+<New Project>+<Visual Basic>+<Windows
6266 Form>
6267 <Project Name>
6268
6269 Name the project "VS VB Simple Class Proj"
6270 <OK>
6271
6272 Right_Click an empty spot on the form and choose
6273 properties.
6274 Set the text property for the form to "VS VB Simple
6275 Class Proj"
6276 and set Start-up Location to Ceter Screen then add the
6277 following controls to the form;
6278
6279 ***7 textboxes*** named txtBoxCarMaker, txtBoxModel,
6280 txtBoxCarType, txtBoxEngine, txtBoxCost,
6281 txtBoxCarColor and txtBoxModelYr.
6282
6283 ***8 labels*** corresponding to the textboxes, set property
6284 "enabled" False.
6285

6286 **4 buttons** named btnSave, btnDisplay, btnClear and
6287 btnExit.
6288
6289 Set the other properties to your own taste . . .i.e.
6290 Font, BackColor etc.
6291
6292 Drag the controls to a location on the form as you see
6293 fit.
6294
6295 On the top task bar <View><Tab Order>
6296
6297 **Note**: White rectangles will appear on each control
6298 showing the tab order number. Click on the tab order
6299 for the first control (textBox) where the user will enter
6300 information i.e. Car manufacturer, Model etc
6301 etc . . .One at a time until the tab order is in the
6302 sequence that the user will enter the information we
6303 need. Tab order determines what order the cursor
6304 moves from control to control if the user presses the
6305 tab key.
6306
6307 One other function of **MVS** to be aware of and use to
6308 your advantage is **intellisense**. As you use "Dot
6309 Notation" to "set" or "get" properties of your class . . .
6310 you will see all available properties listed in a drop-
6311 down menu after typing the "dot", click on the
6312 property of your choice and it will be entered into
6313 code for you exactly as you defined the property in
6314 your class.
6315 Using this feature of MVS helps prevent typos and
6316 other errors. It also means you don't have to rely on
6317 memory to be sure you use all the properties.
6318

6319 Our finished project will produce a screen that looks
6320 like this after a user has entered information, saved
6321 and displayed it . . .
6322

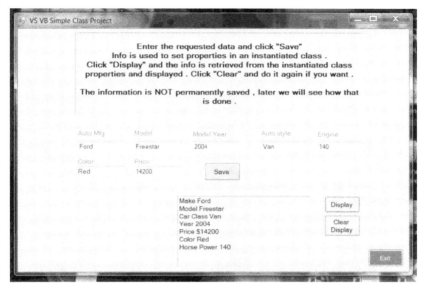

6323
6324                              **Screen 3**
6325
6326 Before we write the event handler code blocks let's
6327 define the "class" that we will reference in our event
6328 handlers.
6329
6330 In the *Solution Explorer* "right_click" on the *<project*
6331 *name>* and choose *<Add>*. A menu pops up and then
6332 click *<New Item>*. Next Click "*<Class>*", name the
6333 class *<Automobile Class>*,click *<Add>*.
6334
6335 In a few seconds, the AutomobileClass will appear as
6336 a file in the Solution Explorer . . . Double_Click the
6337 class name. Now you should be inside a skeletal code
6338 block for the AutomobileClass.
6339

6340  We will define seven (7) properties for the class. *Car*
6341  *Manufacturer, Car Model, Car Type, Model Year,*
6342  *Engine Horse Power, Color,* and *Price.* There are
6343  several more that would be used in reality, but, for our
6344  example 7 is fine.
6345  Enter this code . . .
6346
6347  ***NOTE***: The ***comments*** are super ***important*** . . .
6348  They keep us aware of which "property" we are
6349  working on and make finding and correcting errors
6350  much easier.
6351

```
6352 Public Class AutomobileClass '// Public i.e.
6353 Accessible from
6354     '// elsewhere in the project.
6355     '// ###################### HorsePower
6356     Private intHorsePower As Integer
6357     '// Private . . . Accessible inside this class
6358     ''---------------------------------
6359     Public Property intEngineHP() As Integer
6360        '// When we reference this property we will
6361 use the Public
6362        '// property name . . .parenthese maean can
6363 accept or return
6364        '// a value. References will use "dot"
6365 notation i.e.
6366        '// AutomobileClass.intEngineHP
6367        Get '// Handles requests "Calls" for the
6368 value
6369           Return intHorsePower '// Sends back to
6370 "call" for value
6371        End Get
6372        '//
6373        Set(value As Integer) '// Accepts and
6374 assigns
6375           '// parameter in "call" to "Set" value in
6376 the special
6377           '// variable value automaticall generated
6378 by MVS
```

```
6379                '// "As Integer" must be added by our
6380 code
6381              intHorsePower = value
6382          End Set
6383      End Property
6384      '// Every property follows this pattern,
6385 Integer or decimal is used
6386      '// when the in-comnig parameter is a number
6387      '//
6388
6389      '// next "Property" is much the same
6390      '// #################### Car Class
6391      Private strCarClass As String
6392      ''------------------------------------
6393      Public Property strCarType()
6394          Get
6395              Return strCarClass
6396          End Get
6397          '//
6398          Set(value) '// string is the default "value"
6399 variable type
6400              strCarClass = value
6401          End Set
6402      End Property
6403      '//-------------------------------
6404      '// #################### Car Class
6405      Private decCarPrice As Decimal
6406      ''------------------------------------
6407      Public Property decCarCost() As Decimal
6408          Get
6409              Return decCarPrice
6410          End Get
6411          '//
6412          Set(value As Decimal)
6413              decCarPrice = value
6414          End Set
6415      End Property
6416      '// #################### Car Manufacturer
6417      Private strcCarManufacturer As String
6418      ''------------------------------------
6419      Public Property strCarMaker() As String
6420          Get
```

```
6421              Return strcCarManufacturer
6422         End Get
6423         '//
6424         Set(value As String) '// String is default,
6425  entered for
6426             '// clarity only
6427             strcCarManufacturer = value
6428         End Set
6429     End Property
6430     '// #################### Car Model
6431     Private strCarModel As String
6432     ''---------------------------------
6433     Public Property strCarModelDesc() As String
6434        Get
6435             Return strCarModel
6436        End Get
6437        '//
6438        Set(value As String)
6439            strCarModel = value
6440        End Set
6441     End Property
6442     '//
6443     '// next Property . . .
6444     '// #################### Car Model
6445     Private strCarYear As String
6446     ''---------------------------------
6447     Public Property strCarYr() As String
6448        Get
6449             Return strCarYear
6450        End Get
6451        '//
6452        Set(value As String)
6453            strCarYear = value
6454        End Set
6455     End Property
6456     '// #################### Car Model
6457     Private strCarColor As String
6458     ''---------------------------------
6459     Public Property strCarPaint() As String
6460        Get
6461             Return strCarColor
6462        End Get
```

```
6463        '//
6464        Set(value As String)
6465            strCarColor = value
6466        End Set
6467     End Property
6468 End Class
6469
```

6470 **Now that our class is defined we can return to the**
6471 **form and enter the event handler code. Click**
6472 **<Form1> in Solution Explorer and use the <Design**
6473 **view>.**

6474

6475 Double_Click btnSave and enter the event handler
6476 code.

```
6477
6478 '// Note: we are using "Public" here to make info
6479 available
6480 '// elsewhere
6481
6482 Public Sub btnSave_Click(sender As System.Object,
6483 e As System.EventArgs) Handles btnSave.Click
6484     '// instantiate an active "class" from
6485 AutomobileClass
6486     Dim myCls As AutomobileClass = New
6487 AutomobileClass()
6488 '//
6489 '// Set the strCarMaker property value of
6490 myClass.strCarMaker
6491 '// The string variable matches the property
6492 "variable type" used
6493 '// in the AutomobileClass property
6494 definition . . .Same for all
6495 '// that follows. If the expected variable in the
6496 class is integer, '// use integer here. If the
6497 expected variable in the class is
6498 '// string, use string here Variable types must
6499 match.
6500 '//
6501     Dim strMfg As String = txtBoxMfg.Text
```

```
6502    myCls.strCarMaker = strMfg
6503    '//
6504    Dim decCost As Decimal = txtBoxPrice.Text
6505    myCls.decCarCost =
6506 Convert.ToDecimal(txtBoxPrice.Text)
6507    '//
6508    Dim myModel As String = txtBoxModel.Text
6509    myCls.strCarModelDesc = myModel
6510    '//
6511    Dim myModelYear As String = txtBoxModelYr.Text
6512    myCls.strCarYr = myModelYear
6513    '//
6514    Dim intMyEngine As Integer = txtBoxEngine.Text
6515    myCls.intEngineHP = intMyEngine
6516    '//
6517    Dim myCarColor As String = txtBoxColor.Text
6518    myCls.strCarPaint = myCarColor
6519    '//
6520    Dim myStyle As String = txtBoxAutoStyle.Text
6521    myCls.strCarType = myStyle
6522    '//
6523    myName = myCls
6524    myCls = Nothing
6525 End Sub
6526
```

6527 That's it for setting values of properties in our
6528 "instantiated" class "myClass". Next we write code to
6529 retrieve the property vales we just "Set".

6530

6531 In Solution Explorer
6532 <Form1> + <Design View>

6533

6534 Double_Click <btnDisplay>
6535 Enter event handler code.

6536

```
6537 Private Sub btnDisplayProperties_Click(sender As
6538 System.Object, e As System.EventArgs) Handles
6539 btnDisplayProperties.Click
6540
```

```
6541 '// We are using a "label" to display our property
6542 values.
6543 '// make sure the Autosize property for the label
6544 is "False"
6545 '//
6546 '// Note that we are "concatenating" strings for
6547 the text
6548 '// property of the label. We are adding "Visual
6549 Basic"
6550 '// "Carriage Returns" and "New Line" characters
6551 to format
6552 '// one property per line in the label.
6553 '//
6554 '// Also notice the "Space" following the literal
6555 string
6556 '// inside the quotation marks to separate the
6557 property value '// from the literal string.
6558 '//
6559 '// This makes the displayed info more readable.
6560 '//
6561    lblDisplayProperties.Text = "Make "
6562       + myName.strCarMaker
6563    lblDisplayProperties.Text =
6564 lblDisplayProperties.Text
6565       + vbCrLf + "Model " + myName.strCarModelDesc
6566    lblDisplayProperties.Text =
6567 lblDisplayProperties.Text
6568       + vbCrLf + "Car Class " + myName.strCarType
6569    lblDisplayProperties.Text =
6570 lblDisplayProperties.Text
6571       + vbCrLf + "Year " + myName.strCarYr
6572    lblDisplayProperties.Text =
6573 lblDisplayProperties.Text
6574       + vbCrLf + "Price " + "$" +
6575 Convert.ToString(myName.decCarCost)
6576    lblDisplayProperties.Text =
6577 lblDisplayProperties.Text
6578       + vbCrLf + "Color " + myName.strCarPaint
6579    lblDisplayProperties.Text =
6580 lblDisplayProperties.Text
6581       + vbCrLf + "Horse Power " +
6582    Convert.ToString(myName.intEngineHP)
```

```
6583     '// Make sure the label is visible.
6584     lblDisplayProperties.Visible = True
6585     '//
6586 End Sub
```

6587

6588 That's it!! Run the program, enter some info and save,
6589 then display the properties you set. Later we will learn
6590 to "Save"
6591 The information permanently, one step at a
6592 time . . .Patience!

6593

6594 ***Take a break*** . . . you've earned it!!!

6595

6596 A complete copy of the *VB code* is in Appendix I.

6597

6598 *C# Code* is in Appendix J.

6599

# 6600 Project 18—Next Up . . . Structs (for
# 6601 Structures)

6602

6603 A somewhat less complicated and easier to use
6604 storage device compared to a class is a "*Struct*",
6605 another user defined variable. It has many of the same
6606 capabilities of a class like handling variables of
6607 different types i.e. integers and strings can co-exist in
6608 a struct. Structs can also be defined "***inside***" a class
6609 code block if so desired or they can be placed in their
6610 own code container, just as we did with a class before.
6611 They can be copied and saved to the hard drive much
6612 like other variables.

6613

6614 We are going to place our Struct in its own "Class-
6615 like" container and name it "StructurePropertyDemo".

6616 We will define the Struct first, the add controls and
6617 event handler code blocks to our form. That makes it
6618 easier to write the code for the form because *MVS*
6619 *Intellisense* references the Struct for properties as we
6620 need them.
6621
6622 *VB* Code
6623
6624 Start MVS . . .
6625 <Tools> + <Options> + <Projects and Solutions>
6626 Set the location as your VS VB Projs folder.
6627 <OK>
6628 --------------------------------------------------------------------
6629 ---
6630 <File> + <New Project> + <Visual Basic> +
6631 <Windows Form> Name the project . . . VS VB Struct
6632 <OK>
6633
6634 When the empty form appears,ignore it for a few
6635 minutes.
6636 In Solution Explorer, Right_Click the project name
6637 then . . .
6638
6639 <Add> + <New Item> + <Class>
6640 Name the class StructurePropertyDemo
6641 <Add>
6642
6643 When the class file appears inside the Solution
6644 Explorer, Double_Click the *file name* to get inside the
6645 Code block.
6646
6647 Delete all, *I repeat* "ALL" of the skeletal code in the
6648 new class code block then . . . Enter this code.

```
6649
6650 Public Structure StructurePropertyDemo
6651     '//
6652     Private CarCost As Integer '//# 1
6653     Private Model As String '// 2
6654     Private Mfg As String '// # 3
6655     Private EngHP As Integer '//# 4
6656     Private Banker As String '//# 5
6657     Private Ownership As String '// # 6
6658     Private CarPaint As String '// # 7
6659     Public Price As Integer
6660     Dim Color As String
6661
6662 '// Define the properties, there are 7
6663 '//
6664     Public ReadOnly Property Financing() As String
6665         Get
6666             Banker = "CapitolOne"
6667             Return Banker
6668         End Get
6669     End Property '// . . . Property #1 Financing
6670     '//
6671     Public Property CarPrice() As Integer
6672         Get
6673             Return CarCost
6674         End Get
6675         Set(value As Integer)
6676             CarCost = value
6677         End Set
6678     End Property '// . . . Property #2 CarPrice
6679     '//
6680     '//
6681     Public Property CarOwner() As String
6682         Get
6683             Return Ownership
6684         End Get
6685         '//
6686         Set(ByVal value As String)
6687             Ownership = value
6688         End Set
6689     '//
```

```
6690      End Property '// . . . Property #3 CarOwner
6691      '//
6692      Public Property CarColor() As String
6693         Get
6694            Return CarPaint
6695         End Get
6696         '//
6697         Set(ByVal value As String)
6698            CarPaint = value
6699         End Set
6700         '//
6701      End Property '// . . . Property #4 CarColor
6702      '//
6703      '//
6704      Public Property CarModel() As String
6705         Get
6706            Return Model
6707         End Get
6708         '//
6709         Set(ByVal value As String)
6710            Model = value
6711         End Set
6712         '//
6713      End Property '// . . . Property #5 CarModel
6714      '//
6715      '//
6716      Public Property CarMaker() As String
6717         Get
6718            Return Mfg
6719         End Get
6720         '//
6721         Set(ByVal value As String)
6722            Mfg = value
6723         End Set
6724         '//
6725      End Property '// . . . Property #6 CarMaker
6726      '//
6727      Public Property CarEngine() As Integer
6728         Get
6729            Return EngHP
6730         End Get
6731         '//
```

```
6732        Set(ByVal value As Integer)
6733           EngHP = value
6734        End Set
6735        '//
6736     End Property '// . . . Property #7 CarEngine
6737 End Structure
6738
```

6739 **We are now ready to code the event handlers for**
6740 **the form.**

6741

6742 **You can** *test your work* **to this point by Clicking**
6743 **"Build"Icon on the MVS taskbar at the top of the**
6744 **screen. You will receive a "Sucessful" report at the**
6745 **bottom of the MVS screen if there are no errors.**
6746 **This will help to minimize error when coding for**
6747 **the form. If you get an error report,** *REVIEW* **and**
6748 **try again.**

6749

6750 **When you're ready, Add eight (8) labels and two**
6751 **(2) buttons to the form. In the "Form ", we're done**
6752 **with the Struct code.**

6753

6754 **<ToolBox><8 Label Double_clicks> and then**
6755 **<2 Button Double_Clicks >**

6756

6757 Drag your controls into position and set the properties
6758 for each in their property windows.

6759

6760 Name the labels as;
6761 lblInstruct, lblMfg, lblModel, lblEngine, lblColor,
6762 lblOwnership,lblFinancier and lblCost

6763

6764 Name the buttons as btnChangeOwner and btnExit.
6765

6766  Change the text property of the form to
6767  **VB Struture_Property_Form**
6768
6769  Now **Double_Click** an empty spot on the form and
6770  we will enter the **Form1_Load event handler block.**
6771  We will use the Load_Event to define and initialize
6772  the Struct and display the contents of the properties in
6773  the labels we added to the form.
6774
6775  Near the very top of the screen, just *below* this line;
6776  `Public Class Structure_Property_form`
6777
6778  *add* this line of code . . .
6779  `'// Instantiate a working instance of our struct`
6780  `Public newStruct As New StructurePropertyDemo`
6781
6782  *Inside* the *Form1_Load event handler* add the
6783  following code;
6784
6785  `'// This line should already exist;`
6786  `'// Public Sub Structure_Property_form_Load(sender`
6787  `As`
6788  `'// System.Object, e As System.EventArgs) Handles`
6789  `'// MyBase.Load`
6790  `//`
6791  `    '// Set newStruct Properties using`
6792  `"Dot"notation`
6793  `    '// to access the properties of newStruct`
6794  `    //`
6795  `    newStruct.CarMaker = "Ford" ' // #1`
6796  `    newStruct.CarModel = "2004" ' // #2`
6797  `    newStruct.CarEngine = 140 '//CarEngine #3`
6798  `    newStruct.CarColor = "Red"`
6799  `    newStruct.Color = "Maroon" ' // #4`
6800  `    newStruct.CarOwner = "Personal" ' // #5`
6801  `    '//newStruct.Financing = "CapitalOne" . . .Read`
6802  `Only this`

```
6803     '//will generate an error.. we cannot ""re-Set"
6804  it here.
6805     '// It was "Set" as we defined the struct . . . #6
6806     newStruct.CarPrice = 14200 ' // #7
6807     '//
6808     '// Display properties of newStruct
6809     '//
6810     lblMfg.Text = newStruct.CarMaker '// # 1
6811     lblModel.Text = newStruct.CarModel '// # 2
6812     '// newStruct property "Engine" is an integer,
6813  it must be
6814     '// Converted to a string for label displaying
6815     lblEngine.Text =
6816     Convert.ToString(newStruct.CarEngine) '// # 3
6817     lblColor.Text = newStruct.Color '// # 4 Using
6818  public
6819     '// string variable Color from newStruct
6820     lblColor.Text = newStruct.CarColor '// # 4
6821  Using Property
6822     '// CarColor . . .either works
6823     lblOwnership.Text = newStruct.CarOwner '// # 5
6824     lblFinancier.Text = newStruct.Financing '// # 6
6825     '// newStruct CarPrice is an integer, it must be
6826     '// converted to a string to display in a label
6827     lblCost.Text =
6828  Convert.ToString(newStruct.CarPrice) '// # 7
6829  End Sub
6830  '//
```

6831 Again we can test for error by doing MVS Toolbar
6832 <Build>.
6833 Since we did a build on the Struct, we can be
6834 reasonably sure that any errors generated are coming
6835 from the code for Form1.
6836
6837 **Now we are ready to add the event handler for the**
6838 **btnChangeOwner_Click Event. A property within**
6839 **a Struct can be changed by your event handling**
6840 **code like any other variable as long as it is**
6841 **declared as a Public property.**

6842

**6843 Double_Click the btnChangeOwner and code the
6844 handler.**

6845

6846 We have coded two options for Ownership . . .
6847 "Personal" and "Commercial". Whatever the current
6848 option is it will be changed to the other option. We do
6849 this by testing the option's value with "if" statements
6850 and change based on the results.

6851

```
6852 Private Sub btnChangeOwner_Click(sender As
6853 System.Object, e As System.EventArgs) Handles
6854 btnChangeOwner.Click
6855     If (newStruct.CarOwner = "Commercial") Then
6856         newStruct.CarOwner = "Personal"
6857         lblOwnership.Text = newStruct.CarOwner
6858         Return '// Note the return. If we don't' do
6859 this the
6860         '// option will be changed twice, ending up
6861 as it
6862         '// was to start with.
6863     End If
6864     '//
6865     If (newStruct.CarOwner = "Personal") Then
6866         newStruct.CarOwner = "Commercial"
6867         lblOwnership.Text = newStruct.CarOwner
6868         Return'// Note the return. If we don't' do
6869 this the
6870         '// option will be changed twice, ending up
6871 as it
6872         '// was to start with.
6873     End If
6874 End Sub '//
```

6875

6876 Now run the program . . .the results should look like
6877 this.

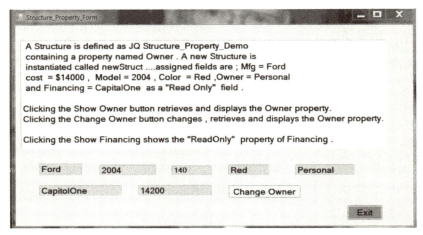

**Structure_Property_Form**

A Structure is defined as JQ Structure_Property_Demo
containing a property named Owner . A new Structure is
instantiated called newStruct ....assigned fields are ; Mfg = Ford
cost = $14000 , Model = 2004 , Color = Red ,Owner = Personal
and Financing = CapitalOne as a "Read Only" field .

Clicking the Show Owner button retrieves and displays the Owner property.
Clicking the Change Owner button changes , retrieves and displays the Owner property.

Clicking the Show Financing shows the "ReadOnly" property of Financing .

| Ford | 2004 | 140 | Red | Personal |

| CapitolOne | 14200 | | Change Owner |

Exit

6878

6879                    **Screen 4**

6880

6881 If you get an error, *REVIEW!!!*
6882 If you didn't congratulations, you've accomplished
6883 a lot!!

6884

6885 # C# Structs

6886

6887 C# structs are quite different from VB Structs.
6888 They don't define properties as VB does (no "get"
6889 or "set"), but, they define "fields" or variables that
6890 can be retrieved in a similar manner.

6891

6892 C# Structs are different. They don't use "get" or
6893 "set". You will see them often if you pursue
6894 programming so you need to understand what they
6895 are and are not.

6896

6897 Being completely honest, I don't see a great deal of
6898 benefit from using "structs" as C# defines them.
6899 The same job can be done using simple variables,
6900 and done more easily. In more demanding cases, a

6901 **"Class", without a form, works better for me. It is**
6902 **easy to instantiate the class and retrieve it's**
6903 **properties using "dot" notation. Remember our**
6904 **Automobile class?**
6905 **(C# code—AutomobileClass Code in Appendix J).**
6906
6907 **But . . . here we go.**
6908
6909 **Declaring a struct with C# looks like this;**

```
6910 // Declaring a C# Struct and "fields" within the
6911 struct
6912 struct Date
6913 {
6914    // C# version of a "property" using "fields"
6915 public Date(int mm, int dd, int ccyy)
6916    // accepts parameters as integers
6917    {
6918       year = ccyy-1900;
6919       month = mm;
6920       day = dd-1;
6921    }
6922    // Declare provate variables
6923    private int year;
6924    private int month;
6925    private int day;
6926    //
6927 }
```

6928
6929 **When our code is complete it will produce results**
6930 **like the screen below . . .**
6931

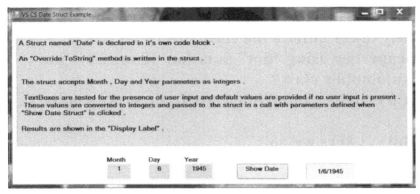

6932

6933                          **Screen 5**

6934

6935 **This is how it's done in C#.**

6936

```
6937 // Declaring a C# Struct and "fields" within the
6938 struct
6939 struct Date
6940 {
6941    // C# version of a "property" using "fields"
6942    public Date(int mm, int dd, int ccyy) //
6943 accepting parameters
6944    // as integers
6945    {
6946       year = ccyy-1900;
6947       month = mm;
6948       day = dd-1;
6949    }
6950    // Declare private variables
6951    private int year;
6952    private int month;
6953    private int day;
6954    //
```

6955 **Having defined the struct, we need a way to get the**
6956 **information it can provide in a usable format.**
6957 **Using the normal "ToString" conversion method**
6958 **simply returns the name of the Struct. Fortunately,**
6959 **we can provide our own "override"** *ToString*

6960 **method that returns a string containing the Struct**
6961 **fields as strings.**
6962
6963 **This method is included in the stand-alone Struct**
6964 **code block just** *before* **the last curly brace as**
6965 **follows;**
6966
```
6967 // The "Override" tostring method, returns a
6968 string to the calling
6969 // statement.
6970     public override string ToString()
6971     {
6972         return month + "/" + (day + 1) + "/" + (year
6973 + 1900);
6974     }
6975
```
6976 **C# . . . Complete Code for a C# Struct is in**
6977 **Appendix L**
6978 **Break Time!!!**
6979

# 6980 Project 19—Next Up Collections (In
# 6981 this case form control collections)

6982
6983 Objects can contain other obects. A "Collection" is a
6984 list of the Objects contained within the parent object.
6985 This concept will be applied when we get into
6986 Database programming. We will want to examine
6987 controls from a form and "write" their content into a
6988 database i.e Names, phone numbers, order numbers
6989 etc, etc.
6990
6991 This will become much more important as you get
6992 deeper into programming. VB and C# are "Event
6993 driven-Object Orientated" Programming languages.

6994  You will hear the acronymn used as OOP -or- OOPs,
6995  meaning Object Oriented Programming. Almost
6996  everything used in VB or C# programs are objects.
6997  Objects have properties, methods and events that are
6998  useful to us.
6999
7000  To illustrate, create a new project . . . "VS VB View
7001  and Count Collections" and add 4 buttons, 1 listBox
7002  and 1 label to the form. You can leave the name of
7003  three of the button as default button1, button2 and
7004  button3, their purpose is just to be there for counting
7005  them as objects. Name the 4$^{th}$ button
7006  "btnShowCollection". Set the other properties as you
7007  see fit, backcolor etc. Make the label "Autosize"
7008  property false for the label and position it near the top
7009  of the screen. Set the label's "enabled" property to
7010  "False". Enter instructions for the user as the text
7011  property.
7012
7013  The same project is presented shortly in C# . . . as
7014  "VS CS View and Count Collections". Coding is a
7015  little different for each language. Let's do VB View
7016  and Count Collections.
7017
7018  Double_Click btnShowCollection and code the even
7019  handler.
7020
7021  The only thing really new here is the reference to the
7022  Form's control collection. Each Control in the
7023  collection is called an "Item" by numbers 0 to the last
7024  item, which is 5 in this case, for a total of 6.
7025  Collections are directly visible to a user. The item

7026 count and properties must be retrieved and displayed
7027 in a visible control.
7028
7029 **When we are done, the resulting screen the user**
7030 **see's looks like this;**
7031

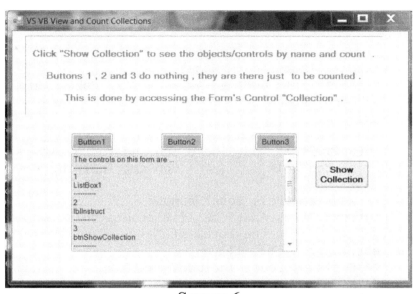

7032
7033                    **Screen 6**
7034
7035 *VB* **. . . Viewing and counting Collection items.**
7036
```
7037 Private Sub btnShowCollection_Click(sender As
7038 System.Object, e As System.EventArgs) Handles
7039 btnShowCollection.Click
7040    Dim myCtrl As Control '// Will hold control s
7041 ierate collection
7042    Dim X As Integer = 0
7043    Dim Y As Integer = 0
7044    '//
7045    Y = Me.Controls.Count-1 '// Count items in the
7046 conrols collection
7047    ListBox1.Items.Add("The controls on this form
7048 are . . .")
```

```
7049    ListBox1.Items.Add("---------------")
7050    '//
7051    For X = 0 To Y '// for item 0 to the last
7052 control (item Y) in the collection
7053    myCtrl = Me.Controls.Item(X) '// X is used at
7054 the index of each item in the collection
7055    Dim myName As String '// Will hold the
7056 control's name
7057    myName = myCtrl.Name() '// Retrieve control's
7058 name
7059    ListBox1.Items.Add(Convert.ToString(X + 1))
7060    ListBox1.Items.Add(myName)
7061    ListBox1.Items.Add("----------")'// Makes info
7062    '// more readable
7063    Next
7064    '//
7065    ListBox1.Items.Add("There are the following
7066 number of controls . . . " + Convert.ToString(Y +
7067 1))
7068    '// adds controls total number
7069    ListBox1.Items.Add("The list counts this
7070 listBox . . . for the Total of " +
7071 Convert.ToString(Y + 1))
7072    '// Explains count includes listBox
7073    '//
7074 End Sub '// End click event
7075 '//
7076
```

## 7077 *C#* Viewing and counting Form Controls 7078 Collection

7079

**7080 When we are done, the results will look like this;**

7081

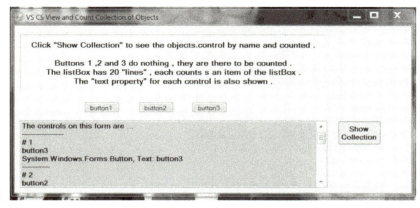

7082

7083                    **Screen 7**

7084

7085 **Look familiar??**

7086

7087 One new method is used for counting the controls . . .
7088 i.e. "foreach" is a modified version of the "for"
7089 looping method. It allows us to perform actions
7090 "foreach" object in a collection of objects. When it
7091 reaches the end of the collection, it terminates. We
7092 also use a type of variable we have not seen before . . .
7093 the "Control" variable. We create a Control object
7094 named "c" for each object in the collection, one by
7095 one (Foreach).

7096
```
7097 private void btnShowCollection_Click(object
7098 sender, EventArgs e)
7099 {
7100     int myCtrlCount = 0;
7101     //
7102     listBox1.Items.Add("The controls on this form
7103 are . . . ");
7104     listBox1.Items.Add("---------------");
7105     foreach (Control c in this.Controls)
7106     {
7107         string strCtrlName = "";
7108         //if (c.Name!= "listBox1")
```

```
7109        {
7110            myCtrlCount += 1;
7111            strCtrlName = c.Name;
7112            listBox1.Items.Add("#
7113 "+Convert.ToString(myCtrlCount));
7114            listBox1.Items.Add(strCtrlName);
7115            listBox1.Items.Add(Convert.ToString(c));
7116            listBox1.Items.Add("----------");
7117        }//End if
7118    }//End foreach
7119    myCtrlCount = this.Controls.Count;
7120    listBox1.Items.Add("There are the following
7121 number of controls . . . " +
7122 Convert.ToString(myCtrlCount));
7123    listBox1.Items.Add("The list counts this
7124 listBox . . . for Total of " +
7125 Convert.ToString(myCtrlCount));
7126 } //End Click
7127
```

7128 **So, hopefully, you're beginning to wonder "OK,**
7129 **but what good is this if all of it goes away when the**
7130 **program stops running"? That's a fair question . . .**
7131 **it deserves an answer.**

7132

7133 *Saving collections of objects permanently.*

7134

7135 **OK, the waiting is over! Now that we know a little**
7136 **about instantiating classes and Structs . . . How do**
7137 **we get the information to a permanent file? We**
7138 **need a way to save the information to the hard**
7139 **drive and have the program re-load the same**
7140 **information the next time it starts running.**

7141

7142 **The answer lies in the Struct itself and the concept**
7143 **of collections.**

7144

7145 **Remember that we said "controls" are "objects".**
7146 **The next step was that Objects can have collections**
7147 **of other objects. Each "Child" object of the**
7148 **"parent" object is a member of a *collection*, a list**
7149 **of the child objects owned by the "parent" object.**
7150
7151 **Each child object in a collection is assigned an**
7152 **"index", a number defining it's position within the**
7153 **collection. The "INDEX" is the key to saving, re-**
7154 **loading and manipulating the child objects and**
7155 **their properties.**
7156
7157 ***Read the preceeding 2 paragraphs several times***
7158 ***until it becomes clear to you what the concept of***
7159 ***parent, child and index means.***
7160
7161 Once you get that idea firmly within your grasp the
7162 rest is easy, just more of what you've already learned.
7163 You will see very soon that the visible text
7164 information shown to a user is important to the user,
7165 but not to our program's code.
7166
7167 Start MVS . . . <Tools> + <Options> + <Solutions
7168 and Projects>
7169
7170 Set the location to your VS VB Projects folder. <OK>
7171
7172 <File> + <New Project> + <Language(VB)> +
7173 <Windows Form>
7174
7175 *Name* the project "***VS VB Structs with File IO***", IO
7176 meaning "Input—Output". Input means "Reading
7177 from file", Output means writing (or saving) to file.

7178

7179 &lt;OK&gt;

7180

7181 **We are going to do a new version of the *Automobile***

7182 **information, save (write) it to file and re-load**

7183 **(read) it from file, using "Struct" objects, listBox**

7184 **objects and a new (to us anyway) arrayList**

7185 **control. This object is "invisible" to the user, but**

7186 **key to our program because it can have as it's**

7187 ***"collection"*, *"objects"*, like our structs.**

7188

7189 **Each one (struct objects) will have a numerical**

7190 **index assigned to it . . . the first will be "0" and the**

7191 **rest 1, 2, 3, 4, etc, etc for as many structs as we**

7192 **want to create.**

7193

7194 **By now, you should have a new project created**

7195 **and a blank form belonging to the project.**

7196

7197 When we are done, we will produce results that look

7198 similar to this;

7199

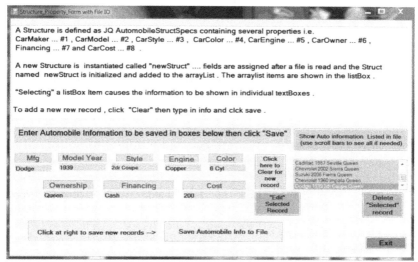

Screen 8

First, we will *define* our *struct*.

In Solution Explorer Right_Click <Project Name> +
<Add>
+ <New Item> + <Class>.
Name the Class "AutomobileStructSpecs". <Add>

When the "class" appears in the solution explorer,
*Double_Click* the *class name* and we will be in the
code block for the skeletal class. Delete everything
in the code block, I REPEAT, "EVERY THING"
in the code block.

(The code is explained by the comments entered
directly in the code block).

Enter the following code;

```
'// Public for access from the form class
```

```
7222 Public Structure AutomobileStructSpecs
7223 '//
7224 '// All the private varibles are assigned by the
7225 '// "Set" code in this class and returned to the
7226 '// "call" command inside the form event handler
7227 '// code blocks as needed.
7228 '// NOTE: I number items in comments to know where
7229 I am
7230 '// and to be sure I address each and every struct
7231 property.
7232 '//
7233 '// I try to do things in the same order each time
7234 I use
7235 '// the properties. It makes finding and
7236 correcting errors
7237 '// much easier.
7238 '//
7239    Private Mfg As String '//# 1
7240    Private Model As String '//# 2
7241    Private Style As String '//# 3
7242    Private EngHP As String '//# 4
7243    Private CarPaint As String '//# 5
7244    Private Banker As String '//# 6
7245    Private Ownership As String '//# 7
7246    Private CarCost As String '//# 8
7247    '//
7248    Public Property CarMaker() As String
7249       Get
7250          Return Mfg
7251       End Get
7252       '//
7253       Set(ByVal value As String)
7254          Mfg = value
7255       End Set
7256       '//
7257    End Property '// . . . Property #1 CarMaker
7258    '//
7259    Public Property CarModel() As String
7260       Get
7261          Return Model
7262       End Get
7263       '//
```

```
7264        Set(ByVal value As String)
7265            Model = value
7266        End Set
7267        '//
7268    End Property '// . . . Property #2 CarModel
7269    '//
7270    Public Property CarStyle() As String
7271        Get
7272            Return Style
7273        End Get
7274        '//
7275        Set(ByVal value As String)
7276            Style = value
7277        End Set
7278        '//
7279    End Property '// . . . Property #3 CarStyle
7280    '//
7281    Public Property CarEngine() As String
7282        Get
7283            Return EngHP
7284        End Get
7285        '//
7286        Set(ByVal value As String)
7287            EngHP = value
7288        End Set
7289        '//
7290    End Property '// . . . Property #4 CarEngine
7291    '//
7292    '//
7293    Public Property CarColor() As String
7294        Get
7295            Return CarPaint
7296        End Get
7297        '//
7298        Set(ByVal value As String)
7299            CarPaint = value
7300        End Set
7301        '//
7302    End Property '// . . . Property #5 CarColor
7303    '//
7304    '//
7305    Public Property Financing() As String
```

```
7306          Get
7307             Return Banker
7308          End Get
7309          Set(ByVal value As String)
7310             Banker = value
7311          End Set
7312       End Property '// . . . Property #6 Financing
7313       Public Property CarOwner() As String
7314          Get
7315             Return Ownership
7316          End Get
7317          '//
7318          Set(ByVal value As String)
7319             Ownership = value
7320          End Set
7321          '//
7322       End Property '// . . . Property #7 CarOwner
7323       Public Property CarPrice() As String
7324          Get
7325             Return CarCost
7326          End Get
7327          Set(value As String)
7328             CarCost = value
7329          End Set
7330       End Property '// . . . Property #8 CarPrice
7331       '//
7332 End Structure
7333
```

7334 **Now for the form and *event handling code*.**

7335

7336 **It really doesn't matter which order you choose to**
7337 **write the**
7338 **Event handlers in. But, within a code block, it's**
7339 **easier if you handle the properties in the same**
7340 **order each time and number them in comments.**

7341

7342 **BUT, at Times, there are "invisible" errors in**
7343 **strings.**

7344 **When typing, you might hit a "control" character,**
7345 **that you cannot see displayed.**
7346
7347 **If a code block fails and you see no error in the**
7348 **strings, delete the string and copy it from a place**
7349 **where it does function correctly -or- as a last**
7350 **resort, re-type the**
7351 **entire string "including" surrounding parenthese**
7352 **and quotation marks.**
7353
7354 **Finding and correcting errors is the hardest part**
7355 **of programming. Numbering items as you process**
7356 **them makes it easier, especially strings being**
7357 **processed that are populated from various object**
7358 **properties.**
7359
7360 **Name the form . . . Use the underscore symbol**
7361 **(don't leave spaces in the name)**
7362 **"Structure_Property_with_File_ IO". Put the**
7363 **same name in the form text property.**
7364
7365 **Add these controls to the form and name as**
7366 **shown;**
7367 *8* **textBoxes,** *10* **labels,** *6* **buttons,** *1* **listBox.**
7368
7369 **Arrange the controls on the form similar to the**
7370 **photo you saw -or- if you have a better idea, use**
7371 **it!! The** *labels* **are for** *hints* **to what the** *user* **should**
7372 *enter* **or** *click* **and one large**
7373 **Explanation/Instruction label for the project, in**
7374 **general.**
7375
7376 *8 textBoxes*          *6 buttons*          *10 labels*

7377

7378 txtBoxMfg             btnDisplay        Name as you like
7379 txtboxModel           btnSaveToFile
7380 txtBoxStyle           btnClear
7381 txtBoxEngine          btnDelete
7382 txtBoxColor               btnEditSelectedRecord
7383 txtBoxFinancer            btnSaveEdits
7384 txtBoxOwner           ArrayList
7385 txtBoxCost            myArryLst

7386

7387 *listBox1* leave name as default "listBox1"

7388

7389 We will create the ArrayList control in our code, it
7390 is not visible to the user. It is a storage device for
7391 our Structs.

7392

7393 Once the controls are added to the form, <View>
7394 on the MVS toolbar. <Tab Order>. Rectangles will
7395 appear on the form controls contaiing default tab
7396 order numbers. Clicking the rectangle changes the
7397 tab order number.

7398

7399 The preferred order of gathering information and
7400 processing information is;

7401

7402 (1) Manufacturer, (2) Model Year, (3) Style, (4)
7403 Engine, (5) Color, (6) Financer, (7) Owner and (8)
7404 Cost. The textboxes and related labels should be
7405 arranged this way. Vertically -or- Horizontally if
7406 you prefer, but in this order and tab order.

7407

7408 Click the <rectangle> by the textbox Mfg until it is
7409 a zero(0). Click the <rectangle> on the next

7410 **control, textBoxModel, until it is One (1). Continue**
7411 **doing this until the 8 textboxes for Auto**
7412 **information are in sequential tab order numbers (0**
7413 **to 7).**
7414
7415 **Get into the *routine* of handling items in this order**
7416 **and you will, I promise, *minimize*(s) your *errors*.**
7417
7418 **This will make it convenient for the user to go, in**
7419 **order, from control to control by hitting the tab**
7420 **key. Sounds simple, but it's a major plus for the**
7421 **user. Everything counts, especially if you are being**
7422 **paid for it or "paying"for it.**
7423
7424 **I chose to code the btnDisplay event handler first.**
7425 **Double_Click btnDisplay and add this code.**
7426
7427 **Normally, after setting up the original records, I**
7428 **think the user will want to see what records are in**
7429 **the file before doing anything else.**
7430
7431 **Occasionally, a user might "Add", "Save" or**
7432 **Delete a record. The same is true of editing**
7433 **records, but probably less often.**
7434
7435 **Let's code;**
7436 **By now you know how to get here.**
7437
7438 **The top portion of this class should look like this;**
7439 `Imports System`
7440 `Imports System.Array`
7441 `Imports System.IO`
7442 `Imports System.IO.DirectoryNotFoundException`
7443 `Public Class Structure_Property_form`

```
7444 Public newStruct As New AutomobileStructSpecs
7445 Public myArryLst As ArrayList
7446 Public myObjIdx As Integer = 0
7447 Public intIdxSelected As Integer
7448 Public intSelectedEditIdx As Integer
7449 '//
7450 '// Some variables are declared as Public so we
7451 can use
7452 '// them throughout the program.
7453
7454 '// btnDisplay event
7455 Private Sub btnDisplay_Click(sender As
7456 System.Object, e As System.EventArgs) Handles
7457 btnDisplay.Click
7458 '// Declare and initialize the StreamReader
7459    Dim myRdr As StreamReader
7460    myRdr = New StreamReader("C:\\App Target Files
7461 AutomobileStructSpecs.txt")
7462
7463 '// Be certain this is the exact, correct path
7464 (name) of the file
7465 '//, spaces, Capital Letter etc., as needed. This
7466 is a very
7467 '// common place to make errors and very hard-to-
7468 discover
7469 '// at times.
7470 '//
7471
```

7472 **For example;**
```
7473 '// myFileTest =
7474 My.Computer.FileSystem.FileExists("C:\\App '//
7475 Target Files\\AutomobileStructSpecs.txt")
7476    '//
7477 ("C:\\ App Target
7478 Files\\AutomobileStructSpecs.txt")
7479    '// This is a good way to compare two
7480 strings . . . ..
7481    '//place one below the other in a comment
7482    '//
```

7483 **The first command might be fine and execute**
7484 **correctly, returning "True", because you**
7485 **"KNOW" the file exists.**
7486
7487 **The next command might fail, because you have an**
7488 **invisible control character embedded in the string.**
7489 **i. e.,**
7490
```
7491 '// If (myFileTest = True) Then
7492 '//    My.Computer.FileSystem.DeleteFile("C:\\App
7493 Target
7494 '// Files\\AutomobileStructSpecs.txt")
7495 '// End If
```
7496

7497 **If "*myFileTest*" is "*True*", the second command**
7498 **should execute correctly. If it doesn't, replace the**
7499 **first string. Yes, it happens!!! Results of the error?**
7500 **You end up with garbage in your files or**
7501 **sometimes, two copies of the same information in**
7502 **file, which is also garbage.**
7503

7504 **OK, having said all that, let's be careful. Get the**
7505 **strings right.**
7506
```
7507 '// btnDisplay event
7508 Private Sub btnDisplay_Click(sender As
7509 System.Object, e As System.EventArgs) Handles
7510 btnDisplay.Click
7511 '// Declare and initialize the StreamReader
7512    Dim myRdr As StreamReader
7513    myRdr = New StreamReader("C:\\App Target Files
7514 AutomobileStructSpecs.txt")
7515    '// Read the file in and set the struct
7516 properties
7517    '//
7518    Dim myStrFromFile As String = " . . ." '//
7519 Prevent "While"
```

```
7520  '// from failing because of an empty string.
7521  '// Declare an integer variable to count the
7522  records we read
7523     Dim intRecordCount As Integer = 0
7524     ''
7525     While myStrFromFile <> "" '// Start file
7526  reading
7527        '// <> means "not" equal, "" means empty.
7528        '// "English" . . . While myStrFromFile is
7529  not empty
7530        '// do the following commands.
7531     '// Declare and read a string.
7532     '// I know CarBuilder is first, that's how we
7533  wrote to the file.
7534        Dim myCarBuilder As String = "" '// property #1
7535        '// Note the numbering of the property.
7536        myCarBuilder = myRdr.ReadLine()
7537        '//
7538        '// Check for end of file, Stop when we
7539  reach the end.
7540        If (myCarBuilder = "" Or myCarBuilder =
7541  Nothing) Then
7542            myRdr.Close()
7543            myRdr.Dispose()
7544            Exit Sub '// exit when we get an empty
7545  string
7546        End If '// end if
7547     '// Assign string "myCarBuilder" to
7548  newStruct."CarMaker"
7549     '// property.
7550        newStruct.CarMaker = myCarBuilder
7551        '//
7552        '//CarBuilder is first Line read from file
7553  for each record
7554        '// We know we read in 8 lines for each
7555  record and assign
7556        '// each one to the correct Struct property.
7557  We must be
7558        '// sure of the order in which we wrote to
7559  the file.
7560        '//
7561        '// Model is next etc, etc.
```

```
7562        Dim myAutoMod As String = "" '// property #2
7563        myAutoMod = myRdr.ReadLine()
7564        newStruct.CarModel = myAutoMod
7565        '//
7566        Dim myAutoStyle As String = "" '// property #3
7567        myAutoStyle = myRdr.ReadLine()
7568        newStruct.CarStyle = myAutoStyle
7569        '//
7570        Dim myAutoColor As String = "" '// property #4
7571        myAutoColor = myRdr.ReadLine()
7572        newStruct.CarColor = myAutoColor
7573        '//
7574        Dim myCarHP As String = "" '// property #5
7575        myCarHP = myRdr.ReadLine()
7576        newStruct.CarEngine = myCarHP
7577        '//
7578        Dim myAutoOwner As String = "" '//property #6
7579        myAutoOwner = myRdr.ReadLine()
7580        newStruct.CarOwner = myAutoOwner
7581        '//
7582        Dim myLoan As String = "" '// property #7
7583        myLoan = myRdr.ReadLine() '
7584        newStruct.Financing = myLoan
7585        '//
7586        Dim myAmt As String = "" '// property #8
7587        myAmt = myRdr.ReadLine()
7588        newStruct.CarPrice = myAmt
7589        '//
7590        '// completed reading in 1 record from file
7591 8 lines.
7592        Dim myListing As String = "" '// Created
7593 right here,
7594        '// not read in from file.
7595        '// concatenate a string to display in our
7596 listBox
7597        '//from strings we read from file.
7598        myListing = myCarBuilder & " " & myAutoMod &
7599 " " & myAutoOwner
7600        '//
7601        '// increment the Record from file counter
7602        '// "intRecordCount"
7603        intRecordCount = intRecordCount + 1
```

```
7604        '// Add object/Struct to ArrayList
7605        myArryLst.Add(newStruct)
7606        '//Add listing to the listBox1.
7607        ListBox1.Items.Add(myListing)
7608     End While '// End "While" . . . Completed
7609 reading a record
7610     '// If didn't get an empty string, go back to
7611 While
7612     '// and repeat the loop.
7613     '// Exit "While"loop after all records have
7614 been read.
7615     '// The reading actually stopped a little
7616 earlier if/when we
7617     '// tried to read in another string and got ""
7618 empty
7619     '// as the contents of the string.
7620     '//
7621 End Sub '// end btnDisplay event handler
7622 '//
7623 '// At this point the screen with a populated
7624 listBox1 becomes
7625 '// visible to the user.
7626
7627 '// The user can now view records, Save a record,
7628 but not
7629 '// delete a record. We need to add that
7630 capability.
7631
```

7632 **For another button added on the form named**
7633 ***btnDelete*, set the *text property* to "*Delete Selected***
7634 ***Record*". I suggest that the "*Back Color property*" be**
7635 **set to "*Red*", this sort of alerts the user to the**
7636 **significance of what they are doing.**
7637

7638 **Get into the event handler code block for**
7639 **"btnDeleteSelectedRecord". Enter this code.**
7640
```
7641 '// Delete a "selected" record
```

```
7642     Private Sub
7643 btnDeleteSelectedRecord_Click(sender As
7644 System.Object, e As System.EventArgs) Handles
7645 btnDeleteSelectedRecord.Click
7646 '// intIdxSelected is a public variable, is
7647 already declared at the '// top of the program. If
7648 the user did NOT select a record
7649 '// by clicking the item in listBox1, -1 is
7650 returned.
7651 '//
7652     intIdxSelected = ListBox1.SelectedIndex
7653 '// Advise the user to select record to delete in
7654 a messageBox.
7655     If (intIdxSelected = -1) Then
7656 '// The first String inside the parenthese is the
7657 actual message.
7658 '// The string following the comma is for the
7659 title bar of the
7660 '// messageBox.
7661 '//
7662         MessageBox.Show("No record selected to
7663 delete. Click a record and then Click ''Delete ''
7664 ", "Delete attempt failed")
```

7665 **The user sees this:**

7666

7667                     **Screen 9**

7668

7669 **They click "OK" and return the original screen.**

7670 **The messageBox is one of a group of controls**

7671 **referred to as "dialog controls". We can and will**

7672 **display more options for the use to click than just**

**7673 OK. We can use code to determine which option**
**7674 was clicked and act accordingly. Our next**
**7675 messageBox will make use of that ability.**
7676
**7677 For now, the user tried clicking "Delete" without**
**7678 choosing (Selecting) a record item. We advised the**
**7679 user and returned them to the starting screen with**
**7680 some instructions to follow.**
7681
```
7682        Return '// exits this event handler. The
7683 user must select
7684        '// a record to delete.
7685    End If
7686    '//
7687    '// Now, assuming a record to delete was
7688 selected
7689    '// purge the file of the old record . . .after
7690 the user
7691    '// confirms the intent to delete the record.
7692    '//
7693    '// Next we are going to rerieve the index of
7694 the Selected
7695    '// Item from the listBox1 and remove that
7696 object from the
7697    '// ArrayList and the listBox1.
7698    '//
7699    '// Then we are going to delete the OLD
7700    '// AutomobileStructSpecs.txt file with the
7701 record
7702    '// the user wants deleted in it.
7703    '//
7704    '// Finally, we will retrieve the properties of
7705 the
7706    '// remaining "Keeper" Objects in the Array
7707 list and
7708    '// Write their prpperties to a "New"
7709    '// AutomobileSructSpecs.txt file.
7710    '//
```

```
7711      '// THIS is where knowing-the-order of items
7712 being
7713      '// read from or written to file is crucial!!!
7714      '// This is another instance and example of the
7715      '// "IMPORTANCE" of "INDEX" numbers.
7716      '//
7717      '// First we know the index of the item
7718 selected, it needs
7719      '// to be "RemovedAt" that index in both the
7720 listBox1
7721      '// and the ArrayList. It has the same index in
7722 both
7723      '// controls because it was added to both, at
7724 the same time.
7725      '// Items are added to both controls one-for-
7726 one.
7727      '//
7728      ListBox1.SelectedIndex = intIdxSelected '//
7729 Assures that we
7730      '// have the right item selected before
7731 deleting anything.
7732      Dim strMyStrMfg As String =
7733 ListBox1.SelectedItem
7734      '// Using MessageBox to get User input
7735 Example . . .
7736      '// Specify the buttons to be shown in the
7737 MessageBox
7738      '// . . . verify "Delete" or "Cancel" before
7739 Delete is done.
7740      '//
7741      If MessageBox.Show(strMyStrMfg & " is located
7742 at index " & Convert.ToString(intIdxSelected) &
7743 "." & " Click OK to remove this item. Click Cancel
7744 to keep this item ", _
7745      " 'DELETE' verification ",
7746 MessageBoxButtons.OKCancel, _
7747      MessageBoxIcon.Information,
7748 MessageBoxDefaultButton.Button1) _
7749      = Windows.Forms.DialogResult.OK Then
7750      '//
7751      '// IF . . . the user clicked "OK" proceed to
7752 delete the
```

```
7753     '// record. This takes several lines of code.
7754     '// Proceed by clearing the txtBoxes and
7755 removing the
7756     '// item from the ArrayList On the otherhand,
7757 if the user
7758     '// Clicks "cancel" only one command is needed.
7759     '// Exit Sub, you'll see this in just a bit.
7760     '//
7761     '// Remove the items from ArrayList and
7762 ListBox.
7763         ListBox1.Items.RemoveAt(intIdxSelected)
7764         myArryLst.RemoveAt(intIdxSelected)
7765         '// Blank out the textboxes.
7766         '//
7767         txtBoxMfg.Text = "" '//        #1
7768         txtBoxModel.Text = "" '//       #2
7769         txtBoxStyle.Text = "" '//       #3
7770         txtBoxEngine.Text = "" '//      #4
7771         txtBoxColor.Text = "" '//       #5
7772         txtBoxFinancer.Text = "" '// #6
7773         txtBoxOwner.Text = "" '//       #7
7774         txtBoxCost.Text = "" '//        #8
7775         '// Now, go re-create the file with only the
7776 "Keeper"
7777         '// items.
7778         ReCreateFile()'// This calls an outside
7779 Sburoutine to
7780         '// write the file.
7781         Else '// Meaning the user did NOT click
7782 "OK".
7783         Exit Sub '// IF . . . the user clicked
7784 "Cancel" abort the
7785                 '// Delete operation!!!!
7786     End If '// End If
7787 End Sub '// End btnDeleteSelectedRecord Click
7788 '//
```

7789 **That's it!! Either we deleted the record or aborted**
7790 **the attempt. *Next*, I'll show you the Re-Create()**
7791 **Sub Routine.**

7792

**PS . . . All of the comments and explanations included here are not actually in the actual code blocks. This subroutine (Sub) is called from the btnDeleteSelectdRecord_Click Event. It is not visible or even known to the user.**

```
'//
Public Sub ReCreateFile()
'//Remember this sub was called from the
'// btnDeleteSelectedRecord_Click event
'// A this point the targeted items has been
removed frm the
'// ArrayList and the listBox1
'// All that remains are records we want to
retain . . .
'//
   Dim myFileTest As Boolean = False
'// Boolean is a "Logocal variable", True means
the Condition
'// tested for exists.
'//
'// CK file, delete old file if it exists
   myFileTest =
My.Computer.FileSystem.FileExists("C:\\App Target
Files\\AutomobileStructSpecs.txt") '// Evaluates
'// as True if the file exists.
("C:\\ App Target
Files\\AutomobileStructSpecs.txt")
   '//
   '// This is a good way to compare two
strings . . . .
   '// place one below the other in a comment and
look
   '// for any differences
   '//
   '// CK file, delete old file if it exists
   If (myFileTest = True) Then
      My.Computer.FileSystem.DeleteFile("C:\\App
Target Files\\AutomobileStructSpecs.txt")
   End If
   '// Create info we need to re-write the
```

```
7833     '// AutomobileStructSpecs.txt file.
7834     Dim ArrayListItemCount As Integer =
7835 myArryLst.Count—1
7836     '// ArrayListItemCountItemCount says how many
7837     '// objects are in the ArrayList (0 to whatever)
7838     '// the count was -1 because it there are 16
7839 items
7840     '// we number them 0 thru 15.
7841     '//
7842     '// get properties from objects (Structs)in the
7843 ArrayList
7844     '// and write them to file
7845     '// Declare two (2) variables to do the work
7846 with.
7847     Dim myObj As Object
7848     Dim XX As Integer = 0 '// This will be our
7849 indexer as we
7850     '// ask for each Object in the ArrayList.
7851     '//
7852     For Each myObj In myArryLst
7853     '//
7854     newStruct = myArryLst.Item(XX)
7855     '// "0" is the first indexer used.
7856     '// Note numbering of properties in comments.
7857     '//
7858     '// Assiging property vaues to strings.
7859     Dim myStr1 As String = newStruct.CarMaker '// #1
7860     Dim myStr2 As String = newStruct.CarModel '// #2
7861     Dim myStr3 As String = newStruct.CarStyle '// #3
7862     Dim myStr4 As String = newStruct.CarEngine '// #4
7863     Dim myStr5 As String = newStruct.CarColor '// #5
7864     Dim myStr6 As String = newStruct.CarOwner '// #6
7865     Dim myStr7 As String = newStruct.Financing '// #7
7866     Dim myStr8 As String = newStruct.CarPrice '// #8
7867     '// re-create (Write) the file
7868 "AutomobileStructSpecs.txt"
7869     Dim myWrt As StreamWriter = New
7870 StreamWriter("C:\\App Target
7871 Files\\AutomobileStructSpecs.txt", True)
7872     '// Remember "True" here means create a file if
7873 it doesn't
7874     '// exist, append it if it does.
```

```
7875    myWrt.WriteLine(myStr1) '// #1
7876    myWrt.WriteLine(myStr2) '// #2
7877    myWrt.WriteLine(myStr3) '// #3
7878    myWrt.WriteLine(myStr4) '// #4
7879    myWrt.WriteLine(myStr5) '// #5
7880    myWrt.WriteLine(myStr6) '// #6
7881    myWrt.WriteLine(myStr7) '// #7
7882    myWrt.WriteLine(myStr8) '// #8
7883    '// One record written to file.
7884    '// Release the system resources and the file
7885    '//
7886    myWrt.Close()
7887    myWrt.Dispose()
7888    '// Increment our object index number, "For
7889 each" doesn't
7890     '// do this for us automatically.
7891    XX = XX + 1
7892    Next '// End point of 1st For each
7893 "object" . . . .
7894     '//Go on to next Struct object in ArrayList.
7895     '//retrieve it's properties and write them to
7896 file.
7897     '//
7898 End Sub'// End Sub Re-createFile after last
7899 Object's properties
7900        '// are written to file.
7901
```

**7902 So far we have programmed two functions for the**
**7903 user,**
**7904 Display and Delete. We included the ReCreate**
**7905 Subroutine for clarity on what Deleting entails.**
7906
**7907 Now we will do the "Add new records" code.**
**7908 The button name for this event is**
**7909 "bntnSaveToFile".**
**7910 The event is . . . btnSaveToFile_Click. It assumes a**
**7911 user**
**7912 Clicked "Click here to clear for new record" then**

7913 **entered the information for a new vehicle record in**
7914 **the textBoxes and is clicking "Save Automobile**
7915 **info to file file".**
7916 **btnClear_Click is very simple;**
7917
```
7918 Private Sub btnClear_Click(sender As
7919 System.Object, e As System.EventArgs) Handles
7920 btnClear.Click
7921     txtBoxMfg.Text = "" '// Blanks this textBox
7922     txtBoxModel.Text = ""
7923     txtBoxStyle.Text = ""
7924     txtBoxEngine.Text = ""
7925     txtBoxColor.Text = ""
7926     txtBoxCost.Text = ""
7927     txtBoxFinancer.Text = ""
7928     txtBoxOwner.Text = ""
7929     ListBox1.Items.Clear()'// Empties the IistBox1.
7930 End Sub '// end btnClear click event
```
7931
7932 **I don't think, at this point, that event needs any**
7933 **further explanation. But, take the time to look it**
7934 **over carefully. make sure you understand what it**
7935 **does.**
7936
7937 **After "Saving" a new record, the user needs to re-**
7938 **load**
7939 **(re-Display) the information from file. This causes**
7940 **all records (including the new one) to be added**
7941 **one-at-a-time to the ArrayList as structure objects**
7942 **and a listing for the listBox1 items created during**
7943 **the loading process.**
7944
7945 **Now let's code the btnSaveToFile_Click event.**
7946 **This assumes the user entered the information for**
7947 **a new vehicle in the textboxes and clicks "Save**
7948 **Autobile Info to file ".**

```vb
7949
7950 '// btnSaveToFile
7951    Private Sub btnSaveToFile_Click(sender As
7952 System.Object, e As System.EventArgs) Handles
7953 btnSaveToFile.Click
7954    '// Declare a string, get the info from the
7955 textbox
7956    '// and assign the string to the property of
7957 the newStruct.
7958    '// Repeat for each property of the 8 we
7959 defined.
7960    '//
7961    Dim myMfg As String = "" '// #1 Mfg
7962    myMfg = txtBoxMfg.Text
7963    newStruct.CarMaker = myMfg
7964    '//
7965    Dim myAutoModel As String = "" '// #2 Model
7966    myAutoModel = txtBoxModel.Text
7967    newStruct.CarModel = myAutoModel
7968    '//
7969    Dim myAutoStyle As String = "" '// #3 Style
7970    myAutoStyle = txtBoxStyle.Text
7971    newStruct.CarStyle = myAutoStyle
7972    '//
7973    Dim myAutoEngine As String = "" '// #4 Engine
7974    myAutoEngine = txtBoxEngine.Text()
7975    newStruct.CarEngine = myAutoEngine
7976    '//
7977    Dim myAutoColor As String = "" '// #5 Color
7978    myAutoColor = txtBoxColor.Text()
7979    newStruct.CarColor = myAutoColor
7980    '//
7981    Dim myAutoOwner As String = "" '// #6 Owner
7982    myAutoOwner = txtBoxOwner.Text()
7983    newStruct.CarOwner = txtBoxOwner.Text
7984    '//
7985    Dim myAutoFinancer As String = "" '//#7
7986 Financer
7987    myAutoFinancer = txtBoxFinancer.Text()
7988    newStruct.Financing = myAutoFinancer
7989    '//
```

```
7990      Dim myAutoCost As String = ""
7991      myAutoCost = txtBoxCost.Text() '// #8 Cost
7992      newStruct.CarPrice = myAutoCost
7993      '//
7994      '// All 8 properties are defined, write them to
7995 file.
7996      '//
7997      '// Create StreamWriter
7998      Dim myWrt As StreamWriter
7999      myWrt = New StreamWriter("C:\\App Target
8000 Files\\AutomobileStructSpecs.txt", True)'// Be
8001 sure the string is '// right.
8002      '//
8003      '// Write info to file for new record
8004      '//
8005      myWrt.WriteLine(myMfg) '//           #1 mfg
8006      myWrt.WriteLine(myAutoModel) '//     #2 model
8007      myWrt.WriteLine(myAutoStyle) '//     #3 Style
8008      myWrt.WriteLine(myAutoEngine) '//    #4 Engine
8009      myWrt.WriteLine(myAutoColor) '//     #5 Color
8010      myWrt.WriteLine(myAutoOwner) '//     #6 Owner
8011      myWrt.WriteLine(myAutoFinancer) '// #7 Financer
8012      myWrt.WriteLine(myAutoCost) '//      #8 Cost
8013      '//
8014      '// ----------------------- Release resources
8015 and file
8016      myWrt.Close()
8017      myWrt.Dispose()
8018      '//
8019 End Sub '// ------------ End btnSaveToFile event
8020 '//
```

8021 This is a good time to make sure the big label has
8022 good instruction for the user. Here is what I wrote.
8023 Got a better idea? If so, use it.

8024

8025 lblInstruct text property . . .

8026

8027 A Structure is defined as JQ AutomobileStructSpecs
8028 containing several properties i.e.

8029 CarMaker . . . #1, CarModel . . . #2, CarStyle . . . #3,
8030 CarColor . . . #4, CarEngine . . . #5, CarOwner . . . #6,
8031 Financing . . . #7 and CarCost . . . #8.
8032
8033 A new Structure is instantiated called
8034 "newStruct" . . . . fields are assigned after a file is read
8035 and the Struct named newStruct is initialized and
8036 added to the arrayList. The arraylist items are shown
8037 in the listBox.
8038
8039 "Selecting" a listBox Item causes the information to
8040 be shown in individual textBoxes.
8041
8042 To EDIT a record Click the item in the listBox, re-
8043 type you changes and Click "Save Edits"
8044
8045 To add a new rew record, click "Clear" then type in
8046 info and clck save. After Saving a new record click
8047 "Show Auto information" to see "ALL" of the records
8048 including the new one.
8049
8050 Like I said, if you have a better idea, use it.
8051

8052 **OK, we've written code for Display, Delete and**
8053 **Save plus the ReCreateFile subroutine. Next we do**
8054 **Edit. This assumes the user displayed the records,**
8055 **selected one and decided to edit the record. Next**
8056 **the *user clicks "Edit Selected record"*.**
8057

8058 **Double Click *"Edit Selected record"*. Enter the**
8059 **event handler code.**
8060 `'//`
8061 `Public Sub btnEdit_Click(sender As System.Object,`
8062 `e As System.EventArgs) Handles btnEdit.Click`

```
8063 '//
8064 '// First things first. Get the index for the item
8065 selected.
8066 '//
8067    intSelectedEditIdx = ListBox1.SelectedIndex
8068 '//
8069 '// If nothing is selected advise and instruct the
8070 user.
8071 '// An index of -1 means no selection has been
8072 made.
8073 '//
8074    If (intSelectedEditIdx = -1) Then
8075 MessageBox.Show("You must first select a listing
8076 to EDIT", "NO ITEM SELECTED!! ")
8077    '// Re-set backcolors of controls
8078    lblMfg.BackColor = Color.Cyan
8079    '// Choose any color you like
8080    txtBoxMfg.BackColor = Color.Cyan '//        #1
8081    lblModel.BackColor = Color.Cyan
8082    txtBoxModel.BackColor = Color.Cyan '//      #2
8083    lblStyle.BackColor = Color.Cyan
8084    txtBoxStyle.BackColor = Color.Cyan '//      #3
8085    lblEngine.BackColor = Color.Cyan
8086    txtBoxEngine.BackColor = Color.Cyan '//     #4
8087    lblEngine.BackColor = Color.Cyan
8088    txtBoxColor.BackColor = Color.Cyan '//      #5
8089    lblColor.BackColor = Color.Cyan
8090    txtBoxFinancer.BackColor = Color.Cyan '//   #6
8091    lblFinancier.BackColor = Color.Cyan
8092    txtBoxOwner.BackColor = Color.Cyan '//      #7
8093    lblOwnership.BackColor = Color.Cyan
8094    txtBoxCost.BackColor = Color.Cyan '//       #8
8095    lblCost.BackColor = Color.Cyan
8096    '//
8097    ListBox1.BackColor = Color.Cyan
8098    btnSaveEdits.Visible = True '// Show the Save
8099 Edits button '// and advise and instruct the user.
8100    MessageBox.Show("To makes CHANGES—RE-TYPE the
8101 information in the desired TEXTBOX(s) then CLICK—
8102 SAVE EDITS ", "Edit Instruction")
8103    '// The first string is the actual message
8104 body,
```

```
8105     '// The string after the comma is the
8106   messageBox Title
8107     '//
8108     '// Create an instance (working copy) of the
8109   Struct
8110     '// object stored in our arraylist.
8111     '//
8112     newStruct = myArryLst.Item(intSelectedEditIdx)
8113     '//
8114     '// Set textbox text properties to the actual
8115   contents
8116     '// of the Struct properties by populating
8117   strings then
8118     '// putting the string in the textbox text
8119   properties.
8120     '//
8121     '// Change the textbox backcolor to draw
8122   attention
8123     '// to the "being edited" situation and
8124   priority.
8125     '//
8126     '//
8127     Dim strEditMfg As String = newStruct.CarMaker
8128     '//                                          #1
8129     txtBoxMfg.Text = strEditMfg
8130     txtBoxMfg.ForeColor = Color.Red
8131     Dim strEditMod As String = newStruct.CarModel
8132     '//                                          #2
8133     txtBoxModel.Text = strEditMod
8134     txtBoxModel.ForeColor = Color.Red
8135     Dim strEditStyle As String = newStruct.CarStyle
8136     '//                                          #3
8137     txtBoxStyle.Text = strEditStyle
8138     txtBoxStyle.ForeColor = Color.Red
8139     Dim strEditEng As String = newStruct.CarEngine
8140     '//                                          #4
8141     txtBoxEngine.Text = strEditEng
8142     txtBoxEngine.ForeColor = Color.Red
8143     Dim strEditColor As String = newStruct.CarColor
8144     '//                                          #5
8145     txtBoxColor.Text = strEditColor
8146     txtBoxColor.ForeColor = Color.Red
```

```
8147     Dim strEditBanker As String = newStruct.Financing
8148     '//                                              #6
8149     txtBoxFinancer.Text = strEditBanker
8150     txtBoxFinancer.ForeColor = Color.Red
8151     Dim strEditOwner As String = newStruct.CarOwner
8152     '//                                              #7
8153     txtBoxOwner.Text = strEditOwner
8154     txtBoxOwner.ForeColor = Color.Red
8155     Dim strEditCost As String = newStruct.CarPrice
8156     '//                                              #8
8157     txtBoxCost.Text = strEditCost
8158     txtBoxCost.ForeColor = Color.Red
8159     '//
8160 End Sub '// End btnEdit_Click
8161 '//
```

8162 **Now it's up to the user to re-type the information**
8163 **they want changed. After that is done, the user will**
8164 **click . . .**
8165 **"Save Edits". So, Double click "save Edits" and**
8166 **let's write the code.**

```
8167
8168 '//
8169     Public Sub btnSaveEdits_Click(sender As
8170 System.Object, e As System.EventArgs) Handles
8171 btnSaveEdits.Click
8172     Dim strChangedMfg = txtBoxMfg.Text
8173     '//                                              #1
8174     txtBoxMfg.ForeColor = Color.MistyRose
8175     '// Change textbox backcolor to show that the
8176 edits have
8177     '// been saved. It's a small thing, but small
8178 things matter.
8179     '// Pick a color you like.
8180     '//
8181     Dim strChangedMod As String = txtBoxModel.Text
8182     '//                                              #2
8183     txtBoxModel.ForeColor = Color.MistyRose
8184     '//
8185     Dim strChangedStyle As String = txtBoxStyle.Text
8186     '//                                              #3
```

```
8187        txtBoxStyle.ForeColor = Color.MistyRose
8188        '//
8189        Dim strChangedEng As String = txtBoxEngine.Text
8190        '//                                              #4
8191        txtBoxEngine.ForeColor = Color.MistyRose
8192        '//
8193        Dim strChangedColor As String = txtBoxColor.Text
8194        '//                                              #5
8195        txtBoxColor.ForeColor = Color.MistyRose
8196        '//
8197        Dim strChangedBanker As String = txtBoxFinancer.Text
8198        '//                                              #6
8199        txtBoxFinancer.ForeColor = Color.MistyRose
8200        '//
8201        Dim strChangedOwner As String = txtBoxOwner.Text
8202        '//                                              #7
8203        txtBoxOwner.ForeColor = Color.MistyRose
8204        '//
8205        Dim strChangedCost As String = txtBoxCost.Text
8206        '//                                              #8
8207        txtBoxCost.ForeColor = Color.MistyRose
8208        '//
8209        '//
8210        '// Delete old Object from ArrayList and
8211 listing in ListBox1
8212        '//
8213        myArryLst.RemoveAt(intSelectedEditIdx)
8214        ListBox1.Items.RemoveAt(intSelectedEditIdx)
8215        '//
8216        '// Re-define edited values to newStruct
8217        '//
8218        Dim myMfg As String = "" '//            #1 Mfg
8219        myMfg = txtBoxMfg.Text
8220        newStruct.CarMaker = myMfg
8221        '//
8222        Dim myAutoModel As String = "" '//   #2 Model
8223        myAutoModel = txtBoxModel.Text
8224        newStruct.CarModel = myAutoModel
8225        '//
8226        Dim myAutoStyle As String = "" '//   #3 Style
8227        myAutoStyle = txtBoxStyle.Text
8228        newStruct.CarStyle = myAutoStyle
```

```
8229     '//
8230     Dim myAutoEngine As String = "" '//   #4 Engine
8231     myAutoEngine = txtBoxEngine.Text()
8232     newStruct.CarEngine = myAutoEngine
8233     '//
8234     Dim myAutoColor As String = "" '//   #5 Color
8235     myAutoColor = txtBoxColor.Text()
8236     newStruct.CarColor = myAutoColor
8237     '//
8238     Dim myAutoOwner As String = "" '//   #6 Owner
8239     myAutoOwner = txtBoxOwner.Text()
8240     newStruct.CarOwner = txtBoxOwner.Text
8241     '//
8242     Dim myAutoFinancer As String = "" '// #7 Financer
8243     myAutoFinancer = txtBoxFinancer.Text()
8244     newStruct.Financing = myAutoFinancer
8245     '//
8246     Dim myAutoCost As String = ""
8247     myAutoCost = txtBoxCost.Text() '//   #8 Cost
8248     newStruct.CarPrice = myAutoCost
8249     '// Add newStruct to myArryLst . . . with
8250 edited information
8251     myArryLst.Add(newStruct)
8252     '// Call Sub CreateEditedFile to erase old info
8253 and save
8254     '// the new info
8255     CreateEditedFile() '// Calls an outside subroutine to
8256               '// re-write the file. It keeps this
8257               '// code block simple and easy to
8258               '// read and trouble shoot.
8259 End Sub '// End Save Edits
8260 '// Here is the Subroutine called from inside
8261 "Save Edits".
8262 '//
8263 Public Sub CreateEditedFile()
8264     '// Remember this sub was called from the
8265     '// btnSaveEdits_Click event.
8266     '//
8267     '// At this point the targeted item has been
8268 removed from
8269     '// the ArrayList and listBox1
8270     '//
```

```
8271    '// A new object has been added to myArryLst
8272    '// containing updated info. All Objects now have
8273    '// properties we want to keep . . .
8274    '//
8275    '// This code writes those items to file.
8276    '// One object at a time, 8 properties per
8277 object.
8278    '// CK file, delete old file if it exists
8279    Dim myFileTest As Boolean = False '// Boolean
8280 is a
8281    '// "Logocal variable", True means the
8282 Condition tested for
8283    '// existed.
8284    myFileTest = My.Computer.FileSystem.FileExists
8285    '//("C:\\App Target
8286 Files\\AutomobileStructSpecs.txt")
8287    '//("C:\\ App Target
8288 Files\\AutomobileStructSpecs.txt")
8289    '//
8290    '// This is a good way to compare two strings
8291 when coding.
8292    '// Errors are hard to find in long
8293 strings . . . .
8294    '// place one below the other in a comment.
8295    '//
8296    '// BUT, at Times, there are "invisible" errors
8297 in strings.
8298    '// When typing, you might hit a "control"
8299 character, that
8300    '// you do not see displayed.
8301    '// If a code block fails and you see no error
8302 in the strings,
8303    '// delete the string and copy it from a place
8304 where it does
8305    '// function correctly -or- as a last resort,
8306 re-type the
8307    '// entire string "including" surrounding
8308 parenthese and
8309    '// quotation marks.
8310    '//
8311    '// BELIEVE ME IT HAPPENS!!!
8312    '//
```

```
8313    '// CK file, delete old file if it exists
8314    If (myFileTest = True) Then
8315        My.Computer.FileSystem.DeleteFile("C:\\App
8316 Target Files\\AutomobileStructSpecs.txt")
8317    End If
8318    '// Create info we need to re-write the
8319    '// AutomobileStructSpecs.txt file.
8320    Dim ArrayListItemCount As Integer =
8321 myArryLst.Count-1
8322    '// ArrayListItemCountItemCount says how many
8323 objects in
8324    '// the ArrayList (0 to whatever) the count was -1
8325    '// to get properties from and write them to
8326 file
8327    '// because they are numbered "0" to??
8328    '//
8329    '// Remember, The old object was deleted, the
8330 new info
8331    '// object added to the myArryLst
8332    '//
8333    Dim myObj As Object
8334    Dim XX As Integer = 0
8335    '//. . . . . . . . . . . . . . For Each Loop
8336    For Each myObj In myArryLst
8337    '//
8338    newStruct = myArryLst.Item(XX)
8339    '//
8340    Dim myStrEdited1 As String = newStruct.CarMaker
8341    '//                                          #1
8342    Dim myStrEdited2 As String = newStruct.CarModel
8343    '//                                          #2
8344    Dim myStrEdited3 As String = newStruct.CarStyle
8345    '//                                          #3
8346    Dim myStrEdited4 As String = newStruct.CarEngine
8347    '//                                          #4
8348    Dim myStrEdited5 As String = newStruct.CarColor
8349    '//                                          #5
8350    Dim myStrEdited6 As String = newStruct.CarOwner
8351    '//                                          #6
8352    Dim myStrEdited7 As String = newStruct.Financing
8353    '//                                          #7
8354    Dim myStrEdited8 As String = newStruct.CarPrice
```

```
8355     '//                                              #8
8356     '// re-create (Write) the file
8357 "AutomobileStructSpecs.txt"
8358     Dim myWrt As StreamWriter = New
8359 StreamWriter("C:\\App Target
8360 Files\\AutomobileStructSpecs.txt", True)
8361     '// Remember "true" here means create a file if it
8362     '// doesn't exist, append it if it does.
8363     myWrt.WriteLine(myStrEdited1) '// #1
8364     myWrt.WriteLine(myStrEdited2) '// #2
8365     myWrt.WriteLine(myStrEdited3) '// #3
8366     myWrt.WriteLine(myStrEdited4) '// #4
8367     myWrt.WriteLine(myStrEdited5) '// #5
8368     myWrt.WriteLine(myStrEdited6) '// #6
8369     myWrt.WriteLine(myStrEdited7) '// #7
8370     myWrt.WriteLine(myStrEdited8) '// #8
8371     '// One record written to file.
8372     '// Release the system resources and the file
8373     myWrt.Close()
8374     myWrt.Dispose()
8375     '// Increment our object index number,
8376 "Foreach"
8377     '// doesn't do this for us automatically.
8378     XX = XX + 1
8379     Next '// End point of 1st Foreach
8380 "object" . . . .
8381     '// Go on to next Struct object in ArrayList.
8382 End Sub
8383 '//
```

8384 One last Event . . . Selecting an Item in the listBox1
8385 When the user Selects a listBox item . . . the Selected
8386 IndexChanged event occurs. The information for that
8387 item appears in the textboxes. This code that makes
8388 that happen.

```
8389 '//
8390 Private Sub ListBox1_SelectedIndexChanged(sender
8391 As System.Object, e As System.EventArgs) Handles
8392 ListBox1.SelectedIndexChanged
8393 '// This event occurs when user selects (Clicks
8394 on) an
```

```
8395 '// item in the listBox.
8396 '// Note: We are NOT readubg from a file here, we
8397 are using
8398 '// properties of our selected Object from the
8399 ArrayList.
8400 '//
8401 '// HERE IS THE HEART BEAT of our program . . . .
8402 '// getting the index for the item the user selected
8403 '// from the listBox display. Each time we read in a
8404 '// record (8 lines from file) we created a string
8405 to display
8406 '// in our listBox -AND- we added an object
8407 (newStruct)
8408 '// to our ArryLst. Since the addition to the
8409 listBox
8410 '// and ArryLst occur at the sametime . . . they
8411 both are assigned
8412 '// the same numerical index.
8413 '//
8414 '// If the user selects Item 2 (or whatever) in
8415 the list box, I know '// I can use the index of 2
8416 (or whatever) to
8417 '// access the correct object in the ArrayList.
8418 Remember,
8419 '// indexes start with "0" and add one to "0"
8420 '// for the second item added etc, etc
8421 '//
8422 '// Get the correct object from the ArrayList
8423     Dim myObjCount As Integer = myArryLst.Count
8424     myObjIdx = ListBox1.SelectedIndex
8425     If (myObjIdx = -1 Or myObjIdx > myObjCount-1) Then
8426         Return '// means exit this event handler
8427         block of code
8428     End If
8429 '// Set the newStruct object to our selected
8430 ArrayList object
8431     newStruct = myArryLst.Item(myObjIdx)
8432 '//
8433 '// Use the property content from the Struct
8434 (newStruct)
8435 '// properties to populate the text property of
8436 the textBoxes
```

```
8437  '//
8438     txtBoxMfg.Text = newStruct.CarMaker '//        #1
8439     txtBoxModel.Text = newStruct.CarModel '//      #2
8440     txtBoxStyle.Text = newStruct.CarStyle '//      #3
8441     txtBoxEngine.Text = newStruct.CarEngine '//    #4
8442     txtBoxColor.Text = newStruct.CarColor '//      #5
8443     txtBoxOwner.Text = newStruct.CarOwner '//      #6
8444     txtBoxFinancer.Text = newStruct.Financing '//#7
8445     txtBoxCost.Text = newStruct.CarPrice '//       #8
8446     '//
8447  End Sub '// End btnDisplay Click event
8448  '//
8449
```

8450  **That's it!!**

8451

8452  **The user can create, display, delete or edit records.**
8453  **Complete, less commented *VB* code is in *Appendix***
8454  ***N.***

8455

8456  **OK, *Break time* . . . do something away from the**
8457  **computer for a while!!! All work and no play**
8458  **makes . . . etc, etc.**

8459

8460  # C# Struct With File IO

8461

8462  **Every program has weak points . . . mine, yours**
8463  **and even Microsoft's applications. One case and**
8464  **point is Microsoft Visual Studio. It has some**
8465  **"bugs", or at least weaknesses, in it too. You have**
8466  **probably stumbled some of them over getting to**
8467  **this point. One in particular is this . . . When an**
8468  **erroneous statement is typed into the code, you get**
8469  **the "Red Line of Error" under the line of code.**
8470  **When this happens the error line flag should**
8471  **disappear as soon as you retype the statement**
8472  **correctly. Frequently, this does not happen.**

8473

8474 **If you have checked your spelling and**
8475 **capitalization carefully and still get an error**
8476 **indication . . . even after re-typing the code,** *use the*
8477 *build command or click the icon* **on the MVS**
8478 **toolbar. This usually clears the error flag.**

8479

8480 **An even more difficult one to find occurs when the**
8481 **form you're working on becoming invisible. This is**
8482 **usually a matter of finding a mis-matched curly**
8483 **brace or renaming something in the program. Still**
8484 **another, is deleting a complete line of code when it**
8485 **is highlighted by pressing some key accidentally.**
8486 **The correction for that is simply pressing or**
8487 **clicking the the undo iconon the toolbar. The line**
8488 **re-appears as it was before.**

8489

8490 **Another example is the difficulty of locating**
8491 **matching curly braces. It is strictly up to you to**
8492 **find the problem and correct it.Often the error(s)**
8493 **are not actually in the line underscored by the**
8494 **error flag. There are several more, one must**
8495 **persist snf believe in their self . . . Try hard enough**
8496 **and long enough and you wil find it!**
8497 **Now for the C# version of Structs with File IO.**

8498

8499 **Even with these and some other short comings . . .**
8500 **MVS is still a powerful, invaluable tool for**
8501 **programming. Learn to use it well. It is the best-**
8502 **suited tool for C# and VB coding I am aware of at**
8503 **this time.**

8504

8505 **As you work save your code frequently. It's really**
8506 **frustrating to do a lot of work and lose it if you**
8507 **have a power failure or something similar.**
8508 **<File><Save All> -or just hit the "Save" icon on**
8509 **the MVS taskbar.**
8510
8511 **Remember the comments about how C# Structs**
8512 **are not clear or conducive to writing Structs with**
8513 **properities you can "get" or "set"? We want to**
8514 **manipulate and save records to file. This time we**
8515 **will build the struct inside the code for the form**
8516 **itself. It's much easier to access from there.**
8517
8518 **Add these controls to the form and name as**
8519 **shown;**
8520 *8* **textBoxes,** *10* **labels,** *6* **buttons,** *1* **listBox.**
8521
8522 **Arrange the controls on the form similar to the**
8523 **photo you saw -or- if you have a better idea, use**
8524 **it!! The** *labels* **are for** *hints* **to what the** *user* **should**
8525 *enter* **or** *click* **and one large**
8526 **Explanation/Instruction label for the project, in**
8527 **general.**
8528
8529 **My example looks like this;**

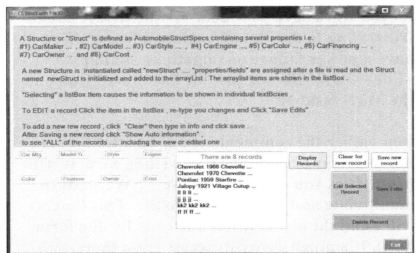

8530

8531                    **Screen 10**

8532

8533 *8 textBoxes*          *6 buttons*          *10 labels*

8534

8535 **txtBoxMfg**          **btnDisplay**          *Name as you like*

8536 **txtboxModel**        **btnSaveToFile**

8537 **txtBoxStyle**        **btnClear**

8538 **txtBoxEngine**       **btnDelete**

8539 **txtBoxColor**            **btnEditSelectedRecord**

8540 **txtBoxFinancer**         **btnSaveEdits**

8541 **txtBoxOwner**        **ArrayList**

8542 **txtBoxCost**         **myArryLst**

8543

8544 *listBox1* leave name as default "listBox1"

8545

8546 **We will create the ArrayList control in our code, it**

8547 **is not visible to the user. It is a storage device for**

8548 **our Structs.**

8549

8550 **This is a pretty long block of code. I again** *caution*

8551 *against* **copying and pasting from the text.** *Copy*

8552 *and paste from the example files. Do* this when you
8553 are *refreshed* and can *concentrate* for at least *two*
8554 *hours.* Losing your train of thought can be a real
8555 issue in this exercise.
8556
8557 **The first step for an actual user would be creating**
8558 **some records. Let's code it. Double_Click the**
8559 **"Save new Record" button and enter the event**
8560 **handler.**

```
8561 //
8562 private void btnSaveRecord_Click(object sender,
8563 EventArgs e)
8564 {
8565     AutoStruct newStruct = new AutoStruct();
8566     //
8567     string myMfg = "";//                    #1 Mfg
8568     myMfg = txtBoxMfg.Text;
8569     newStruct.CarBuilder = myMfg;
8570     //
8571     string myAutoModel = "";//              #2 Model
8572     myAutoModel = txtBoxModel.Text;
8573     newStruct.CarModel = myAutoModel;
8574     //
8575     string myAutoStyle = "";//              #3 Style
8576     myAutoStyle = txtBoxStyle.Text;
8577     newStruct.myCarStyle = myAutoStyle;
8578     //
8579     string myAutoEngine = ""; //            #4 Engine
8580     myAutoEngine = txtBoxEngine.Text;
8581     newStruct.myCarEng = myAutoEngine;
8582     //
8583     string myAutoColor = ""; //             #5 Color
8584     myAutoColor = txtBoxColor.Text;
8585     newStruct.myCarsColor = myAutoColor;
8586     //
8587     string myAutoOwner = "";//              #6 Owner
8588     myAutoOwner = txtBoxOwner.Text;
8589     newStruct.myCarRealOwner = txtBoxOwner.Text;
8590     //
```

```
8591      string myAutoFinancer = ""; //        #7 Financer
8592      myAutoFinancer = txtBoxFinancer.Text;
8593      newStruct.myCarsBanker = myAutoFinancer;
8594      //
8595      string myAutoCost = "";
8596      myAutoCost = txtBoxCost.Text; //       #8 Cost
8597      newStruct.myCarPrice = myAutoCost;
8598      //
8599
8600      // Calls "myWriteToFile" method to do the
8601 actual "save-to-file-function"
8602      // The "call" must include all of the
8603 information needed for the item.
8604      //
8605      // This is another place where things get
8606 dropped, take your time!!!
8607      // Aren't you glad we "numbered" the items?
8608      //
8609      myWriteToFile(myMfg, myAutoModel, myAutoStyle,
8610 myAutoEngine, myAutoColor,
8611      myAutoOwner, myAutoFinancer, myAutoCost);
8612      //
8613      // Now the info is saved to hard disk. We still
8614 need the item to be listed in listBox1
8615      // and be pkaced into the myArrylist.
8616      //
8617      // Add listing to listBox1 and myArrylst . . . .
8618      //
8619      string myListing = "";
8620      myListing = myMfg + " " + myAutoModel + " " +
8621 myAutoStyle;
8622      listBox1.Items.Add(myListing);
8623      myArrylst.Add(newStruct);
8624      //
8625      // Inform the user of the status of the records
8626 in file.
8627      //
8628      intCountOfRecords = myArrylst.Count;
8629      lblDisplayedRecords.Text = "There are "+
8630 Convert.ToString(intCountOfRecords)+"
8631      records";
```

```
8632  } /// End Save record --- Works with btnSave_click
8633  calls WriteToFile OK!!!
8634  //
8635  // "WriteToFile" works with btnSave_Click Event.
8636  //
8637  // Now that the records have been established, we
8638  need the everyday
8639  // record manipulation functions to be added.
8640  //
8641
```

**8642  As before, start with displaying records.**
**8643  Double_Click <Display> . . . Enter the event**
**8644  handler code like so;**

```
8645
8646  //--------- Start Display records -----------
8647  public void btnDisplay_Click(object sender,
8648  EventArgs e)
8649  {
8650      // Empty the ListBox1 and Araylist
8651      listBox1.Items.Clear();
8652      myArrylst.Clear();
8653      // instantiate the "Struct"
8654      AutoStruct newStruct = new AutoStruct();
8655      // instantiate a StreaReader
8656      StreamReader myRdr; // Double check the
8657  complete file name
8658      myRdr = new StreamReader("C:\\App Target
8659  Files\\AutomobileStructSpecs.txt");
8660      //Define String variables and Read the file in
8661  and set the struct properties
8662      //
8663      // I number all critical items in complex
8664  programs using comments added to help
8665      // locate and correct errors(debugging).
8666      //
8667      string myStrFromFileMaker = ". . ."; //    #1
8668      string myStrFromFileMod = ". . .";//       #2
8669      string myStrFromFileStyle = ". . .";//     #3
8670      string myStrFromFileEng = ". . .";//       #4
8671      string myStrFromFileColor = ". . .";//     #5
8672      string myStrFromFileFinance = ". . .";//   #6
```

```
8673     string myStrFromFileOwner = ". . .";//      #7
8674     string myStrFromFileCost = ". . .";//       #8
8675     //
8676     string myStrFromFile = ". . .";// String read
8677 in from file and count records read in.
8678     while (myStrFromFile!= null && myStrFromFile!=
8679 null)// // Start file reading
8680     {
8681         intCountOfRecords = 0; // keep records read in.
8682         //
8683         // Read the first string of the first -or-
8684             next record from file
8685         // "Every string" --- read will be tested in
8686             case partial
8687         // records are found. Assign strings i.e.
8688             "myCarBuilder" etc to
8689         // newStruct i.e."CarMaker" property of
8690             struct I know the Manufacturer
8691         // is first because that's the order in
8692             which we wrote info to the file.
8693         // So, we read and assign each string to the
8694             correct
8695         // "instantiated Struct property"
8696         //
8697         myStrFromFileMaker = myRdr.ReadLine();// #)1
8698         //MessageBox.Show("#1—Line 160 Got 1 Line
8699 Mfg " + myStrFromFileMaker,"btnDisplay_ Click");
8700         if (myStrFromFileMaker == "" ||
8701 myStrFromFileMaker==null)
8702         {
8703             intCountOfRecords = myArrylst.Count;
8704             lblDisplayedRecords.Text = "";
8705             lblDisplayedRecords.Text =
8706             "There are"
8707 +Convert.ToString(intCountOfRecords)+"records";
8708             myRdr.Close();
8709             myRdr.Dispose();
8710             return;
8711         }
8712         if (myStrFromFileMaker!= null &&
8713         myStrFromFileMaker!= null)// #)1
8714         {
```

```
8715                newStruct.CarMaker(myStrFromFileMaker);
8716          }
8717      // If the first string (line from file) is
8718          good (contains info), there are 7
8719      // more for this record unless it is a
8720          faulty, partial record. In that case we
8721      // want to return to the user screenen and
8722          advise the user.
8723      //
8724      // -----------------------------Start #2
8725      myStrFromFileMod = myRdr.ReadLine();
8726      if (myStrFromFileMod == "" ||
8727 myStrFromFileMod == null)
8728          {
8729              myRdr.Close();
8730              myRdr.Dispose();
8731              MessageBox.Show(" Line 185 . . . Partial
8732 record found in file, aborted display!", "Partial
8733 record found!");
8734              return;
8735          }
8736      if (myStrFromFileMod!= null &&
8737 myStrFromFileMod!= "")
8738          {
8739              newStruct.CarMods(myStrFromFileMod);
8740          }
8741      // ------------------------------ Start #3
8742      myStrFromFileStyle = myRdr.ReadLine();// #)3
8743      if (myStrFromFileStyle == "" ||
8744 myStrFromFileStyle == null)
8745      // this means either empty -or- null. They
8746          amount to
8747      // the same effect on the code.
8748          {
8749              myRdr.Close();
8750              myRdr.Dispose();
8751              MessageBox.Show("Line 185 . . . Partial
8752 record found in file, aborted display!", "Partial
8753 record found!");
8754              return;
8755          }
```

```
8756            if (myStrFromFileStyle!= "" &&
8757  myStrFromFileStyle!= null)
8758            {
8759                newStruct.CarStyles(myStrFromFileStyle);
8760                //MessageBox.Show("Line 206 . . . Partial
8761  record found in file, aborted display!", "Partial
8762  record found!");
8763            }
8764            //------------------------------- Start #4
8765            myStrFromFileEng = myRdr.ReadLine();// #)4
8766            if (myStrFromFileEng == "" ||
8767  myStrFromFileEng == null)
8768            {
8769                myRdr.Close();
8770                myRdr.Dispose();
8771                MessageBox.Show("Line 214 . . . Partial
8772  record found in file, aborted display!", "Partial
8773  record found!");
8774                return;
8775            }
8776            if (myStrFromFileEng!= "" &&
8777  myStrFromFileEng!= null)
8778            {
8779                newStruct.myCarsEngine(myStrFromFileEng);
8780            }
8781            //------------------------------- Start #5
8782            myStrFromFileColor = myRdr.ReadLine();// #)5
8783            if (myStrFromFileColor == "" ||
8784  myStrFromFileColor==null)
8785            {
8786                myRdr.Close();
8787                myRdr.Dispose();
8788                MessageBox.Show("Line 228 . . . Partial
8789  record found in file, aborted display!", "Partial
8790  record found!");
8791                return;
8792            }
8793            if (myStrFromFileColor!= "" &&
8794  myStrFromFileColor!= null)
8795            {
8796                newStruct.myCarsColors(myStrFromFileColor);
8797            }
```

```
8798          //------------------------------ Start #6
8799          myStrFromFileFinance = myRdr.ReadLine();// #)6
8800          if (myStrFromFileFinance == "" ||
8801 myStrFromFileFinance == null)
8802          {
8803              myRdr.Close();
8804              myRdr.Dispose();
8805              MessageBox.Show("Line 242 . . . Partial
8806 record found in file, aborted display!", "Partial
8807 record found!");
8808              return;
8809          }
8810          if (myStrFromFileFinance!= "" &&
8811 myStrFromFileFinance!= null)
8812          {
8813              newStruct.myCarsFinancer(myStrFromFileFinance);
8814          }
8815          //------------------------------ Start #7
8816          string myStrFromFileCarOwner =
8817 myRdr.ReadLine();
8818          newStruct.CarsRealOwner(myStrFromFileCarOwner);
8819          if (myStrFromFileCarOwner == "" ||
8820 myStrFromFileCarOwner == null)
8821          {
8822              myRdr.Close();
8823              myRdr.Dispose();
8824              MessageBox.Show("Line 257 . . . Partial
8825 record found in file, aborted display!", "Partial
8826 record found!");
8827              return;
8828          }
8829          if (myStrFromFileCarOwner!= "" &&
8830 myStrFromFileCarOwner!= null)
8831          {
8832              newStruct.CarsRealOwner(myStrFromFileCarOwner);
8833          }
8834          myStrFromFileCost = myRdr.ReadLine();// #)8
8835          if (myStrFromFileCost == "" ||
8836 myStrFromFileCost == null)
8837          {
8838              myRdr.Close();
8839              myRdr.Dispose();
```

```
8840              MessageBox.Show("Line 270 . . . Partial
8841 record found in file, aborted display!", "Partial
8842 record found!");
8843           return;
8844       }
8845       // If the record is good, we will process it
8846          further.
8847       //
8848       if (myStrFromFileCost!= "" &&
8849 myStrFromFileCost!= null)
8850       {
8851           newStruct.CarsCost(myStrFromFileCost);
8852           intCountOfRecords += 1;
8853           lblDisplayedRecords.Text = "";
8854           lblDisplayedRecords.Text =
8855 Convert.ToString(intCountOfRecords);
8856       }
8857       // --- 8 lines --- 1 Record Read in complete
8858       // --- Create Listing to Add to listBox1 ---
8859       string myListing = "";
8860       myListing = myStrFromFileMaker + " " +
8861 myStrFromFileMod + " " + myStrFromFileStyle + " "
8862 + myStrFromFileOwner;
8863       listBox1.Items.Add(myListing);
8864       /* --------- Add to myArrylst --------- */
8865       intSelectedIdx = listBox1.SelectedIndex;
8866       myArrylst.Add(newStruct);
8867       /* -- Item added to listBox and Array --- */
8868       } //. . . Matching up with "if!= "",!= null"
8869    } //. . .—Ends While Loop --- Starts Loop again
8870 } //. . . End of btnDisplay_ Click --- //
8871 //
8872
```

8873 That's a pretty long block of code. I again *caution*
8874 *against* copying and pasting from the text. Copy
8875 from the example files.

8876

8877 By now, possibly, you can imagine other ways to
8878 do this work. That's great! This way is chosen to
8879 use simple, stright-forward methods that we have

8880 **learned to this point. You can and will learn of**
8881 **more complex, more efficient ways to do the same**
8882 **thing later on.**
8883
8884 **As before with Visual Basic we will deal early with**
8885 **deleting unwanted records from file. It amounts to**
8886 **("clear")ing out the old listing in the listBox1 and**
8887 **the myArrylist, then rewriting the file. But, the**
8888 **natural thing a user is likely to do is Click on an**
8889 **item in the listBox1, so we will handle that event**
8890 **next, then do delete.**
8891

```
8892 //
8893 public void listBox1_SelectedIndexChanged(object
8894 sender,
8895 EventArgs e)
8896 {// OK!!!! . . . I put this comment here to check
8897 out the
8898     // matching sets of curly braces, I do this a
8899         first step
8900     // before coding long blocks to avoid confusion.
8901     //
8902     XX = listBox1.SelectedIndex;
8903     // MessageBox.Show(myStrSender);
8904     // To populate the textBoxes we need a Struct
8905         instantiated
8906     // to get the properties we want to display for the
8907     // particular item chosen by the user.
8908     intSelectedIdx = listBox1.SelectedIndex;
8909     if (intSelectedIdx == -1) {intSelectedIdx = 0;}
8910     int intArrayCount = 0;
8911     intArrayCount = myArrylst.Count; //
8912     /*-------------------------------------------------*/
8913     Object myObj; // cannnot create a struct
8914         directly from
8915     // the ArrayList.
8916     //
8917     // --- This is the first Struct in this event
8918         handler block.
```

```
8961      txtBoxEngine.Text = myNewStrCarEng;// ----- #4)
8962      txtBoxColor.Text = myNewStrCarColor;// ---- #5)
8963      txtBoxFinancer.Text = myNewStrCarFinancer;// - #6)
8964      txtBoxOwner.Text = myNewStrCarOwner;// ---- #7)
8965      txtBoxCost.Text = myNewStrCarCost;// ------ #8)
8966      //
8967 } // End SectedIndexChanged OK!!!! --- Curly Brace
8968 check
8969
```

8970 If you need a short break, get it now . . . . But hurry
8971 back, while the logic is still fresh in your mind. Note
8972 the line number so you won't waste time later looking
8973 for where you stopped.
8974

8975 *Now for deleting* . . . **the first issue is knowing**
8976 **which "Item" is to be deleted. The user had to first**
8977 **display the records then select one *but* if they did**
8978 ***not* we also need to remind them. It is also a good**
8979 **idea to let them confirm the deletion before**
8980 **actually doing it.**
8981

```
8982 //
8983 private void btnDelete_Click(object sender,
8984 EventArgs e)
8985 {
8986 // Get the properties we need to identify the
8987 correct Lines to delete from File
8988 // Advise user if no item selected
8989 intSelectedIdx = listBox1.SelectedIndex;
8990      //
8991      if (intSelectedIdx == -1)
8992      {
8993          MessageBox.Show("No item selected to delete,
8994 Select an item the click delete . . .","No item
8995 selected advisor");
8996      }
8997      //
```

```
8998    // --- Now we know "which item" was selected
8999        from the listBox1 --- to be
9000    // deleted If item selected, proceed to get the
9001        properties needed
9002    Object myObj;
9003    myObj = new Object();
9004    AutoStruct newStruct = new AutoStruct();
9005    myObj = myArrylst[intSelectedIdx];
9006    // -Now we know "which item" "Struct/Object" -
9007    // convert into "newStruct"
9008    newStruct = (AutoStruct)Convert.ChangeType(myObj,
9009  typeof(AutoStruct));
9010    // --- Confirm decision "before" deleting
9011
9012    string strMyStrMfg =
9013  listBox1.SelectedItem.ToString();
9014
9015    // Now this is a heck of an "if" statement,
9016        take some time to understand it . . . .
9017    //
9018    if (MessageBox.Show(strMyStrMfg + "is located
9019  at index" + Convert.ToString(intSelectedIdx) + "."
9020  + "Click OK to remove this item. Click Cancel to
9021  keep this item", "'DELETE' verification",
9022  MessageBoxButtons.OKCancel,
9023  MessageBoxIcon.Information,
9024  MessageBoxDefaultButton.Button1) ==
9025  DialogResult.OK);
9026    {
9027        // IF . . . user clicked "OK" delete record.
9028        // Clear txtBoxes Remove item ArrayList
9029        // --- Use "textBox.text" properties!!!!!
9030        //
9031        // "if" user clicks "Cancel" . . . abort and
9032            return to the screen.
9033        //
9034        string txtBoxMfgInfo=txtBoxMfg.Text; // #1
9035        string txtBoxModelInfo = txtBoxModel.Text; // #2
9036        string txtBoxStyleInfo = txtBoxModel.Text; // #3
9037        string txtBoxEngineInfo = txtBoxEngine.Text; // #4
9038        string txtBoxColorInfo = txtBoxColor.Text; // #5
```

```
9039          string txtBoxFinancerInfo =
9040  txtBoxFinancer.Text; // #6
9041          string txtBoxOwnerInfo = txtBoxOwner.Text; // #7
9042          string txtBoxCostInfo = txtBoxCost.Text; // #8
9043          // Blank the textBoxes --- Blank the textBoxes
9044          txtBoxMfg.Text = "";// #1- Blank the textBox
9045          txtBoxModel.Text = "";// #2- Blank the textBox
9046          txtBoxStyle.Text = ""; // #3- Blank the textBox
9047          txtBoxEngine.Text = ""; // #4- Blank the textBox
9048          txtBoxColor.Text = ""; // #5- Blank the textBox
9049          txtBoxFinancer.Text = "";// #6- Blank the
9050  textBox
9051          txtBoxOwner.Text = ""; // #7- Blank the textBox
9052          txtBoxCost.Text = ""; // #8- Blank the textBox
9053          //
9054          // --- Object is NOT Removed from myArraylst
9055             or listBox1 YET!!
9056          //
9057          listBox1.Items.RemoveAt(intSelectedIdx);
9058          myArrylst.RemoveAt(intSelectedIdx);
9059          // Now, re-write the file.
9060          // --- Call ReCreateFile()
9061          ReCreateFile();
9062          listBox1.SelectedIndex = 0;
9063      } // --- End if clicked OK Delete messageBox
9064  button
9065  } // -------------------- End
9066  btnDeleteSelectedRecord Click
9067  //
9068
```

9069 **At this time the user can *display*, *select* an item for**
9070 **details and *delete* an item.**
9071 **Next we need the ability to edit an item rather than**
9072 **delete it and re-enter the whole set of information.**

```
9073
9074  //
9075  private void btnEdit_Click(object sender,
9076  EventArgs e)
9077  {//------------------------------------------ OK!!!!
9078     intSelectedEditIdx = listBox1.SelectedIndex;
```

```
9079     if (intSelectedEditIdx == -1)
9080     {MessageBox.Show("You must first select a
9081 listing to EDIT", "NO ITEM SELECTED!! ");}
9082     // Re-set backcolors of controls
9083     lblMfg.BackColor = Color.Cyan;
9084     txtBoxMfg.BackColor = Color.Cyan; //          #1
9085     lblModel.BackColor = Color.Cyan;
9086     txtBoxModel.BackColor = Color.Cyan; //        #2
9087     lblStyle.BackColor = Color.Cyan;
9088     txtBoxStyle.BackColor = Color.Cyan; //        #3
9089     lblEngine.BackColor = Color.Cyan;
9090     txtBoxEngine.BackColor = Color.Cyan; /        #4
9091     lblEngine.BackColor = Color.Cyan;
9092     txtBoxColor.BackColor = Color.Cyan; //        #5
9093     lblColor.BackColor = Color.Cyan;
9094     txtBoxFinancer.BackColor = Color.Cyan; //     #6
9095     lblFinancer.BackColor = Color.Cyan;
9096     txtBoxOwner.BackColor = Color.Cyan; //        #7
9097     lblFinancer.BackColor = Color.Cyan;
9098     txtBoxCost.BackColor = Color.Cyan; //         #8
9099     lblCost.BackColor = Color.Cyan;
9100     //
9101     listBox1.BackColor = Color.Cyan;
9102     btnSaveMyEdits.Visible = true;
9103     MessageBox.Show("To makes CHANGES—RE-TYPE the
9104 information
9105     // in the desired TEXTBOX(s) then CLICK—SAVE
9106 EDITS ", "Edit Instruction");
9107     //
9108     Object myObj = new Object();
9109     AutoStruct newStruct = new AutoStruct();
9110     myObj=myArrylst[intSelectedEditIdx];
9111     newStruct =
9112 (AutoStruct)Convert.ChangeType(myObj,
9113 typeof(AutoStruct));
9114     myObj = myArrylst[intSelectedEditIdx];
9115     //
9116     string strEditMfg = newStruct.CarBuilder;
9117     // --- #1)
9118     txtBoxMfg.Text = strEditMfg;
9119     txtBoxMfg.ForeColor = Color.Red;
9120     string strEditMod = newStruct.CarModel;
```

```
9121        // --- #2)
9122        txtBoxModel.Text = strEditMod;
9123        txtBoxModel.ForeColor = Color.Red;
9124        string strEditStyle = newStruct.myCarStyle;
9125        // --- #3)
9126        txtBoxStyle.Text = strEditStyle;
9127        txtBoxStyle.ForeColor = Color.Red;
9128        string strEditEng = newStruct.myCarEng;
9129        // --- #4)
9130        txtBoxEngine.Text = strEditEng;
9131        txtBoxEngine.ForeColor = Color.Red;
9132        string strEditColor = newStruct.myCarsColor;
9133        // --- #5)
9134        txtBoxColor.Text = strEditColor;
9135        txtBoxColor.ForeColor = Color.Red;
9136        string strEditBanker = newStruct.CarsLien;
9137        // --- #6)
9138        txtBoxFinancer.Text = strEditBanker;
9139        txtBoxFinancer.ForeColor = Color.Red;
9140        string strEditOwner = newStruct.myCarRealOwner;
9141        // --- #7)
9142        txtBoxOwner.Text = strEditOwner;
9143        txtBoxOwner.ForeColor = Color.Red;
9144        string strEditCost = newStruct.CarCost;
9145        // --- #8)
9146        txtBoxCost.Text = strEditCost;
9147        txtBoxCost.ForeColor = Color.Red;
9148        //
9149 } // End btnEdit_Click OK!!!
9150 //
9151
```

9152 **That's it!**

9153

9154 This is a fairly complex application. I deliberately
9155 used a lot of file and Struct related code . . . for the
9156 purpose of learning. There are other ways to construct
9157 the program but do this for now . . . it's is the
9158 simplest, most comprehendible code that we could
9159 write. I hope you really go through the code line by

9160  line and make sure you understand the commands one
9161  by one.
9162
9163  Also, if you are learning both C# and VB . . . it
9164  presents the opportunity to contrast the two programs,
9165  almost line for line. Pay attention to the definition of
9166  the "in-line" construction of the Struct and what is
9167  needed to get access to the properties defined there.
9168
9169  **A complete, un-commented (to the extent used**
9170  **above) of the C# code in *appendix P*.**
9171
9172  ***Break time***!!!!!!!!!!! Get away, do something fun with
9173  your friends or family. Let this digest, be refreshed.
9174  Then come on back afterwards . . . when you're ready.
9175
9176  With the knowledge and experience gained so far
9177  you're ready to tackle a more complex and very
9178  different type of programming i.e. accessing and
9179  manipulation a database. ***Take your time*** . . . review
9180  this project until you're sure you understand every
9181  part of it. ***Review, Review, Review***!!
9182
9183  ***NOTE TO YOU . . . THE READER***!!!!!
9184
9185  This unit . . . even more so than the others, requires
9186  line-by-line explanation. Inside the code block is
9187  where I put a ***great deal*** of the ***explanation***. Right
9188  there beside the statement it applies to.
9189
9190  ***READ THE CODE . . . READ THE CODE . . . etc***
9191  ***etc***!!!!!
9192

9193 # Project 20—. . . Accessing and
9194 # Manipulating databases
9195
9196 **This project is divided into two parts . . . Accessing**
9197 **a database with Visual Basic.. proj. 20a and**
9198 **accessing a database with C# . . . proj. 20b**
9199
9200 **Visual Basic is first.Visual basic is different from**
9201 **C# in several ways when using the data acess tools.**
9202 **There is no good way to do a line by line**
9203 **comparison that yields a better or clearer**
9204 **understanding in my opinion. I think Microsoft**
9205 **developers did a better job with implementing the**
9206 **data access tools in C# versus the team doing the**
9207 **same for Visual Basic, but that's just my**
9208 **opinion.You form your own.**
9209
9210 **We will start by looking carefully at the basic**
9211 **capabilities and mechanics of SqlServer 2010**
9212 **Express and the database management tool, SQL**
9213 **Visual Manager Studio from Microsoft.**
9214
9215 **I am *"NOT"* going to try (right now at least) to**
9216 ***teach* you to how to *"create" complex databases*.**
9217
9218 That is worthy of it's own book, there are dozens
9219 around. There are thousands of databases in existence,
9220 just learn how to *use* them. This exercise depends on
9221 being able to do a few, relatively simple functions
9222 with a database.
9223
9224 This is a VERY BRIEF, to-the-point tutorial that will
9225 get you started.

9226  If you're dying of curiosity, try reading;
9227
9228  **"Discovering SQL for Beginners"**
9229  **by Alex Kriegel . . . WROX publishing**
9230  **-or-**
9231  **"Mastering Microsoft Visual Basic 2010"**
9232  **by Evangelos Petroutsos, Wiley Publishing . . .**
9233
9234  **These books have a section on SQL that is pretty**
9235  **well done . . .**
9236  **you can translate almost word-for-word from the**
9237  **VB code to C# code.**
9238
9239  **Still another book I use is;**
9240
9241  **"Murach's Database Programming with Visual**
9242  **Basic 2010"**
9243  **by Anne Boehm and Ged Mead from Murach**
9244  **publishing.**
9245
9246  Honestly, I had to dig through several books to piece
9247  together an explanation I could understand and use.
9248  Maybe it's just me and perhaps you'll have better luck
9249  or the authors will have become clearer and more
9250  focused by now.
9251
9252  I like *"Do this"* . . .instruction, not philosophy or
9253  history of programming topics.
9254
9255  *If you did not acquire the tools for the database*
9256  *project outlined in the beginning of the book, do so*
9257  *now*. **Otherwise, this unit is going to be of very**
9258  **limited value to you in terms of the ability to**

9259 **programmatically access and manipulate**
9260 **databases.**
9261
9262 You can get everything you need directly from
9263 Microsoft for free. These free programs are "Express
9264 Editions". They are more than adequate for learning
9265 purposes. If you are *NOT* using SQL Express there
9266 are slight differences in the products. But, the
9267 differences don't matter for this learning experience.
9268
9269 The express editions lack some bells and whistles of
9270 the full product, but they are good, I use them
9271 intensely before buying the full products. This is an
9272 excellent program from Microsoft and I'm quite sure
9273 it leads to many, many sales of the more robust
9274 products.
9275 You need not worry about the "Folder" issue for the
9276 database, C# will find the database when we ask for it,
9277 wherever it is.
9278
9279 Be sure you put these C# or VB examples (not the
9280 database) in the correct *VB and C# folders* just like
9281 the others for the *language* you're using so that
9282 you're organized and find them when they're needed.
9283
9284 *OK, let's go*!!!
9285
9286 /* ---- This is a comment line in the code blocks
9287 you're going to see a lot of them in the C# project */
9288 The words between the /* and */ are the
9289 comments . . . .the compiler ignores them, they are
9290 there to explain how or why something is being done
9291 in the actual code.

9292 // So is this but only for one line at a time, just in a
9293 different format. Visual Basic comments start with the
9294 apostrophe technialy, I use '// to make them more
9295 easily seen.
9296
9297 One further suggestion, ***Keep a notebook handy*** while
9298 doing this execise.
9299
9300 Jot down things like what you're working on, where
9301 in the book and in you editor, code line numbers, lists
9302 of variables you are using etc . . . it will save lots of
9303 time and confusion as you do iterations of properties
9304 from textboxes, database dataTable column names
9305 etc. If you do not you will find yourelf scrolling back
9306 through the code trying to find them.
9307
9308 **An option is to use "Note pad" . . . in "Windows**
9309 **Accessories", to do the jotting down.**
9310 **I even put an "Icon for note pad" on my desk top**
9311 **because I use it so often and, I use it intensely.**
9312 **Also, create a folder for programming notes and**
9313 **make use of it to remember how to do certain**
9314 **"methods". Again, this is something I do a lot.**
9315
9316 Here we go!!!!
9317
9318 A database is ***similar*** in ***design*** to a ***spreadsheet***.
9319
9320 **It is a "software entity" with the database "name"**
9321 **and files containing tables (and many others we**
9322 **are not concerned with right now).**
9323
9324 The data ***tables*** . . . are where the action and focus are.

9325

9326 Tables are organized into groups of "***Rows***"
9327 containing "***Columns/Cells***", where the "***values***" are
9328 stored.

9329

9330 ***Each "Row"* contains one complete set of data**
9331 **items("*Cells*") describing "*ONE*" *item*, a customer**
9332 **in our case.**

9333

9334 **This is usually referred to as one "*Record*".**

9335

9336 There might be more detailed information about this
9337 particular item in yet another "***related***" table. In this
9338 exercise we will restrict our activities to one (1)
9339 table . . . "Customers".

9340

9341 **A relationship is defined by using "Dot Notation"**
9342 **i.e.**

9343

9344 **table1.Mfg -and- table2.Mfg" are variables that**
9345 **contain the same information, BUT, in different**
9346 **tables.**

9347

9348 That is how a relationship is defined . . . literally
9349 much like we use regular variables. Hence the term
9350 you will see very often, "***Relational Database***".

9351

9352 Usually in one database, multiple "***tables***" are
9353 "***related***". That means they have at least one data item
9354 that contains the same information as the some of the
9355 other tables.

9356

9357 **This allows for *"Normalized"* data structuring.**
9358 **"Normalized" means minimal duplication of data**
9359 **in multiple tables and the data is accessed only**
9360 **when needed by *"relating"* the tables when making**
9361 ***"queries"* or reports.**
9362
9363 Related, normalized database tables improve system
9364 performance enormously. The required computer
9365 processing time is kept as low as possible by
9366 processing *"only"* the data needed for any given user
9367 request ("Query").
9368
9369 With very large commercial applications, this is a
9370 major issue. Millions of requests per day are
9371 processed. For example, stock market database users
9372 make millions and millions of requests (queries) per
9373 each minute or even per second. Auto parts companies
9374 are another example and there are thousands more.
9375
9376 **In the "Base" -or- "Master" table, at times the**
9377 **terminology uses the words "Master" and "Slave",**
9378 **The related (relatable) information is called a**
9379 **"Primary Key".**
9380
9381 A "Primary Key" is unique in each table per data item
9382 (Record) and no other record can have the same
9383 Primary Key.
9384
9385 ***But*,** variables in the related tables contain the same
9386 information (although the variable "names"*could* be
9387 different).
9388

9389 In the *"related"* table this information is called a
9390 *"Foreign Key"*.
9391
9392 **Remember that we said "Objects" have the ability**
9393 **to own a collection of "child-objects"?**
9394
9395 **As C# and VB look at it EACH "Column" in**
9396 **EACH Row("*Cell*") is actually a separate *"object"*.**
9397
9398 **Databases have "Table" objects. Table "Objects"**
9399 **have Row objects -and- Rows have "Column"**
9400 **objects.**
9401
9402 **The Column Objects contain the "values" that are**
9403 **stored in the database tables.**
9404
9405 That's the hierarchy "tree" of a database.
9406
9407 Column objects and Row objects each have their own
9408 set of *properties* that can be manipulated from code
9409 i.e. Color, Width, Heigth etc. and *"value"* -or-
9410 "content" that can be retrieved.
9411
9412 **Each *"Cell Object"* (one Column within one Row)**
9413 **can contain *only* a *"Specific" type and size* of**
9414 ***value(variable)* that is defined at design time.**
9415
9416 For example, a *string*, an *integer* or even some *object*
9417 like a picture. Each *"Row"* is also seen as an *object*, it
9418 has a *"Collection"* of objects, there I go again, of
9419 *"Columns"* as it's *"child"* objects.
9420

9421 *Columns are indentfied by a name or index*
9422 *numbers.*
9423
9424 Considerable thought is required to create a database
9425 table that does the job you want efficiently.
9426
9427 Man!!! That was an ear full. *Read* and *re-read* those
9428 paragraphs . . . The concepts are very important, in
9429 fact, *super important*!!
9430
9431 **There's no way around it!! Stay with it until you**
9432 **have them straight in your mind. They are the**
9433 **foundation on which all that follows is built. Make**
9434 **sure they're firmly embedded in you mind.**
9435
9436 Those concepts are applicable to *ALL* programming
9437 languages and database products. They will be *very*
9438 *valuable* to you.
9439
9440 **You can conceptualize a database "*data table*" as**
9441 **looking like this;**
9442
9443 **A data Table . . . with a name i.e. AutoStructSpecs.**
9444 **It also has an index number, starting with "0"**
9445 **Databases can have many tables . . . usually they**
9446 **do.**
9447 **The first datatable has a numerical index of "0".**
9448

| Mfg | Model | Style | Engine | Color | Finance r | Owner | Cost | 8 Columns With indexes And names <<< | 1 Row With Index 0 |
|------|-------|-------|--------|-------|-----------|-------|-------|--------|--------|
| Col 0 | Col 1 | Col 2 | Col 3 | Col 4 | Col 5 | Col 6 | Col 7 | | |
| Index 0 | Index 1 | Index 2 | Index 3 | Index 4 | Index 5 | Index 6 | Index7 | | |

| Ford | 1980 | Comet | V6 | Red | BOA | Jones | 1800 | 8 Columns With Indexes And names | 1 Row with index 1 <<< |
|------|------|-------|-----|-----|-----|-------|------|------|------|
| Index 0 | index 1 | Index 2 | Index 3 | Index 4 | Index 5 | Index 6 | index 7 | | |

9449

9450 The above *"table"* contains two *"Rows/Records"*. The
9451 *"Rows"* have 8 *"Columns"*, containing 8 data
9452 items/*"variable/value"*, one in each cell.

9453

9454 The data item "Comet" is contained by
9455 *"Cell"* (0,2) (*"Row"* 0, *"Column"* 2)

9456

9457 The data item "V6" is contained by
9458 *"Cell"* **(0,3) ("Row" 0, "Column" 3)**

9459

9460 I could also have stated it this way;

9461

9462 Data item or value "Comet" is contained by
9463 *"Cell"* (0,"*Style*") -or- (0, 3)

9464

9465 The data item "V6" is contained by
9466 *"Cell"* (0,"*Engine*") -or- (0,3).

9467

9468 So what's the big deal? It all amounts to the same
9469 thing . . . *"except"* . . .

9470

9471 When you want to *iterate(look at each one, one-at-a-*
9472 *time)* through a collection with a "for" or "while" loop
9473 and use an index number to control the loop, you need
9474 an index number.

9475

9476 Remember how we did that in the last example for our
9477 collection of AutoStructs?
9478
```
9479 For Each myObj In myArryLst
9480    newStruct = myArryLst.Item(XX)
9481 Next
```
9482 XX is the numerical index for the object.

9483
9484 IF NOT . . . review!!!
9485 At the top of the table are the "Column" names.
9486 Each "Row" has the Complete set of information for
9487 one automobile.
9488
9489 Each "Column" in a row has one data item ("*value*").
9490 One whole row equals one record. Rows have index
9491 numbers.
9492 ***"Rows" have only an index number, NOT a names.***
9493
9494 Each "*Column*" has a "*name*" and an "*index*"
9495 number.
9496
9497 When you refer to a "particular" ***Column within*** a
9498 "particular" ***Row*** . . . you are referring to a "***Cell***". The
9499 "***Cell***" is referred to numerically with "***Two***" ***indexes***
9500 i.e. (0,2), meaning Row 0,Column 2.
9501
9502 You can also ***refer*** to a "***Cell***" by using the "***Row***"
9503 ***index*** number and the "***Column***" ***name*** . . . i.e (Row
9504 0, Mfg). Get comfortable with this format/syntax, it
9505 will be used many times.
9506
9507 ***Re-read*** the past few ***paragraphs*** and the ***table***
9508 illustration several times until you firmly grasp the
9509 ideas. They are very ***basic***, but ***very important***.

9510
9511 When you're ready we'll move on.
9512
9513 Some, in fact, most databases have multiple "*tables*".
9514 They are "*Related*" but contain different sets of
9515 information. For example, we could build another
9516 table that has specific, detailed information needed on
9517 "only" some occasions, but *"related"* to a *specific*
9518 automobile.
9519
9520 When I look into a detailed, related table, I have to
9521 know what automobile I'm interested in to make
9522 sense from the data.
9523
9524 **This means the detailed table must contain some of**
9525 **the information included in the first table i.e. Mfg**
9526 **and Model year etc. Or, a unique indenifier like a**
9527 **VIN number. That unique identifier might be a**
9528 **Primary Key in the "Master Table" -or- Base**
9529 **Table, when it is used in the "Child or Related**
9530 **Table it is referred to as the Foreign Key".**
9531
9532 **For example I might want to look up the warranty**
9533 **information on a specific car.**
9534
9535 The info I choose from the first table for this purpose
9536 is called a *Primary Key*. When I include that same
9537 data in the second table it is called a "*Foreign Key*".
9538
9539 When the *two sets* of data items chosen are *equal in*
9540 *both tables* . . . I have defined a "*Relationship*" for
9541 the two tables.
9542

9543 I can give the chosen columns in both tables the same
9544 name if I want. Since they reside in different tables,
9545 there is no conflict in the names. In actual practice this
9546 makes the coding easier.
9547
9548 Dot notation is used to refer to the two columns each
9549 in a different table, for example;
9550 **_Table1.Mfg_** and **_Table2.Mfg_** are **_acceptable_**.
9551
9552 When I use a comparision like . . .
9553
9554 VB
9555 `if(Table1.Mfg = Table2.Mfg) then`
9556 `    do so`
9557 `    do so again`
9558 `end if`
9559
9560 **-or-**
9561
9562 C#
9563 `if(Table1.Mfg == Table2.Mfg)`
9564 `    {`
9565 `        do so;`
9566 `        do so again;`
9567 `    }`
9568 **. . . that is perfectly fine. There is no conflict in the**
9569 **names.**
9570
9571 The **_purpose_** of **_relationships_** is to let us **_join data_** . . .
9572 meaning get data from **_two_** or **_more tables when we_**
9573 **_need_** it, about the same item.
9574
9575 OK, enough on **_relationships_** for the moment.
9576

9577 **I have been using the Automobile example for the**
9578 **discussion to this point because it helps "relate"**
9579 **what we have already done to what we're doing**
9580 **now. But actually, the database used for this unit is**
9581 **from Microsoft and called "Northwind" and it's**
9582 **free.**
9583
9584 **You can download it from several different**
9585 **websites including Microsoft.**
9586
9587 **"Northwind" has become sort of a standard for**
9588 **writers addressing database programming. Almost**
9589 **any book you read on the subject of database**
9590 **access from VB or C# refers to Northwind. I've**
9591 **read and paid for 72 of them, so I'm pretty**
9592 **comfortable saying that.**
9593
9594 To you, this means that "*if*" you decide to follow up
9595 into more detailed and advanced programming (and
9596 Boy, there's plenty of it) . . . the material will make
9597 more sense, more easily and more quickly.
9598 **I hope you do. Later, I make some suggestions in**
9599 **that regard.**
9600 **There is plenty of instruction available online**
9601 **about downloading and installing the database**
9602 **tools and the example database "Northwind"**
9603 **online. Some of those come directly from the**
9604 **people that created the items (who better?). So, I**
9605 **won't be-labor that topic here, they are supposedly**
9606 **the experts. Go to the Microsoft home page and**
9607 **search**
9608 -or- just do a general search from your browser.
9609

9610 **Again, right now I am "NOT" trying, to teach you**
9611 **to how to *create* databases. That topic is worthy of**
9612 **it's own book, there are dozens around. There are**
9613 **thousands of databases in existence, just learn how**
9614 **to access and use them. However, you do need to**
9615 **be aware of a few of the "SQL", *S*tandard *Q*uery**
9616 ***Language*, command statements.**
9617
9618 **SQL is a NOT a programming language. It is a**
9619 **"STANDARD" created for database products.**
9620 **Most companies support and use the standard or**
9621 **parts of it. It allows software writers to access**
9622 **almost any database . . . using standard statements.**
9623
9624 When we access a database from a VB or C#
9625 program, we embed SQL statements/commands inside
9626 our progam. Probably the most commomly used SQL
9627 command is "*SELECT*". When we use it . . . we tell
9628 the database what information we want to get back
9629 from the database using the database name and table
9630 name.
9631
9632 SQL uses something called a "Wildcard" search
9633 criteria. The asterisk "*" says . . . "I want everything
9634 in the table, give me all the records you have".
9635
9636 This is how it's done using SQL Management
9637 Studio's database editor.
9638 **The query contains these two lines . . . .(NO, don't**
9639 **try to do it just yet, read and learn)**
9640

9641  (We specify the "database" name with the "Use"
9642  command followed by the database name, then ended
9643  with a semi-colon.)
9644
9645  `use Northwind;`
9646  `SELECT * FROM Customers;`
9647
9648  If we want, we can specify what the wanted column
9649  name(s) are and let the database loop through the
9650  "records" returning only the column cell information
9651  (values) we want.
9652
9653  I repeat, SQL uses an asterisk (*) in queries meaning
9654  "get all records" to retrieve everything in the table
9655  without being selective about which records we see,
9656  unless we specify some qualifiers.
9657
9658  The output from this command will look like this

9659
9660                    **Screen 11**
9661
9662  The output has information from every record in the
9663  "customers" table.
9664

9665 **Two "qualifier" words are often used with**
9666 **"Select", "Where" and "*" that are important and**
9667 **frequently used qualifiers. "*" means**
9668 **"everything" . . . "Where" specifies the matching**
9669 **criteria when we want to be a little more selective.**
9670 **We can specify more than one qualifier if desired;**
9671
```
9672 SELECT * FROM AutoStructs WHERE Mfg = 'Ford' AND
9673 ModelYr > 1970;
```
9674
9675 The ">" means *"**Greater Than**"*. *Note:* The single
9676 quotation marks around 'Ford'.
9677
9678 Strings are enclosed in single quotation marks.
9679 Numbers are not.
9680 SQL Management Studio uses English-like formats
9681 for SQL staemens/commands to run queries.
9682
9683 This (below) is how the results look on SQL
9684 Manament studio's screen.
9685

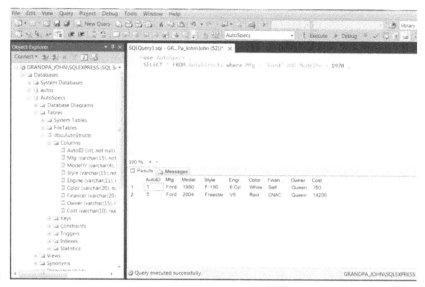

9687                    **Screen 12**

9688

9689 **Above is the SQL Management Studio screen with**
9690 **our query typed in and executed, with the resulting**
9691 **output. Two records met our "WHERE" *AND***
9692 **criteria.**

9693

9694 Our C# commands (in our database access program)
9695 will pass the SQL statements to the SQL database in a
9696 string format, which is how C# is able to accept the
9697 statements as "NOT" being formatted as part of the
9698 normal C# program code.

9699

9700 You can close MVS for a while if you like. We'll use
9701 SQL Management Studio Express for most of this job.

9702

9703 OK, let's give it a shot.

9704

9705 I assume that you have now completed installing
9706 "SQL Management Studio Express" and the example

9707 database "Northwind". If "*NOT*" wait until those
9708 tasks are completed, then do this exercise.
9709
9710 **If you have an Icon on your desktop for Microsoft**
9711 **SQL Management Studio, double_click it.**
9712
9713 **If you don't . . . click the Start Icon for windows,**
9714 **click "All Programs" and look for SQL**
9715 **Management Studio and create a shortcut/icon . . .**
9716 **on the desktop. Remember, drag and drop, then**
9717 **select "create shortcut here".**
9718
9719 Now, double_click the icon and let's go.
9720
9721 **After it gets loaded and running (takes a few**
9722 **seconds) you will see the Startup Screen that looks**
9723 **like this;**

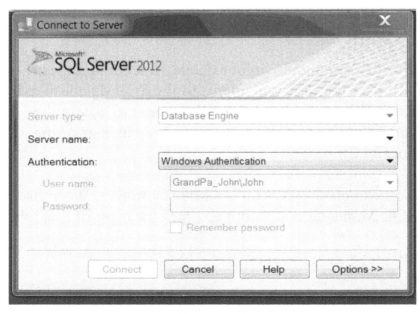

9724
9725                              **Screen 13**

9726
9727 **After connecting, you see this screen.**

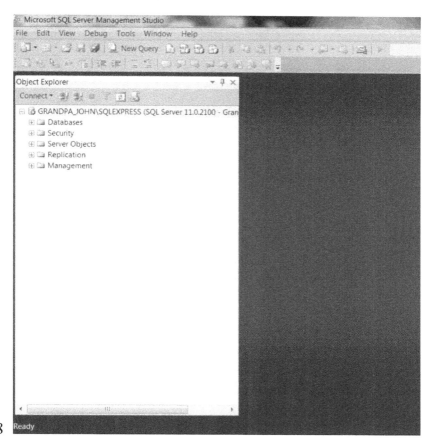

9728
9729                    **Screen 14**
9730
9731 **Click the database "+" button to expand the list of**
9732 **databases for viewing.**
9733
9734 **Now you have this screen . . .**
9735

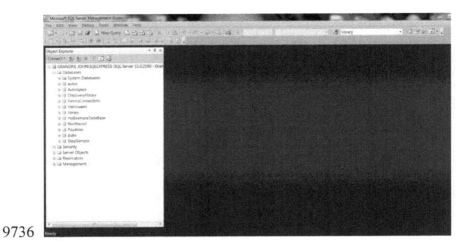

9736
9737                              **Screen 15**
9738
9739 **Now + <+ Beside Northwind> and see this;**
9740

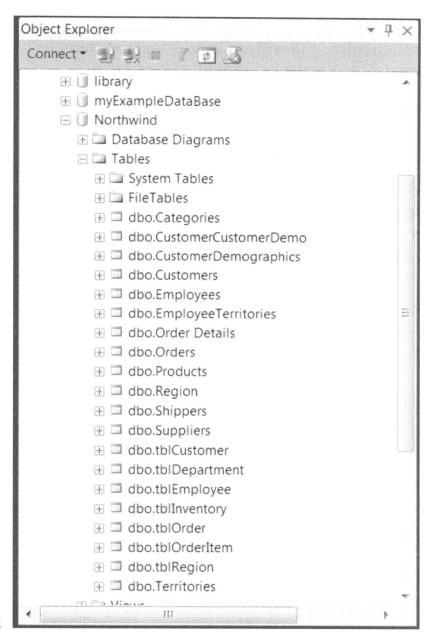

**Screen 16**

9744 **After clicking <Customers> + <Tables> +**
9745 **<Columns>, you will see actual "named columns"**
9746 **used with Northwind, NOTE the names . . .**
9747
9748 **Many are named i.e. "dbo. something". This name**
9749 **is referring to the items as "Objects" belonging to**
9750 **this database table.**
9751
9752 **If you look more closely at the individual**
9753 **items/Objects . . .**
9754 **You'll see the properties of the columns. For**
9755 **example, this tells us the *type of variable* expected**
9756 **as input and the maximum *size* of the variable.**
9757

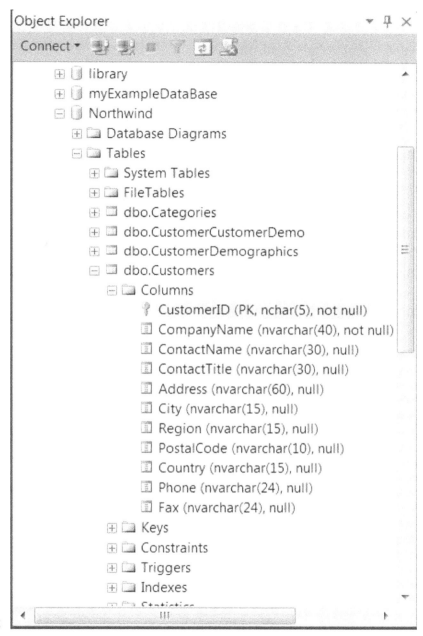

**Screen 17**

9761  You can see that "customerID" is the "Primary
9762  Key (PK)", it is a nchar type variable . . . meaning
9763  It accepts strings as input and
9764  the length of the strings is limited to 5 characters
9765  and it cannot be "null", meaning it cannot be left
9766  empty or it will cause an error and crash the
9767  program.
9768
9769  This is where we can get the information needed
9770  for use in our C# or VB program. *Back up* and
9771  *review* the proceedure. You will use it many times.
9772  While we're here, let's learn how to actually query
9773  the database table.
9774
9775  In the toolbar, look for the "New Query" icon.
9776
9777  The editor screen may already be showing in the
9778  right-hand pane of the screen. If so, we are ready
9779  to write a Query. If not click the icon . . . the editor
9780  looks like this;

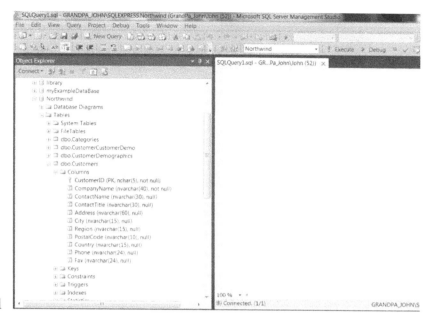

9781

**Screen 18**

9783

9784  **At this point we are finally read to write our**
9785  **query.**
9786  **Click inside the editor and enter these statements;**
9787  **Use Northwind; -- Don't forget the semi-colon.**
9788  **SELECT * FROM customers;**

9789

9790  **PS: -- (dash dash) is the comment line indicator for**
9791  **SQL.**

9792

9793  **Now, Click the <execute query> and watch the**
9794  **results shown appear in the bottom pane of the**
9795  **window.**

9796
9797                    **Screen 19**
9798
9799 **Note the "identity" column shown first as a**
9800 **sequentially numbered list of the actual records in**
9801 **the database. This column does not have a**
9802 **displayed name.**
9803
9804 **The database program generates these numbers**
9805 **automatically when records are entered by the**
9806 **users. This was specified during design by the**
9807 **person that created the database table columns.**
9808
9809 **"Identity" is a term used by the designer creating**
9810 **these table columns.**
9811
9812 **"customerID" is the first data item shown. The**
9813 **column names are automatically displayed with**
9814 **the output for us.**
9815
9816 **Now, lets re-write the query to be selective about**
9817 **the records displayed by using the "WHERE"**
9818 **qualifier.NOTE THE CAPS, SQL prefers**

9819 **CAPITAL LETTERS, but accepts lower case as**
9820 **well.**
9821
9822 `use Northwind;`
9823 `SELECT * FROM customers WHERE customerID LIKE`
9824 `'a%';`
9825
9826 `-- I'm guessing you already understand the`
9827 `command.`
9828 `-- It's very much like plain English . . . except`
9829 `for the "*" and "%" symbols . . . and`
9830 `-- the -- semi-colon at the end. "*" means "get`
9831 `all records", "WHERE" says`
9832 `-- "qualified as" . . . "Any record with customrID`
9833 `starting with the character "a"`
9834 `--, " % "meaning "a" followed by anything".`
9835 `--`
9836 `-- This how it looks in the editor;`

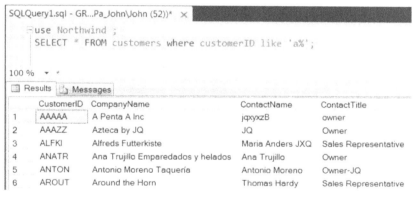

9837

9838                    **Screen 20**
9839

9840 **The results have records starting with "a" followed**
9841 **by whatever comes "after" the character "a".**
9842 **If I wanted results for all records containing an**
9843 **"a" . . . I'd write;**
9844

9845  **SELECT * FROM customers WHERE**
9846  **customerID like '%a';**
9847  **-- reversed the "%" and the "a".**
9848
9849  **Go ahead, Try it!!! Experiment and learn. It won't**
9850  **break, it's only software.**
9851
9852  **So far we've covered;**
9853  **SELECT, WHERE, LIKE . . . and the "USE"**
9854  **statements. Two more, just for fun!!**
9855
9856  **The "INSERT" statement is used to add new**
9857  **records.**
9858
9859  **Have you noticed that all the action is taking place**
9860  **within a *table*? Tables are the focal point of**
9861  **database activity.**
9862
9863  **Here's how "INSERT" looks . . .**

9864

9865                          **Screen 21**
9866
9867  **NOTES:**
9868     **1. A value is provided for every possible**
9869         **column.**

9870   2. A "value" is given to store in every column.

9871   3. Strings are enclosed in " Single Quotation

9872      marks.

9873   4. "INSERT" is followed by the table name.

9874   5. The key word "Values" preceeds the actual

9875      values.

9876   6. The actual values being stored are inside

9877      parentheses.

9878   7. Column names are not used.

9879   8. Actual values are in the *same order as the*

9880      *columns.*

9881   9. A semi-colon terminates the statement.

9882

9883 I used uppercase letters for the Key words. NO, I

9884 intentionally used uppercase letters for the Key

9885 words, it's not a mistake. Capital letters are

9886 expected for Key words. However, SQL will accept

9887 lowercase letters as well.

9888

9889 After I click execute . . . a message appears in the

9890 status bar at the bottom of the screen . . . It says

9891 the query excuted successfully.

9892

9893 Now, check your work . . . Run a select * query,

9894 scroll down to the bottom, or wherever, and locate

9895 the record you just added.

9896
9898

9899 **The records are listed alphabetically, ordered by**
9900 **the customerID.**

9901

9902 **Look ma, it worked!!! Congratulations (to me and**
9903 **you).**

9904

9905 **OK . . . the last one; "DELETE "**

9906

9907 **DELETE is used to remove a record . . . expected?**

9908

9909 **It looks like so;**

```
SQLQuery1.sql - GR...Pa_John\John (52))*  ×
   use Northwind ;
   -- SELECT * FROM customers where customerID like
   -- INSERT into customers Values ('XXXXX','MyCo In
   -- SELECT * FROM customers ;
   DELETE customers WHERE customerID like(%x);



100 %    ▼  ◂
  Messages
   Command(s) completed successfully.




100 %    ▼  ◂
  Query executed successfully.
```

**Screen 23**

**NOTES:**
  1. **DELETE is the first word entered.**
  2. **The table name is the second word entered.**
  3. **WHERE is used.**
  4. **LIKE is entered and used.**

9918    5.  **Parenthese enclose the "%x".**
9919    6.  **I get a message stating that the operation**
9920        **succeeded.**
9921    7.  **"--" on the old statements "Comment" them**
9922        **out.**
9923    8.  **Comments don't get executed or cause**
9924        **errors. I "commented out" the previous**
9925        **commands in case I want to use them again.**
9926        **All I have to do is remove the comment**
9927        **symbol.**
9928    9.  **Like I said, I'm not teaching you to create**
9929        **databases, I'm teaching you (I hope) to use**
9930        **them and manipulate them.**
9931
9932    **However, If you are like me at all, you're**
9933    **wondering how it's done.**
9934
9935    **Here's an example . . . I don't want you losing**
9936    **sleep because you're thinking "How do I create a**
9937    **database ".**
9938
9939    **CREATE database Autoparts;**

```
9940    CREATE TABLE parts
9941    (
9942        pt_id INTEGER IDENTITY(1,1),
9943        pt_name VARCHAR(50) NOT NULL,
9944        pt_SN VARCHAR(50),
9945        CONSTRAINT pt_pk PRIMARY KEY (pt_sn)
9946    );
```

9947

9948    **Notice the designer used the "pt_Column name"**
9949    **format.**
9950

9951    **Actually this is an excellent idea. It makes you**
9952    **aware that each column is part of the "parts" i.e**

9953 "pt_name" table. This would come in handy if we
9954 were trying to relate tables and compare column
9955 values.
9956
9957 That concludes the SQL tutorial. Now, let's turn
9958 our attention to accessing the database from our
9959 C# -or- VB program.
9960
9961 It's a good time for a break if you need one!
9962
9963 Note the line number and come back when you're
9964 ready.
9965 This unit is focused on one thing . . . retrieving and
9966 displaying and manipulating data from a database
9967 from either a C# or Visual basic program.
9968
9969 It does this and it does not do more. We are not
9970 trying to design and construct a new database. It
9971 assumes the installation of the required tools
9972 (software applications) has been completed.
9973
9974 Let's code.
9975

# 9976 Project 20a VB Access to the
# 9977 Northwind database . . .

9978
9979 Several new Objects are going to be introduced in
9980 this example including OleDb and Sqlproviders
9981 data providers;
9982
9983   1. Connection objects
9984   2. Command objects
9985   3. Data Adapters

9986    **4. Data Tables**
9987    **5. Data Sets**
9988    **6. Data grid view controls**
9989    **7. Variables used for database actions**
9990    **8. Defining data sources**
9991    **9. Binding data to controls**
9992
9993    **And away we go (my Jackie Gleason imitation)!**
9994
9995    **Start MVS . . . Configure Project and Solution**
9996    **location.**
9997
9998    **Start VB access to database project . . .**
9999
10000   **This is where we are going in terms of user**
10001   **presentation you can vary the location and**
10002   **arrangement of controls and verbage for**
10003   **instruction/explanation as you like;**

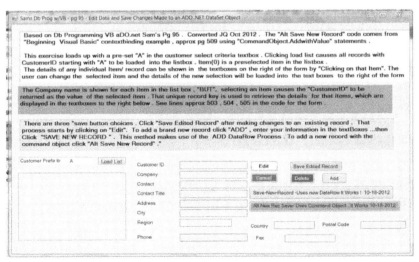

10004

10005       **Screen 30 Accessing a database from Visual Basic**
10006

10007 This program will make use of the CustomerID
10008 column of the Customers table to access all records
10009 beginning with the letter we specify or "all"
10010 records if no letter is specified from the Customers
10011 tale in the Northwind Sql database.
10012
10013 After the records are loaded we will have the
10014 ability to modify, delete or add new records for the
10015 table. Each record has 11 data items or
10016 columns . . . each can be displayed in the boxes
10017 shown for easy reading by clicking that record in
10018 the list of records.
10019
10020 This is a long, but not terribly difficult project. We
10021 will use several data access tools provided in Visual
10022 Basic and "ADO.Net" . . . Access to Data Objects.
10023
10024 I could write forever and you'd learn very little
10025 until you write the code yourself and see it work,
10026 so let's get going.
10027 Again, *I caution against* copying the text from this
10028 page and pasting it into your code . . . instead use
10029 the example project files for actual code in your
10030 event handler code blocks!! This code is simple for
10031 the purose of explanation.
10032
10033 You will need a new project in MVS, specify Visual
10034 Basic as the language and set the <Tools> + <
10035 Options> + <Solution Location> to your VS VB
10036 projects folder.
10037
10038 The controls needed are 12 textBoxes and their
10039 corresponding labels, 1 listbox and 7 buttons.

10040 **Study the Screen 30 photo and arrange the**
10041 **controls for your form as you like them.**
10042
10043 **Textbox names should correspond to the columns**
10044 **of the table in the database . . . this simplifies**
10045 **coding enormously. I always start a texbox name**
10046 **with "txt" for the same reason and it's a little less**
10047 **typing.**
10048
10049 **Lable names should reflect the content of the**
10050 **textbox they are associated with . . . make it easy**
10051 **on yourself. I always start label names with "lbl",**
10052 **again you decide for yourself what your**
10053 **methodology for naming is and stay consistent**
10054 **throughout the code.**
10055
10056 **Take care with the large instruction labels for the**
10057 **user. Make sure you can understand the**
10058 **instructions when you come back later and use this**
10059 **program for a model to build your own**
10060 **applications.**
10061
10062 **I used multiple labels for instructions so I could**
10063 **make the colors different for each type of**
10064 **operation being described.**
10065 **Make it easy on yourself and your users.**
10066
10067 **The first order of business is to import the Visual**
10068 **Basic Libraries we need for the program and then**
10069 **then to write the event handler for clicking the**
10070 **"Load Data" button. We allow the user to specify a**
10071 **letter which is the first letter of the records to be**
10072 **retrieved, then retrieve the records.**

10073

10074 Much of the code for the project was modeled
10075 from examples in "Database Programming with
10076 Visual Basic.NET, Second Edition Copyright
10077 ©2003 by Carsten Thomsen" of Apress publishing.
10078 That is an excellent book and I LEARNED A LOT
10079 FROM IT. I think it would be best used as an
10080 intermediate level book for the subject of accessing
10081 databases with Visual Basic.

10082

10083 For beginners in programming this book provides
10084 a more concise, easier to follow example project in
10085 my opinion.

10086

10087 The *program code explanation is embedded directly*
10088 *in the project example's code with comment lines.*
10089 This makes it easier to understand each line of
10090 code's purpose and effect as it is executed and
10091 without the distraction of switching back and forth
10092 between the textbook and actual executable file.

10093

10094 For the Visual basic Project, use MicrosoftVisual
10095 Studio and open the project . . . read the code!!!! It
10096 is written solely for the purpose of instruction. The
10097 event handlers are appropriate for modeling and
10098 building your own applications as you become
10099 ready. The Project is Proj 20a in the example files.
10100 I will also include a complete copy of the code in
10101 appendix "R". Once more, be cautioned about
10102 copying and pasting from the textbook into your
10103 own executable code . . . . It can and often does
10104 present problems

10105 un-necessarily and sometimes they are quite
10106 difficult to find and remedy.
10107
10108 Now to the C# DataAdpter project for the
10109 Northwind database.
10110

# 10111 Project 20b C# . . . Access to a
# 10112 database . . .

10113
10114 C# is a significantly different program when
10115 accessing databases in the syntax and speficity of
10116 the statements.
10117
10118 I tried to do a line by line comparisonwith Visual
10119 basic and found myself tangled up in semantics . . .
10120 many lines of code are similar, but . . . C# is more
10121 precise and more consistent in the definition and
10122 use of the tools for interacting with databases than
10123 Visual Basic.
10124
10125 I think that is a very large and well deserved
10126 compliment to the development team at Microsoft
10127 for C#.
10128
10129 As I see it, this places the developer in a situation
10130 where you must choose the language you like best
10131 and focus your efforts there when writing database
10132 related programs.
10133
10134 The alternative is to spend significant amounts of
10135 time becoming intimately acquainited with both
10136 languages. Personally, I don't see the point in that.

10137  **Never-the-less, I covered both. You will choose for**
10138  **yourself.**
10139
10140  **Start a new project named "C Sharp data adapter**
10141  **display".**
10142
10143  **Add these controls to the form;**
10144
10145      **A. A data grid view control**
10146      **B. 2 labels**
10147      **C. 2 buttons**
10148
10149  **These are all of the controls we need for now.**
10150
10151  **Don't be mis-led, the amount of code makes up for**
10152  **the scarcity of controls. This is a rather detailed**
10153  **and complex project. Take the time to analyze**
10154  **each step thoroughly. It isn't any more difficult**
10155  **than the other examples, but a lot of it is new.**
10156  **Attention to detail is the Key for success.**
10157
10158  **Below is how the start up screen might appear.**

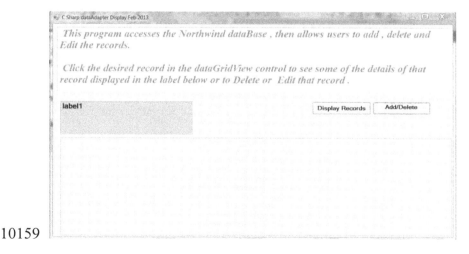

10159

10160                    **Screen 24**

10161

10162 **Here are the step our code will take to complete**

10163 **it's job;**

10164

10165    **1. Define variables and objects needed to access**

10166       **the database i.e dataAdapters, datasets,**

10167       **commands, dataTables etc.**

10168    **2. Connect to the Northwind database**

10169    **3. Read the database tables (mostly**

10170       **"customers" table)**

10171    **4. Fill our data objects with the data read from**

10172       **Northwind**

10173    **5. Display the records in our controls (Bind**

10174       **data)**

10175    **6. Create SQL commands as needed**

10176    **7. Execute tasks to add, edit and delete**

10177       **database records**

10178

10179 **Here is what the form looks like when the records**

10180 **ae populated with data.**

10181

10182                         **Screen 25**

10183

10184  **The content of the instruction label is up to you.**

10185

10186  **A lot of the complexity of the program involves**
10187  **passing variables and commands to the database in**
10188  **the correct format. The actions taken to do the**
10189  **actual record handling are accomplished inside the**
10190  **database, without our help beyond passing the**
10191  **correction information in strings.**

10192

10193  **"SQL Statements/Commands" are actions to be**
10194  **taken by a database on it's data table, more**
10195  **specifically, it's records. Data objects are the**
10196  **software devices that create and pass the**
10197  **commands into the database along with the**
10198  **information (data) to be used.**

10199

10200  **The database server we are using is the "Microsoft**
10201  **SQL Server 2010 Express. This is one of the "Big**
10202  **4" database products in the market today. The**
10203  **others are IBM@, Oracle@ and SAP@. Oracle is**
10204  **the market share leader.**
10205  **I have worked with them all, each has it's strong**
10206  **and weak points. Microsoft SQL offers "Openess**
10207  **in product design" meaning it is designed from the**
10208  **start to work cooperatively with software products**
10209  **from several major software providers, not just**
10210  **products from Microsoft.**

10211

10212  **It also offers a relatively high level of simplicity**
10213  **and easy-to-use tools for managing and working**
10214  **with the database.**

10215
10216 **Some, in fact, just about all of the other product**
10217 **makers are more closed or proprietary in my**
10218 **opinion. The amount of documentation from them**
10219 **is somewhat scarce.**
10220
10221 **Most importantly, Microsoft makes a complete**
10222 **suite of products and services designed to work**
10223 **together compatibly, including hardware**
10224 **manufacturers committed to their software and**
10225 **the Windows operating system. Who should have**
10226 **the most know-how?**
10227
10228 **Set the form's text property to the project name.**
10229
10230 **Name one of the buttons btnAddDelete and the**
10231 **other btnDisplay. Set their text properties as you**
10232 **like along with their other properties i.e.**
10233 **backColor etc.**
10234
10235 **Now we're ready to code the event handler for the**
10236 **"btnDisplayData_ Click" event. Double_Click the**
10237 **button and . . . let's go.**
10238
10239 **At the very top of the editor . . .(scroll up)**
10240
10241 **We specify a class that is to be used for the**
10242 **program that has**
10243 **The definition of the database objects we are using**
10244 **(and others).**
10245 `using System;`
10246 `using System.Collections.Generic;`
10247 `using System.ComponentModel;`

```
10248 using System.Data; // Where all data objects are
10249 defined
10250 using System.Data.SqlClient;
10251 //
10252 // NOTE: we are using SQL client.
10253 // there are others we are not concerned with
10254 right now.
10255 //
10256 using System.Drawing;
10257 using System.Linq;
10258 using System.Text;
10259 using System.Windows.Forms;
10260 //
10261 // prepare the strings we will use to end and
10262 receive data
10263 //
10264 // Note the correlation between the string names
10265 // and the database column names we are interested
10266 in.
10267 //
10268 // This is NOT required but makes coding easier.
10269 // Keeping track of where you are in the code
10270 // IS REQUIRED.
10271 //
10272 // Make it easy on yourself.
10273 //
10274 public partial class frmCSharpDataAdapter: Form
10275 {
10276     public string myCoID = ""; // --------- #1)
10277     public string myCoName = "";// -------- #2)
10278     public string myConName = "";// ------- #3)
10279     public string myConTitle = "";// ------ #4)
10280     public string myAddr = "";// ---------- #5)
10281     public string myCity = "";------------- #6)
10282     public string myRegion = "";----------- #7)
10283     public string myPostalCode = "";------- #8)
10284     public string myCountry = "";---------- #9)
10285     public string myPhone = "";------------ #10)
10286     public string myFax = "";------------- #11)
10287 // --- --- --- --- --- --- --- Yep, got em all.
10288 // --- now we start the form, actually it's done
10289 for us by
```

```
10290 // MVS.
10291 // C# starts setting uo the forn, variables etc.
10292 //
10293     public frmCSharpDataAdapter()
10294     {
10295         InitializeComponent();
10296     }
10297 //
10298 // Finally we begin our event handler code
10299 //
10300     public void btnDisplayData_Click(object sender,
10301 EventArgs e)
10302 //
10303 // The first statement defines a connection a, a
10304 link (of sorts) // to the database engine.
10305 //
10306     {
10307     SqlConnection myConn = new
10308 SqlConnection("Integrated
10309     Security = SSPI; Initial Catalog = Northwind;
10310 Data Source = SQLExpress");
10311 //
10312 // the connection string gives the database and our
10313 // program more specific information about processing
10314 // our request. It is stored as one part of the
10315 // "connection object".
10316 //
10317     myConn.ConnectionString = "Integrated Security
10318 = true;
10319     Initial Catalog=Northwind; Data Source =
10320     LocalHost\\SQLExpress";
10321 //
10322 // The initial catalog is the database,
10323 // the data source is your computer's official
10324 name.
10325 //
10326 // The dataAdapter object contains several
10327 properties,
10328 // one is the command information. It says what
10329 type
10330 // of command we are sending and the actual
10331 command
```

```
10332 // criteria to use i.e.
10333 // "SELECT * FROM "dataTable name ";
10334 //
10335 // The dataAdapter interprets the info returned
10336 // and brings a copy of it back to our program for
10337 // processing and display.
10338 //
10339 // The "using Northwind;" statement is technically
10340 // un-necessary. We told the database manager what
10341 // database to use with the "connection string".
10342 //
10343 // Next we define "instantiate" a working
10344 dataAdapter
10345 // named myAdapter . . . it's easier to type.
10346 // it needs much of the same info seen before.
10347 //
10348 // We also tell it the name of our connection
10349 object
10350 // and pass that info to it by name of the
10351 connection.
10352 //
10353     SqlDataAdapter myAdapter = new
10354     SqlDataAdapter("Integrated Security = SSPI;
10355 Initial
10356     Catalog = Northwind; Data Source =
10357     GrandPa_John\\SQLExpress", myConn);
10358 // Now we tell it what SQK query statement it can
10359 use
10360 //
10361     myAdapter.SelectCommand.CommandText = "Select *
10362         from Customers";
10363 // Then finally, we "open" or activate the
10364 connection to
10365 // the database.
10366 myConn.Open();
10367 //
10368 // Now we define a dataTable to store the data we
10369 get back
10370 // from the database via the dataAdapter.
10371 //
10372 // The data doesn't come back to string we define
10373 directly.
```

```
10374 // we must process the dataTable to get the data
10375 into strings.
10376 //
10377 // The "fill" command tells the dataAdapter where
10378 to put the
10379 // data returned from the database.
10380 //
10381    System.Data.DataTable myTable = new
10382       System.Data.DataTable("myTable");
10383    myAdapter.Fill(myTable);
10384 //
10385 // next, define a dataRow object . . . remember
10386 dataRows??
10387 //
10388 // We choose a name for the dataRow . . . and say
10389 which
10390 // record in the dataTable we want in our dataRow.
10391 // using an "index" number. Remember??
10392 //
10393    DataRow myRow;
10394 //
10395    myRow = myTable.Rows[0];
10396 //
10397    string myStrRow =
10398       Convert.ToString(myTable.Rows[0]);
10399 //
10400 // Now we take 10 data values and create a string
10401 // that we can use for display and put the string
10402 in our label
10403 // for display in a label.
10404 // We use the dataRow name(which we defined
10405 // earlier) and Column names -or- index numbers
10406 either one
10407 // to do this task. If the names are used, they
10408 must be
10409 // enclosed in quotes and MATCH EXACTLY the column
10410 // names used in the database dataTable. EXACTLY!!
10411 //
10412 // Experiment and learn (Make some mistakes!! It's
10413 fine.)
10414 //
10415 // A good way to experiment is to "Comment out" a
```

```
10416 // statement that works and copy & paste the
10417 statement
10418 // on the line below that, then edit the
10419 statement. Try it.
10420 //
10421 // If you new statement fails, just remove the
10422 "Comment
10423 // out" symbols and you're good to go again. Saves
10424 re-typing
10425 // and more importantly time and more errors.
10426 //
10427    string myStrCoID =
10428 Convert.ToString(myRow["customerID"]);
10429    string myStrCoName =
10430 Convert.ToString(myRow["companyName"]);
10431    string myStrCoCont =
10432 Convert.ToString(myRow["ContactName"]);
10433    string myStrConTitle =
10434 Convert.ToString(myRow["ContactTitle"]);
10435    string myStrCoAddr =
10436 Convert.ToString(myRow["Address"]);
10437    string myStrPhone =
10438 Convert.ToString(myRow["Phone"]);
10439
10440 //
10441 // Concatenate a string for displaying in a label
10442 text property.
10443 //
10444    lblDataColumn.Text = "";
10445    lblDataColumn.Text = lblDataColumn.Text +
10446       lblDataColumn.Text + myStrCoID + "\n" +
10447       myStrCoName + "\n" + myStrCoCont +
10448          "\n" + myStrConTitle + "\n" +
10449             myStrCoAddr + "\n" +
10450                "\n"+myStrPhone;
10451 //
10452 // Set Color scheme for DataGridView1 for easier
10453 reading
10454 // View Help search Row Style for details
10455    dataGridView1.RowsDefaultCellStyle.BackColor
10456    = Color.Yellow;
10457    dataGridView1.AlternatingRowsDefaultCellStyle.
```

```
10458      BackColor = Color.Lime;
10459 //
10460 //
10461 // Here's something completely new!!
10462 //
10463 // The dataGridView is tied (Bound/"Bind")
10464 // to the input retrieved from the database
10465 // by specifying it's data source property as the
10466 // "dataTable". It is designed for this purpose,
10467 // it is a data focused control.
10468 //
10469 // It also has other methods you can explore on
10470 // your own like "Sort" . . . and others.
10471 //
10472 // The C# code does the job of finding and filling
10473 // the column titles and the "Cell values" for us.
10474 //
10475 // Bind DataGridView1 Data Source
10476 dataGridView1.DataSource = myTable;
10477 //
10478 // Release the System Resources
10479 // VERY IMPORTANT!!!
10480 // Especially with large, heavy users and
10481 Applications
10482 //
10483      myConn.Close();
10484      myAdapter.Dispose();
10485      myTable.Dispose();
10486      myRow = null;
10487 } // ----- ----- ----- ----- End btnDisplay_Click
10488
```

10489 **Run the program to see that It works.**

10490

10491 **IF NOT . . . . Review and try again!!**

10492

10493 **I just ran (Feb 25 2013) the exact same code and it**
10494 **worked, Check typos in the code, check to see that**
10495 **the control "name" properties match the code etc.**
10496

10497 Occasionally, MVS will throw in an extra event
10498 handler code block which actually contain "NO
10499 CODE".
10500
10501 This usually happens after you re-name a control,
10502 or make a mistake naming it originally, then
10503 correct the name property
10504
10505 It's a good place to check for mistakes if you get a
10506 build error message.
10507
10508 These are all common mistakes, not the
10509 apocalypse. Remember C# is Case sensitive . . .
10510 check spelling and capital letters, where they
10511 *"should"* and *"should not"* be.
10512
10513 Remember what I said wayyyy back there, *"Not*
10514 making any mistakes, you're *NOT* trying hard
10515 enough"!!!! Experiment and learn, make some
10516 mistakes. Occasionally, I make a mistake, just
10517 occasionally . . . to stay humble and to *LEARN*.
10518
10519 Part of learning to program, A *BIG, BIG* part . . .
10520 is making, finding and correcting MISTAKES. DO
10521 IT!!!!!!!!!!!!!!!!!!
10522 OK now for Add, Edit and Delete.
10523
10524 keeping things simple is always a smart idea, and
10525 usually, the job gets done as expected and more
10526 efficiently. The user screen is pretty heavily loaded
10527 with data and controls.
10528

10529 **"Deleting" records will use another form as will**
10530 **"Adding New Records". This keeps thing clean**
10531 **and simple from a user perspective. The**
10532 **programmer, on the other hand, has more work to**
10533 **do . . . such is the life of a programmer, thank**
10534 **goodness!**
10535
10536 // start OK btnAddDelete_ Click . . . .
10537 //
10538 **Well, the first thing that needs to happen . . .**
10539 **happens in the first form's code. When the user**
10540 **clicks "btnAddDelete" the code instantiates a new**
10541 **working copy of the second form, then "Shows"**
10542 **the second form.**
10543
10544 *BUT*, **In-The-Midst of all those goings-on . . . we**
10545 **have to get some info (data) sent over to the second**
10546 **form to work with.**
10547 **It's sitting over there alone,** *in it's own* **class,**
10548 **having no knowledge of what's happening at**
10549 **headquarters (the first form). Do . . . one-thing at a**
10550 **time!**
10551 //
10552 /* ------ Rember this is a comment line -----*/
10553 //
10554 // Gather the information the database will need
10555 to delete a // record from the customers
10556 table . . . It will be sent over
10557 // to the next form when it is displayed/shown as
10558 variables in
10559 // (strings).
10560 //
10561
10562 // ---------- Start btnAddDelete_Click ------- //
10563 public void btnAddDelete_Click(object sender,
10564 EventArgs e)

```
10565  {
10566      // Determine the "user-selected" record/Row
10567      // for deletion // in the datagridview control
10568      // ("get the index" of the Row) just like we did
10569      // with the automobile struct exercise, except we
10570      // were using a listBox, not a dataGridView
10571      // control.
10572      //
10573      int myRowIdx = dataGridView1.CurrentRow.Index;
10574      // Now we have the index number for the
10575  selected Row
10576      //
10577      int myInt = myRowIdx;
10578      // Each column in the selected row contains data
10579      // we want. Retrieve it into string variables!!
10580      //
10581      string myStrCoID = Convert.ToString
10582          (dataGridView1[0, myRowIdx].Value);
10583          // For reasons known only to Microsoft . . .
10584          // They soecify the column index as the first
10585          // index number.i.e column 0 of the selected
10586          // Row is stored . . .
10587          // . . . We know this because we looked at the
10588          // database table Columns in SQL
10589          // Management studio, remember? They are
10590          // always in that order.
10591          // Same for CompanyName, Column 1.
10592      string myStrCoName =
10593          Convert.ToString(dataGridView1[1,
10594              myRowIdx].Value);
10595  // --- --- Now we have customerID,compantName in
10596  // a string we can send to the second form--- ---
10597  Do the
10598  // same thing for the contactname --- using Column 2.
10599      string myStrConName =
10600          Convert.ToString(dataGridView1[2,
10601              myRowIdx].Value);
10602  /* --- --- --- Do the same thing for the
10603  contactTitle, // Column 3, etc etc.
10604      string myStrConTitle =
10605          Convert.ToString(dataGridView1[3,
10606              myRowIdx].Value);
```

```
10607 /* --- --- --- Do the same thing for the street
10608 address --- */
10609     string myStrAddr = Convert.ToString
10610         (dataGridView1[4,myRowIdx].Value);
10611
10612 /* --- --- --- Do the same thing for the city ---
10613 */
10614     string myStrCity = Convert.ToString
10615         (dataGridView1[5,
10616             myRowIdx].Value);
10617 /* --- --- --- Do the same thing for the region --
10618 - */
10619     string myStrRegion = Convert.ToString
10620         (dataGridView1[6, myRowIdx].Value);
10621 /* --- --- --- Do the same thing for the zip code-
10622 -- --- */
10623     string myStrPostalCode =
10624         Convert.ToString(dataGridView1[7,
10625             myRowIdx].Value);
10626 /* --- --- --- Do the same thing for the country -
10627 -- */
10628     string myStrCountry =
10629         Convert.ToString(dataGridView1[8,
10630             myRowIdx].Value);
10631 /* --- --- --- Do the same thing for the phone ---
10632 */
10633     string myStrPhone = Convert.ToString
10634         (dataGridView1[9, myRowIdx].Value);
10635 /* --- --- --- Do the same thing for the fax--- --
10636 - --- */
10637     string myStrFax =
10638         Convert.ToString(dataGridView1[10,
10639             myRowIdx].Value);
10640 //
10641 // Now we have all the info (data items) for 1
10642 Row/Record
10643 // More to the point "The-USER- selected" "Row".
10644 //
10645 // We're ready to display ("Show") the next form
10646 to user
10647 //
10648 // --- ---Instantiate frmSQLUpdate --- --- --- //
```

```
10649 // Notice all the string data we just gathered are
10650 inside the
10651 // parentheses calling the new form to be
10652 displayed "Shown".
10653 //
10654 //
10655     frmSQLUpdate myfrmSQLUpdate = new
10656 // These 4 lines are one continous command, broken
10657 up to fit in
10658 // the Word processing document page of this book.
10659 //
10660     frmSQLUpdate(myStrCoID,myStrConName,myStrConTit
10661 le,myStr
10662         Addr,myStrCity,myStrRegion,myStrPostalCode,
10663            myStrCountry,myStrPhone,myStrFax);
10664            myfrmSQLUpdate.Show();
10665 }// End ---- ---- ---- --- btnAddDelete_Click
10666 //
```

10667 Now the user will see the second form appear.

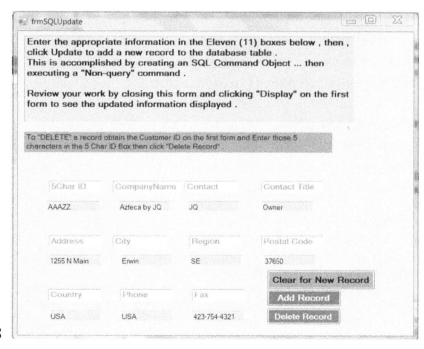

10668

10669                           **Screen 26**

10670
10671 // The user selected record in the dataGridView
10672 information // has been transferred to this form.
10673 Should the user click
10674 // "Delete" . . . the record will be deleted. We need
10675 to add a
10676 // confirmation messageBox to avoid accidental
10677 deletions.
10678 // Confirming decisions that change a database is
10679 most
10680 // always a good idea.
10681 //
10682 The best place to do that is right at the beginning
10683 of the btnDelete_Click event handler code. Don't
10684 waste CPU
10685 time (central processor unit).
10686
10687 I placed the code in Appendix Q . . . if you get
10688 stuck, but try it by yourself first. The help tab on
10689 MVS has some useful information.
10690
10691 This is the routine if you want to add it go ahead,
10692 do so now.
10693 The simplest approach is to exit btnDelete _Click if
10694 the user clicks cancel.
10695 //

```
10696 string myStrCoName = "";
10697 myStrCoName = txtBoxCompanyName.Text;
10698 string myStrCoID = "";
10699 myStrCoID = txtBoxCustomerID.Text;
10700 DialogResult result = MessageBox.Show(myStrCoName
10701     +" . . . " + myStrCoID + " Delete this record?",
10702     // "Delete confirmation",
10703     MessageBoxButtons.OKCancel);
10704     switch (result)
```

```
10705     {
10706        case DialogResult.OK:
10707        {
10708           this.Text = "[OK]";
10709           break;
10710        }
10711        case DialogResult.Cancel:
10712        {
10713           this.Text = "[Cancel]";
10714           return;
10715        }
10716     } End MessageBox Dialog
10717 //
10718 // Editing existing Records
10719
```

10720 **First order of business . . . Knowing which record**
10721 **to edit!**

10722

10723 **When the user has displayed the dabase current**
10724 **records, they may click a record then click <Add**
10725 **/Delede / Edit>and be taken to a new form with ths**
10726 **textboxes already populated with the chosen**
10727 **record's data items.**

10728

10729 **They then have the options of "Add" a new record,**
10730 **"Edit" or "Delete" . . . the pre-selected record. The**
10731 **choice comes "after" they see the new form.**

10732

10733 **Right now, we are going to deal with editing or**
10734 **updating existing records.**

10735

10736 **The assumptions are that the user loaded data with**
10737 **the first form, selected a specific record displayed**
10738 **on that form and then clicked "Add—Delete-Edit".**
10739

10740 **The next user step was clicking "Edit" which**
10741 **enabled allowed the cursor to enter and the user to**
10742 **type in the textboxes, editing the information of the**
10743 **existing record.**
10744
10745 *A copy of more verbosely commented Visual Basic*
10746 *access to database with dataAdapters is included in*
10747 *appendix XX.*
10748
10749 *Next up* . . . Arrays (one and two dimension arrays)
10750
10751 I debated long and hard whether to present arrays or
10752 databases first. I concluded that the most benefit
10753 would come from understanding database applications
10754 which have tables that closely resemble arrays in
10755 structure and access methods.
10756
10757 Once you understand the database code, arrays are
10758 much easier to comprehend and the learning time and
10759 effort are reduced as I see it.
10760
10761 You have seen that you can define a class, add
10762 properties and use the class over and over to
10763 instantiate instances of the class you defined with
10764 different names. In essence, you created a user
10765 defined variable with sub-variables (properties), a
10766 very sophisticated one of great use to programmers.
10767 You learned of a similar control, the Struct and
10768 applied that concept in a working application. We
10769 looked briefly at "Collections" . . . the "collection" of
10770 controls on a form and counted the number of
10771 controls.
10772

10773 There are several variables/objects you can define that
10774 have this "sub-variable" or property capability. One
10775 such variable is an array. The word properties is not
10776 used with the Array control. Instead, the term
10777 *"element"* is used.
10778
10779 Compared to defining and using classes and class
10780 properties or structs, arrays are much less complicated
10781 and easier to use. They are not as flexible as classes
10782 and are limited, in most cases, to having every
10783 property defined as holding the same type of variable
10784 i.e. strings or integers within a particular array. Arrays
10785 are not directly visible to the user. Arrays are
10786 information storage devices.
10787
10788 Visualize an array as a bookshelf . . . Each sub-
10789 variable or "Item(s)" or "elements", as they are
10790 termed, is a storage compartment. Think of them as
10791 "Rows" if you like. Each Item (element) is given an
10792 "Index" . . . 0, 1, 2, 3, 4 etc. I can "Add" Items
10793 (elements) to each compartment (Row). I can "Add" a
10794 string variable, for example, if I created the array as a
10795 "string" array or number, *if* I created an "Integer"
10796 array. All values must be of the same variable type,
10797 strings in this case. But, I can only add as many
10798 "Items or elements" as I created "DIM" the array to
10799 hold.
10800
10801 This code creates an array that *holds five (5)*
10802 *items(elements)* . . . 0 to 4.
10803
10804 *VB* **Array Code**
10805

```
10806 Dim myArray(4) As String
10807 '// We say 4, but in Visual Basic actually get 5
10808 '// i.e. "0" thru "4" elements.
10809 '//
10810    myArray(0) = "John"
10811    myArray(1) = "James"
10812    myArray(2) = "Jesse"
10813    myArray(3) = "Joseph"
10814    myArray(4) = "Jake"
```

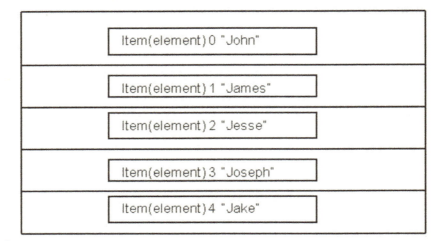

10815
10816  This procedure is called "initializing the array." I
10817  specify the array name, the item(element) index and
10818  set the value equal "=" to a "literal string", characters
10819  enclosed in quotation marks. Since I defined the array
10820  as a "string" array, the values I store must also be
10821  strings. They have no mathematical value and cannot
10822  be used in arithmetic operations.
10823
10824  The array is not visible to a user. To display the
10825  values, I have to retrieve the values and display them
10826  in a visible control, i.e. a textbox or label or listBox or
10827  comboBox etc. This code displays the values in a
10828  listBox;

Simply Programming C# and Visual Basic . . . 317

```
10829
10830    ListBox1.Items.Add(myArray(0))
10831    ListBox1.Items.Add(myArray(1))
10832    ListBox1.Items.Add(myArray(2))
10833    ListBox1.Items.Add(myArray(3))
10834    ListBox1.Items.Add(myArray(4))
10835
```

# 10836 Project 21—Single dimension array

10837

10838 Here is the *complete code* for a form that defines the
10839 array and displays the values in a listBox. It is entered
10840 in the event handler code block for a botton's click
10841 event. In this case, the button is named btnLoadArray;

10842

## 10843 Project 32 Arrays with Visual Basic

10844

```
10845 Imports System
10846 Imports System.Array
10847 Public Class Form1
10848 '//
10849    Private Sub btnLoadArray_Click(sender As
10850 System.Object, e As System.EventArgs) Handles
10851 btnLoadArray.Click
10852        Dim myArray(4) As String
10853        myArray(0) = "John"
10854        myArray(1) = "James"
10855        myArray(2) = "Jesse"
10856        myArray(3) = "Joseph"
10857        myArray(4) = "Jake"
10858        '//
10859        ListBox1.Items.Add(myArray(0))
10860        ListBox1.Items.Add(myArray(1))
10861        ListBox1.Items.Add(myArray(2))
10862        ListBox1.Items.Add(myArray(3))
10863        ListBox1.Items.Add(myArray(4))
10864    End Sub
10865 End Class
10866
```

10867  Start a new project, add a button and listBox to the
10868  form and enter the code in the click event handler for
10869  the button.
10870  Run the program. You should see results that are
10871  similar to this;
10872

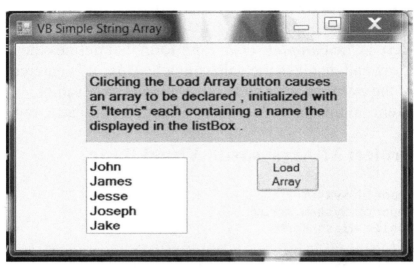

10873
10874                          **Screen 27**
10875  If you don't see these results, REVIEW!!
10876
10877  At this point the values are not stored permanently on
10878  your hard drive. Patience! We'll get to that.
10879
10880  The array we just created is called a ***one-dimension***
10881  array. Each Row holds one item or "***element***". The
10882  next array is called a ***two-dimension*** array. It can hold
10883  two (2) values (Items or elements) per Row. Each
10884  Row has an index (0 to 4) and each Item or "element"
10885  on each Row has an index of it's own i.e. (0) and (1).
10886  Remember, all items or "elements" must be the same
10887  variable type and be the same as the array type you

10888 declared i.e. string or integer. Yes . . . this is
10889 somewhat limiting, but have patience, we'll soon
10890 learn of other controls that do not have this limitation.
10891

# 10892 **Project 22—Two-dimension arrays:**

10893

10894 Re-call that you envisioned a one-dimension array as
10895 a bookshelf. Now apply that idea to a two dimension
10896 array, with the individual shelves divided into two
10897 compartments or "elements".
10898

| Row 0 | Item 0,0 | Item 0,1 |
| | Item 1,0 | Item 1,1 |
| | Item 2,0 | Item 2,1 |
| | Item 3,0 | Item 3,1 |
| Row 4 | Item 4,0 | Item 4,1 |

10899

10900          **Now each element has 2 indexes i.e. 0,0 to 4,1.**

10901

10902 When we refer to a specific element we use both
10903 indexes i.e. myArray(0,0) thru myArray(4,1).
10904 You can think in terms of rows and columns if it helps
10905 to clarify things for you. Defining a two-dimension
10906 array looks like this;
10907

10908 VB
10909 Dim myArray(4,2) as string

```
10910
10911 So, another new project VB Two dimension array.
10912
10913 Public Class Form1
10914 '//
10915    Private Sub btnLoadArray_Click(sender As
10916 System.Object, e As System.EventArgs) Handles
10917 btnLoadArray.Click
10918    '// Define and initialize the array
10919       Dim myArray(4, 2) As String
10920       myArray(0, 0) = "Arthur"
10921       myArray(0, 1) = "Architect"
10922       myArray(1, 0) = "Bill"
10923       myArray(1, 1) = "Banker"
10924       myArray(2, 0) = "Charles"
10925       myArray(2, 1) = "Chef"
10926       myArray(3, 0) = "David"
10927       myArray(3, 1) = "Doctor"
10928       myArray(4, 0) = "Edward"
10929       myArray(4, 1) = "Educator"
10930       '// Display the element values in the
10931 listBox using two indexes for each element.
10932       '// To make the information more readable
10933 add a space between pairs of elements
10934       '//
10935       '// Notice that the listBox adds scroll bars
10936 automatically if
10937       '// it is to small to display the
10938 information as we designed it.
10939       '//
10940       ListBox1.Items.Add(myArray(0, 0))
10941       ListBox1.Items.Add(myArray(0, 1))
10942       ListBox1.Items.Add(" ")
10943       ListBox1.Items.Add(myArray(1, 0))
10944       ListBox1.Items.Add(myArray(1, 1))
10945       ListBox1.Items.Add(" ")
10946       ListBox1.Items.Add(myArray(2, 0))
10947       ListBox1.Items.Add(myArray(2, 1))
10948       ListBox1.Items.Add(" ")
10949       ListBox1.Items.Add(myArray(3, 0))
10950       ListBox1.Items.Add(myArray(3, 1))
```

```
10951          ListBox1.Items.Add(" ")
10952          ListBox1.Items.Add(myArray(4, 0))
10953          ListBox1.Items.Add(myArray(4, 1))
10954          '//
10955       End Sub
10956 End Class
10957
```

10958 Run the program . . . results should look like this;
10959

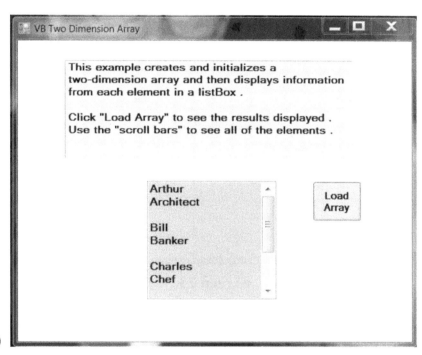

10960
10961                    **Screen 28**
10962
10963 **If not, *Review* and try again!!!**
10964
10965 **Get it right and *take a break*.**
10966
10967 *C# Array Code*
10968

10969 **If you want to "stretch" a little, try converting the**
10970 **VB code to C#. The C# is fundamentally the same**
10971 **except for declaring th array. Use this format for a**
10972 **One Dimension Array**
10973 **It defines and initializes the array in one**
10974 **statement . . .**
10975 **Our results will look like this;**
10976

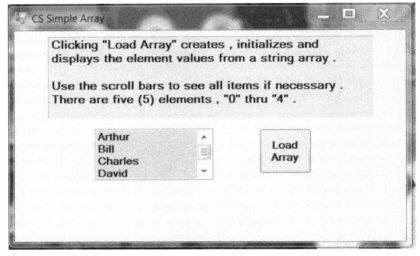

10977
10978                              **Screen 29**
10979
10980 **Looks pretty much the same as before huh?**
10981 **Except, for the text property of the form in the top**
10982 **left of the picture.**
10983
10984 **// *Note* the use of brackets and their location**
10985
```
10986 string[] myArray = {"Arthur", "Bill", "Charles",
10987 "David","Edward"};
10988     listBox1.Items.Add(myArray[0]);
10989
```

10990 (repeat the second line for each element being
10991 added to the listBox).NOTE; C# uses "Brackets" to
10992 specify the indexes, not parentheses.
10993
10994 **For a Two Dimension Array C# Uses this**
10995 **declaration;**
10996
```
10997 string[,] myArray;//Note where the brackets are
10998 placed
10999     myArray= new string[5,2];//Note use of the
11000 "new" word
```
11001
11002 **Adding elements to the listBox is similar except for**
11003 **brackets and semicolons;**
11004
```
11005 listBox1.Items.Add(myArray[0, 0]);
11006 listBox1.Items.Add(myArray[0, 1]);
11007 listBox1.Items.Add(" ");// Spaces make the
11008 information
11009 //more readable
```
11010
11011 **Complete C# code for this project is in Appendix**
11012 **K.**
11013
11014 At this point you should have a vey broad base of
11015 knowledge to build on for both Visual Basic or C#
11016 or the one you chose to start your journey into
11017 programming with . . . It's a strong beginning but,
11018 only a beginning. There is a great deal more to be
11019 learned.
11020
11021 My suggestion would be at this point that you
11022 spend some time and effort on debugging
11023 application code and using the "Try and Catch"
11024 methods of error trapping.
11025

**After that, spend your effort and time on Web programming. There are many great books on the subject and it certainly is a lucrative field.**

# Appendix A . . .

## VB Code for Forms TextBoxes Variables RadioButtons

```
Private Sub btnCalculate_Click(sender As
System.Object, e As System.EventArgs) Handles
btnCalculate.Click
    txtBoxAns.Text = ""
    Dim decAns As Decimal = 0
    Dim dec1 As Decimal = 0
    Dim dec2 As Decimal = 0
    dec1 = Convert.ToDecimal(txtBoxNum1.Text)
    dec2 = Convert.ToDecimal(txtBoxNum2.Text)

    If (radBtnAdd.Checked) Then
        txtBoxAns.Text = ""
        decAns = 0
        decAns = dec1 + dec2
        txtBoxAns.Text = Convert.ToString(decAns)
    End If

    If (radBtnSubtract.Checked) Then
        txtBoxAns.Text = ""
        decAns = 0
        decAns = dec1—dec2
        txtBoxAns.Text = Convert.ToString(decAns)
    End If

    If (radBtnMultiply.Checked) Then
        txtBoxAns.Text = ""
        decAns = 0
        decAns = dec1 * dec2
        txtBoxAns.Text = Convert.ToString(decAns)
    End If
```

```
11065
11066    If (radBtnDivide.Checked) Then
11067        txtBoxAns.Text = ""
11068        decAns = 0
11069        decAns = dec1 / dec2
11070        txtBoxAns.Text = Convert.ToString(decAns)
11071    End If
11072 End Sub
11073
```

# 11074 Appendix B . . . VB "for loop"

```
11075
11076 Private Sub btnLoopAndDecide_Click(sender As
11077 System.Object, e As System.EventArgs) Handles
11078 btnLoopAndDecide.Click
11079    Dim X As Integer = 0
11080    Dim myStr As String = ""
11081    For X = 0 To 20
11082        X += 5
11083        myStr = Convert.ToString(X)
11084        TextBox1.Text = myStr
11085        If (X >= 10) Then ' >= Means is greater than
11086 or equals
11087            TextBox1.Text = "Loop ended" +
11088            " X's Value was " + Convert.ToString(X)
11089            Return
11090        End If
11091    Next X
11092 End Sub
11093 ===================================
```

# 11094 Appendix C . . . VB ToDo, comboBox,
# 11095 file reader project.

```
11096
11097 Imports System
11098 Imports System.IO
11099
11100 Public Class Form1
11101    Private Sub btnReadFile_Click(sender As
11102 System.Object, e As System.EventArgs) Handles
11103 btnReadFile.Click
```

```
11104            Dim myStrToDo As String = " "
11105            Dim myRdr As StreamReader
11106            myRdr = New System.IO.StreamReader("C:\App
11107  Target Files\ToDo.txt")
11108            While myStrToDo <> ""
11109                myStrToDo = myRdr.ReadLine()
11110                If (myStrToDo = "") Then
11111                    Return
11112                End If
11113                ComboBox1.Items.Add(myStrToDo)
11114            End While
11115        End Sub
11116  End Class
11117
```

11118 **This is a complete, tested, working comboBox, VB**
11119 **file IO application for the environment I described.**
11120 **Take this code, change a file name and a few**
11121 **control properties and you have another**
11122 **completely new application for another user and**
11123 **situation.** *Appendix D* **has the** *C#* **code for the same**
11124 **application.**

11125

# 11126 Appendix D . . . C# comboBox, File IO,
# 11127 for "ToDo" items.

```
11128
11129  using System;
11130  using System.IO;
11131  using System.Collections.Generic;
11132  using System.ComponentModel;
11133  using System.Data;
11134  using System.Drawing;
11135  using System.Linq;
11136  using System.Text;
11137  using System.Windows.Forms;
11138  namespace VS_CS_File_IO_ComboBox
11139  {
11140      public partial class Form1: Form
11141      {
```

```
11142          public Form1()
11143          {
11144              InitializeComponent();
11145          }
11146          public int OriginalSelectedIdx;
11147          public string myStrToAdd = "";
11148          public string path = "C:\\App Target
11149 Files\\ToDo.txt";
11150          private void btnReadInfo_Click(object
11151 sender, EventArgs e)
11152          {
11153              cboToDoItems.Items.Clear();
11154              string myStr = " "; // Note the spaces in
11155 myStr
11156              // This prevents the code from seeing
11157 myStr as
11158              // empty (null) at the beginning of the
11159 while loop.
11160              //
11161              string myPath = "C:\\App Target
11162 Files\\ToDo.txt";
11163              // Declare a StreamReader
11164                 StreamReader mySR;
11165              //
11166              // Initialze the StreamReader
11167              mySR = new StreamReader(myPath);
11168              //
11169              // Read lines for the file the file, stop
11170              // when the end is reached.
11171              myStr = "..";
11172              while (myStr!= null)
11173              {
11174                 myStr = mySR.ReadLine();
11175                 // Add the line to the comboBox
11176                 if(myStr!=null && myStr!="")
11177                 {
11178                     cboToDoItems.Items.Add(myStr);}
11179                 }
11180                 // Release the file and resources
11181                 mySR.Close();
11182                 mySR.Dispose();
11183              }//End Read
```

```
11184              public void btnAddInfo_Click(object
11185  sender, EventArgs e)
11186          {
11187              txtBoxAddInfo.Text = "";
11188              txtBoxAddInfo.Visible = true;
11189              btnAddInfo.Visible = true;
11190              // No need to be visible, until needed
11191  for input
11192              txtBoxAddInfo.Focus();
11193              // Focus puts the cursor in that control
11194              // ready to type input
11195              txtBoxAddInfo.Visible = true;
11196              btnSaveInfo.Visible = true;
11197              // not needed until the user
11198              // is ready to type input
11199          }//End Add
11200              private void btnSaveInfo_Click(object
11201  sender, EventArgs e)
11202          {
11203              myStrToAdd = txtBoxAddInfo.Text;
11204              cboToDoItems.Items.Add(myStrToAdd);
11205              StreamWriter mySW = new
11206  StreamWriter(path, true);
11207              // true says if the file exists append it.
11208              //Code determines if that is the case
11209              // automatically, without our help.
11210              mySW.WriteLine(myStrToAdd);
11211              // Release the resources
11212              mySW.Close();
11213              mySW.Dispose();
11214              mySW = null;
11215              // hide the control we don't need anymore
11216              txtBoxAddInfo.Text = "";
11217              txtBoxAddInfo.Visible = false;
11218              btnSaveInfo.Visible = false;
11219              // Show the results
11220              StreamReader mySR = new
11221  StreamReader(path);
11222              cboKeepers.Items.Clear();
11223              string myReadString = " ";
11224              cboToDoItems.Items.Clear();
11225              while (myReadString!= "")
```

```
11226                    {
11227                        myReadString = mySR.ReadLine();
11228                        if (myReadString == null)
11229                        {
11230                            return;
11231                        }
11232                        cboToDoItems.Items.Add(myReadString);
11233                        cboToDoItems.Text = "New Item Added";
11234                    } //End While
11235                    //
11236                    // Release the resources and the file
11237                    mySR.Close();
11238                    mySR.Dispose();
11239                    // Empty the user input textBox
11240                    txtBoxAddInfo.Text = "";
11241                    cboToDoItems.Text = "ToDo Items-Revised";
11242                    // we're done!!!
11243                }//End Save
11244
11245            public void btnDeleteInfo_Click(object
11246 sender, EventArgs e)
11247                {
11248                    // Clear Keepers
11249                    //cboKeepers.Items.Clear();
11250                    //' Select Name to delete
11251                    String strToDelete;
11252                    strToDelete = cboToDoItems.Text; //
11253 Text to Delete
11254                    int intIdxcboItems =
11255 cboToDoItems.SelectedIndex;
11256                    int Y = intIdxcboItems;
11257                    cboToDoItems.Items.RemoveAt(Y);
11258                    //cboKeepers = cboToDoItems; // Doesnt
11259 transfer items
11260                    // content or title
11261                    //
11262                    int XX = 0;
11263                    int intItems =
11264 cboToDoItems.Items.Count-1;
11265                    string strToWrite;//=;// "";
11266                    MessageBox.Show("Read toadd to keepers
11267 cbo");
```

```
11268                    cboKeepers.Items.Clear();
11269                    while (XX <= intItems)
11270                    {
11271                        //MessageBox.Show("Inside for ");
11272                        cboToDoItems.SelectedIndex = XX;
11273                        cboToDoItems.SelectedItem = XX;
11274                        cboToDoItems.SelectedValue = XX;
11275                        //MessageBox.Show("Ready for showing
11276                        // strToWrite ");
11277                        strToWrite= cboToDoItems.Text;
11278                        // MessageBox.Show(strToWrite);
11279                        if (strToWrite!= "" && strToWrite
11280                           != null)
11281                        {
11282                            cboKeepers.Items.Add(strToWrite);
11283                        }
11284                        XX++;
11285                    }
11286
11287                OriginalSelectedIdx =
11288    cboToDoItems.SelectedIndex;//First comboBox Idx of
11289    Delete Item
11290                int intKeepersCount =
11291    cboKeepers.Items.Count;
11292                lblKeepersCount.Text = "There are "+
11293    Convert.ToString(intKeepersCount)+" to store.";
11294                cboKeepers.Text = "Items saved to
11295    file.";
11296            }// End Delete
11297            private void btnExit_Click(object sender,
11298    EventArgs e)
11299            {
11300                Application.Exit();
11301            }
11302
11303            private void btnSaveKeepers_Click(object
11304    sender, EventArgs e)
11305            {
11306                //MessageBox.Show("Inside Save", "Line
11307    149 Inside Save");
11308                int intKeepersCount;
11309                // Dipsplay number of Keepers
```

```
11310                    intKeepersCount =
11311 cboKeepers.Items.Count;
11312                    MessageBox.Show(Convert.ToString
11313 (intKeepersCount), "Line 152 Keepers Count");
11314                    lblKeepersCount.Text = " There were "
11315 + Convert.ToString(intKeepersCount) + " Keeper
11316 names Line 153.";
11317                    //
11318                    //' If it exists, delete the old file
11319 of names bool myboolean;
11320                    myboolean = File.Exists("C:\\App
11321 Target Files\\ToDo.txt");
11322                    if (myboolean == true)
11323                    {
11324                        File.Delete("C:\\App Target
11325 Files\\ToDo.txt");
11326                    }
11327                    MessageBox.Show("Keeper Names File.tx
11328 was deleted", "Deleting old Keeper Names File");
11329                    //
11330                    //-- Write the Keeper items into a new
11331 file
11332                    //
11333                    intKeepersCount =
11334 cboKeepers.Items.Count;
11335                    int intStart = 0;
11336                    int intStop = cboKeepers.Items.Count-1;
11337                    string strToWrite = "";
11338                    while(intStart <=intStop)
11339                    {
11340                        MessageBox.Show("There are "+
11341                        Convert.ToString(intKeepersCount),
11342 "intStart Loop line 180");
11343                        cboKeepers.SelectedIndex =
11344 intStart;
11345                        cboKeepers.SelectedItem = intStart;
11346                        cboKeepers.SelectedValue =
11347 intStart;
11348                        strToWrite =
11349 strToWrite+"\n"+cboKeepers.Text;
11350                        MessageBox.Show(strToWrite +"\n"+ "
11351 Line 178");
```

```
11352                    intStart++;
11353                    //intkeepersCount += 1;
11354                } //End While write to file
11355                StreamWriter myFileWrt = new
11356 StreamWriter("C:\\App Target Files\\ToDo.txt",
11357 true);
11358                myFileWrt.WriteLine(strToWrite);
11359                // Release the resources and file
11360                myFileWrt.Close();
11361                myFileWrt.Dispose();
11362                MessageBox.Show("Line 188 File re-
11363 written ");
11364                // Update the keepers count label
11365                lblKeepersCount.Text = "There are " +
11366                Convert.ToString(intKeepersCount) + "
11367 keeper Items";
11368                // Update the Names Count label
11369                lblNames.Text = "There are " +
11370 Convert.ToString(intKeepersCount) + " Items in the
11371 file now.";
11372                cboToDoItems.Text="ToDo Items-
11373 Revised";
11374                cboKeepers.Text="Items saved to
11375 file.";
11376            }//End while
11377        }//End Save Keepers
11378    } // End partial class
11379
```

11380 That's it a complete, working CS file IO application.
11381 Take this code, change a file name and a few control
11382 properties and you have another completely new
11383 application for another user and situation.
11384

# 11385 Appendix E . . . btnThisMonth

11386

```
11387 private void btnThisMonth_Click(object sender,
11388 EventArgs e)
11389 {
11390     intLastLoaded = 0;
```

```
11391        listBox1.Height = 24;
11392        SetMyCustomFormat();
11393        DateTime myTestDate = DateTime.Now;
11394        //test code MessageBox.Show(Convert.ToString
11395        (myTestDate),"datePicker.Text");
11396        mySeekDay = " ";
11397        mySeekMo = " ";
11398        mySeekYr = " ";
11399        mySeekDateFinal = " ";
11400        intIdxItemFound = 0;
11401        mySeekDay = Convert.ToString(myTestDate.Day);
11402        mySeekMo = Convert.ToString(myTestDate.Month);
11403        mySeekYr = Convert.ToString(myTestDate.Year);
11404        //
11405        int intLenMo = mySeekMo.Length;
11406        if (intLenMo == 1)
11407        {
11408            mySeekMo = "0" + mySeekMo;
11409        }
11410        int intLenDay = mySeekDay.Length;
11411        if (intLenDay == 1)
11412        {
11413            mySeekDay = "0" + mySeekDay;
11414        }
11415        //
11416        //
11417        btnClearToDoItems.Visible = true;
11418        listBox1.Visible = true;
11419        string myStr = " "; // Note the spaces in myStr
11420        // This prevents the code from seeing myStr as
11421        // empty (null) at the beginning of the while
11422 loop.
11423        //
11424        // Declare a StreamReader
11425        StreamReader mySR;
11426        // Initialze the StreamReader
11427        int intStrIdx1 = 0;
11428        int intStrIdx2 = 0;
11429        intIdxItemFound = 0;
11430        // Read lines for the file the file, stop when
11431 the end is reached.
11432        myStrRead = "xx";
```

```
11433      mySR = new StreamReader("C:\\App Target
11434  Files\\ToDo.txt");
11435      listBox1.Items.Clear();
11436      intItemFound = 0;
11437      while (myStrRead!= null && myStrRead!= "")
11438      {
11439          myStrRead = "xx";
11440          myStrRead = mySR.ReadLine();
11441          // test for end of file
11442          if (myStrRead == null || myStrRead == "")
11443  {mySR.Close();mySR.Dispose();return;}
11444          intIdxItemFound =
11445  myStrRead.IndexOf(mySeekDateFinal);
11446          //
11447          if (myStrRead!= null && myStrRead!= "")//
11448  Big IF lOOP
11449          {
11450              // Determine if month and day desired are
11451  in string read from file
11452              //
11453              // Get day and month from known positions
11454  in the read-from-file string
11455              string SubStrMo = myStrRead.Substring(0, 2);
11456              string SubStrYear = myStrRead.Substring(6,
11457  4);
11458              //
11459              // Compare substrings with desired Month
11460  and Day strings
11461
11462              int intCompSubs1;
11463              int intCompSubs2;
11464              intCompSubs1 = string.Compare(mySeekMo,
11465  SubStrMo);
11466              intCompSubs2 = string.Compare(mySeekYr,
11467  SubStrYear);
11468              //
11469              // If both results are "0" i.e. the same,
11470  Add to listbox
11471              if (intCompSubs1!= 0 || intCompSubs2!= 0)
11472  {continue;}
11473              if (intCompSubs1 == 0 && intCompSubs2 ==
11474  0)
```

```
11475                    {
11476                        listBox1.Visible = true;
11477                        intItemFound++;
11478                        listBox1.Height += 24;
11479                        listBox1.Items.Add(myStrRead);
11480                        listBox1.Sorted = true;
11481                    }// End if
11482                }// End Big If Loop
11483            }// End while
11484    }// End This Month
11485
```

## 11486 Appendix F

```
11487
11488    private void btnThisMonth_Click(object sender,
11489    EventArgs e)
11490    {
11491        intLastLoaded = 0;
11492        listBox1.Height = 24;
11493        SetMyCustomFormat();
11494        DateTime myTestDate = DateTime.Now;
11495        //test code MessageBox.Show(Convert.ToString
11496    (myTestDate),"datePicker.Text");
11497        mySeekDay = " ";
11498        mySeekMo = " ";
11499        mySeekYr = " ";
11500        mySeekDateFinal = " ";
11501        intIdxItemFound = 0;
11502        mySeekDay = Convert.ToString(myTestDate.Day);
11503        mySeekMo = Convert.ToString(myTestDate.Month);
11504        mySeekYr = Convert.ToString(myTestDate.Year);
11505        //
11506        int intLenMo = mySeekMo.Length;
11507        if (intLenMo == 1)
11508        {
11509            mySeekMo = "0" + mySeekMo;
11510        }
11511        int intLenDay = mySeekDay.Length;
11512        if (intLenDay == 1)
11513        {
11514            mySeekDay = "0" + mySeekDay;
11515        }
```

```
11516    //
11517    //
11518    btnClearToDoItems.Visible = true;
11519    listBox1.Visible = true;
11520    string myStr = " "; // Note the spaces in myStr
11521    // This prevents the code from seeing myStr as
11522    // empty (null) at the beginning of the while
11523 loop.
11524    //
11525    // Declare a StreamReader
11526    StreamReader mySR;
11527    // Initialze the StreamReader
11528    int intStrIdx1 = 0;
11529    int intStrIdx2 = 0;
11530    intIdxItemFound = 0;
11531    // Read lines for the file the file, stop when
11532 the end is reached.
11533    myStrRead = "xx";
11534    mySR = new StreamReader("C:\\App Target
11535 Files\\ToDo.txt");
11536    listBox1.Items.Clear();
11537    intItemFound = 0;
11538    while (myStrRead!= null && myStrRead!= "")
11539    {
11540        myStrRead = "xx";
11541        myStrRead = mySR.ReadLine();
11542        // test for end of file
11543        if (myStrRead == null || myStrRead == "")
11544 {mySR.Close();mySR.Dispose();return;}
11545        intIdxItemFound =
11546 myStrRead.IndexOf(mySeekDateFinal);
11547        //
11548        if (myStrRead!= null && myStrRead!= "")//
11549 Big IF lOOP
11550        {
11551            // Determine if month and day desired are
11552 in string read from file
11553            //
11554            // Get day and month from known positions
11555 in the read-from-file string
11556            string SubStrMo = myStrRead.Substring(0,
11557 2);
```

```
11558          string SubStrYear =
11559 myStrRead.Substring(6, 4);
11560          //
11561          // Compare substrings with desired Month
11562 and Day strings
11563              int intCompSubs1;
11564          int intCompSubs2;
11565          intCompSubs1 = string.Compare(mySeekMo,
11566 SubStrMo);
11567          intCompSubs2 = string.Compare(mySeekYr,
11568 SubStrYear);
11569          //
11570          // If both results are "0" i.e. the same,
11571 Add to listbox
11572          if (intCompSubs1!= 0 || intCompSubs2!= 0)
11573 {continue;}
11574          if (intCompSubs1 == 0 && intCompSubs2 ==
11575 0)
11576          {
11577              listBox1.Visible = true;
11578              intItemFound++;
11579              listBox1.Height += 24;
11580              listBox1.Items.Add(myStrRead);
11581              listBox1.Sorted = true;
11582          }//End if
11583      } // End Big If Loop
11584   }//End while
11585 }// End This Month
11586
```

# 11587 Appendix F Hiding listBoxes and
# 11588 clearing textboxes

```
11589
11590 private void btnClearToDoItems_Click(object
11591 sender, EventArgs e)
11592 {
11593    listBox1.Visible = false;
11594 }
11595
11596 private void btnClearWordSearch_Click(object
11597 sender, EventArgs e)
```

```
11598 {
11599    txtBoxWordSearch.Visible = true;
11600    txtBoxWordSearch.Text = "";
11601    listBox2.Visible = false;
11602    btnLoadToDoItems.PerformClick();
11603 }
11604
11605 private void btnHideBlockedDates_Click(object
11606 sender, EventArgs e)
11607 {
11608    listBoxBlocked.Visible = false;
11609    btnHideBlockedDates.Visible = false;
11610 }
11611
```

## 11612 Appendix G ... VB code for ToDO
## 11613 dateTimePicker exercise

```
11614
11615 Imports System
11616 Imports System.Collections.Generic
11617 Imports System.ComponentModel
11618 Imports System.IO
11619 Imports System.Data
11620 Imports System.Drawing
11621 Imports System.Linq
11622 Imports System.Text
11623 Imports System.Windows.Forms
11624 '//
11625 Public Class Form1
11626    Public intLastLoaded As Integer
11627    Public intIdxItemFound As Integer
11628    Public intItemFound As Integer = 0
11629    Public myStringToSave As String = "."
11630    Public myStrDate As String = " "
11631    Public myStrNowYear As String = " "
11632    Public myStrNowMonth As String = " "
11633    Public myStrNowDay As String = " "
11634    Public myStrFinalNow As String = " "
11635    Public myStrFinalPicked As String = " "
11636    Public mySeekDateFinal As String = " "
11637    Public mySeekMo As String = " "
```

```
11638      Public mySeekDay As String = " "
11639      Public mySeekYr As String = " "
11640      Public myStr As String = "."
11641      Public myStrRead As String = "."
11642      Public strToDelete As String = "."
11643      '
11644      Private Sub Form1_Load(sender As System.Object,
11645 e As System.EventArgs) Handles MyBase.Load
11646          intLastLoaded = 0
11647          btnLoadToDo.PerformClick()
11648      End Sub
11649
11650      Private Sub DateTimePicker1_ValueChanged(sender
11651 As System.Object, e As System.EventArgs) Handles
11652 DateTimePicker1.ValueChanged
11653          SetMyCustomFormat()
11654          myStrDate = DateTimePicker1.Text
11655          txtBoxAddInfo.Visible = True
11656          btnSaveInfo.Visible = True
11657      End Sub
11658      Public Sub SetMyCustomFormat()
11659          ' Establish today's date string
11660          myStrNowMonth =
11661 Convert.ToString(DateTime.Now.Month)
11662          myStrNowDay =
11663 Convert.ToString(DateTime.Now.Day)
11664          myStrNowYear =
11665 Convert.ToString(DateTime.Now.Year)
11666          myStrFinalNow = myStrNowMonth + "/" +
11667 myStrNowDay + "/" + myStrNowYear
11668          'Get Date picked value
11669          ' Set the Format type and the CustomFormat
11670 string.
11671          DateTimePicker1.Format =
11672 DateTimePickerFormat.Custom
11673          DateTimePicker1.CustomFormat = "MM/dd/yyyy"
11674      End Sub ' End SetmyCustomFormat
11675
11676      Private Sub btnLoadToDo_Click(sender As
11677 System.Object, e As System.EventArgs) Handles
11678 btnLoadToDo.Click
11679          intLastLoaded = 99
```

```
11680          ListBox1.Height = 24
11681          ListBox2.Visible = False
11682          ''//SetMyCustomFormat()
11683          ListBox1.Items.Clear()
11684          ListBox1.Visible = True
11685          Dim intNumItems As Integer = ListBox1.Items.Count
11686          btnHideToDo.Visible = True
11687          '//
11688          '// Declare and initialize StreamReader
11689          '// Read lines for the file the file, stop
11690 when the end is reached.
11691          myStr = "xx" ' // Note: "xx" in myStr
11692 prevents the code from seeing myStr as
11693          ' // empty (null) at the beginning of the
11694 while loop.
11695          Dim mySR As StreamReader
11696          mySR = New StreamReader("C:\\App Target
11697 Files\\ToDo.txt")
11698          While (myStr <> "")
11699             myStr = mySR.ReadLine()
11700             If (myStr = "") Then
11701                mySR.Close()
11702                mySR.Dispose()
11703                Exit While
11704             End If
11705             If (myStr <> "") Then
11706                ListBox1.Height += 24
11707                ListBox1.Items.Add(myStr)
11708                ListBox1.Sorted = True
11709             End If
11710          End While
11711       End Sub ' End Load ToDo items
11712
11713       Private Sub btnLoadTodayItems_Click(sender As
11714 System.Object, e As System.EventArgs) Handles
11715 btnLoadTodayItems.Click
11716          intLastLoaded = 0
11717          ListBox1.Height = 24
11718          SetMyCustomFormat()
11719          Dim myTestDate As DateTime = DateTime.Now()
11720          mySeekDay = " "
11721          mySeekMo = " "
```

```
11722          mySeekYr = " "
11723          mySeekDateFinal = " "
11724          intIdxItemFound = 0
11725          mySeekDay = Convert.ToString(myTestDate.Day)
11726          mySeekMo = Convert.ToString(myTestDate.Month)
11727          mySeekYr = Convert.ToString(myTestDate.Year)
11728          '//
11729          Dim intLenMo As Integer = mySeekMo.Length
11730          If (intLenMo = 1) Then
11731             mySeekMo = "0" + mySeekMo
11732          End If
11733          Dim intLenDay As Integer = mySeekDay.Length
11734          If (intLenDay = 1) Then
11735             mySeekDay = "0" + mySeekDay
11736          End If
11737          '//
11738          '//
11739          mySeekDateFinal = mySeekMo + "/" + mySeekDay
11740 + "/" + mySeekYr
11741          '//MessageBox.Show(mySeekDateFinal,"Seek
11742 Date Final");
11743          btnHideToDo.Visible = True
11744          ListBox1.Visible = True
11745          '// Test Code
11746 MessageBox.Show(myStrFinalPicked,"Date Picked.");
11747          Dim myStr As String = " " '// Note the
11748 spaces in myStr
11749          '// This prevents the code from seeing myStr as
11750          '// empty (null) at the beginning of the
11751 while loop.
11752          '//
11753          '// Declare a StreamReader
11754          Dim mySr As StreamReader
11755          '// Initialze the StreamReader
11756          Dim intStrIdx As Integer = 0
11757          Dim intStrIdx2 As Integer = 0
11758          intIdxItemFound = 0
11759          '// Read lines for the file the file, stop
11760 when the end is reached.
11761          myStrRead = "xx"
11762          mySr = New StreamReader("C:\\App Target
11763 Files\\ToDo.txt")
```

```
11764          ListBox1.Items.Clear()
11765          intItemFound = 0
11766          While (myStrRead <> "")
11767             myStrRead = "xx"
11768             myStrRead = mySr.ReadLine()
11769             If (myStrRead = "") Then
11770                If (intItemFound >= 1) Then
11771                   Dim myMsgStr As String =
11772 Convert.ToString(intItemFound)
11773                   '//test code
11774 MessageBox.Show("Completed Selected Date search."
11775 + " I found " + myMsgStr + " Items for that
11776 date.", "Selected Day Items");
11777                End If
11778                If (intItemFound = 0) Then
11779                   MessageBox.Show("Completed Selected
11780 Date search." + " I found no Items for that
11781 date.", "Selected Day Items")
11782                End If
11783                mySr.Close()
11784                mySr.Dispose()
11785                Return
11786             End If
11787             ''
11788             intIdxItemFound =
11789 myStrRead.IndexOf(mySeekDateFinal)
11790             '//if (intIdxItemFound == -1) {continue;}
11791             '//
11792             If (myStrRead <> "") Then ' // Big IF lOOP
11793                intIdxItemFound =
11794 myStrRead.IndexOf(mySeekDateFinal)
11795                ListBox1.Visible = True
11796             End If
11797             ''
11798             If (intIdxItemFound >= 0) Then
11799                intItemFound = intItemFound + 1
11800                ListBox1.Height += 24
11801                ListBox1.Items.Add(myStrRead)
11802                ListBox1.Sorted = True
11803             End If
11804             If (intIdxItemFound = -1) Then
11805                Continue While
```

```
11806          End If '// End Big If Loop
11807        End While
11808      End Sub '//End Load TodayToDo items
11809      Private Sub btnHideToDo_Click(sender As
11810  System.Object, e As System.EventArgs) Handles
11811  btnHideToDo.Click
11812        ListBox1.Visible = False
11813      End Sub
11814
11815      Private Sub btnSelDayItems_Click(sender As
11816  System.Object, e As System.EventArgs) Handles
11817  btnSelDayItems.Click
11818        intLastLoaded = 0
11819        ListBox1.Height = 24
11820        ListBox1.Visible = True
11821        SetMyCustomFormat()
11822        ' Get selected date from datePicker
11823        Dim myTestDate As DateTime =
11824  Convert.ToDateTime(DateTimePicker1.Text)
11825        '//test code
11826  MessageBox.Show(Convert.ToString(myTestDate),"date
11827  Picker.Text");
11828        mySeekDay = " "
11829        mySeekMo = " "
11830        mySeekYr = " "
11831        mySeekDateFinal = " "
11832        intIdxItemFound = 0
11833        mySeekDay = Convert.ToString(myTestDate.Day)
11834        mySeekMo =
11835  Convert.ToString(myTestDate.Month)
11836        mySeekYr = Convert.ToString(myTestDate.Year)
11837        '//
11838        Dim intLenMo As Integer = mySeekMo.Length
11839        If (intLenMo = 1) Then
11840           mySeekMo = "0" + mySeekMo
11841        End If
11842        Dim intLenDay As Integer = mySeekDay.Length
11843        If (intLenDay = 1) Then
11844           mySeekDay = "0" + mySeekDay
11845        End If
11846        '//
```

```
11847            mySeekDateFinal = mySeekMo + "/" + mySeekDay
11848 + "/" + mySeekYr
11849          '//MessageBox.Show(mySeekDateFinal,"Seek
11850 Date Final")
11851          btnHideToDo.Visible = True
11852          ListBox1.Visible = True
11853          myStrFinalPicked = DateTimePicker1.Text
11854 ''For display with test code
11855          '// Test Code
11856 MessageBox.Show(myStrFinalPicked,"Date Picked.");
11857          Dim myStr As String = " " ' // Note the
11858 spaces in myStr
11859          '// This prevents the code from seeing myStr as
11860          '// empty (null) at the beginning of the
11861 while loop.
11862          '//
11863          Dim intStrIdx As Integer = 0
11864          Dim intStrIdx2 As Integer = 0
11865          intIdxItemFound = 0
11866          '// Read lines for the file the file, stop
11867 when the end is reached.
11868          myStrRead = "xx"
11869          '// Declare a StreamReader
11870          Dim mySR As StreamReader
11871          '// Initialze the StreamReader
11872          mySR = New StreamReader("C:\\App Target
11873 Files\\ToDo.txt")
11874          ListBox1.Items.Clear()
11875          intItemFound = 0
11876          myStrRead = "xx"
11877          While (myStrRead <> "")
11878             myStrRead = mySR.ReadLine()
11879             ' Exit While on null string from file
11880             If (myStrRead = "") Then
11881                mySR.Close()
11882                mySR.Dispose()
11883                Exit While
11884             End If
11885             ''
11886             'If (intItemFound >= 1) Then
```

```
11887                    'MessageBox.Show("Completed Selected
11888 Date search." + " I found " + myMsgStr + " Items
11889 for that date.", "Selected Day Items")
11890           'End If
11891           ''
11892           '' For populated string from file
11893           If (myStrRead <> "") Then '// Big IF lOOP
11894              ''
11895              intIdxItemFound =
11896 myStrRead.IndexOf(mySeekDateFinal)
11897              ' If sought items not in string from file
11898              If (intIdxItemFound = -1) Then
11899                 Continue While
11900              End If '// End Big If Loop
11901              ''
11902              '' If sought item IS in string from file
11903              If (intIdxItemFound >= 0) Then
11904                 intItemFound += 1
11905                 ListBox1.Height += 24
11906                 ListBox1.Items.Add(myStrRead)
11907                 ListBox1.Sorted = True
11908                 '' look for more matches
11909                 Continue While
11910              End If
11911              ''
11912           End If
11913        End While
11914     End Sub '//End SelectedDate Load event
11915
11916     Private Sub btnThisMonth_Click(sender As
11917 System.Object, e As System.EventArgs) Handles
11918 btnThisMonth.Click
11919        intLastLoaded = 0
11920        ListBox1.Height = 24
11921        SetMyCustomFormat()
11922        Dim myTestDate As DateTime = DateTime.Now
11923        '//test code
11924 MessageBox.Show(Convert.ToString(myTestDate),"date
11925 Picker.Text")
11926        mySeekDay = " "
11927        mySeekMo = " "
11928        mySeekYr = " "
```

```
11929          mySeekDateFinal = " "
11930          intIdxItemFound = 0
11931          mySeekDay = Convert.ToString(myTestDate.Day)
11932          mySeekMo = Convert.ToString(myTestDate.Month)
11933          mySeekYr = Convert.ToString(myTestDate.Year)
11934          ''//
11935          Dim intLenMo As Integer = mySeekMo.Length
11936          If (intLenMo = 1) Then
11937             mySeekMo = "0" + mySeekMo
11938          End If
11939          Dim intLenDay As Integer = mySeekDay.Length
11940          If (intLenDay = 1) Then
11941             mySeekDay = "0" + mySeekDay
11942          End If
11943          '//
11944          '//
11945          btnHideToDo.Visible = True
11946          ListBox1.Visible = True
11947          Dim myStr As String = " " ' // Note the
11948 spaces in myStr
11949          '// This prevents the code from seeing myStr as
11950          '// empty (null) at the beginning of the
11951 while loop.
11952          '//
11953          '// Declare a StreamReader
11954          Dim mySR As StreamReader
11955          '// Initialze the StreamReader
11956          Dim intStrIdx1 As Integer = 0
11957          Dim intStrIdx2 As Integer = 0
11958          intIdxItemFound = 0
11959          '// Read lines for the file the file, stop
11960 when the end is reached.
11961          myStrRead = "xx"
11962          mySR = New StreamReader("C:\\App Target
11963 Files\\ToDo.txt")
11964          ListBox1.Items.Clear()
11965          intItemFound = 0
11966          While (myStrRead <> "")
11967             myStrRead = "xx"
11968             myStrRead = mySR.ReadLine()
11969             '// test for end of file
11970             If (myStrRead = "") Then
```

```
11971                    mySR.Close()
11972                    mySR.Dispose()
11973                    Return
11974                End If
11975                intIdxItemFound =
11976 myStrRead.IndexOf(mySeekDateFinal)
11977                '//
11978                If (myStrRead <> "") Then '// Big IF lOOP
11979                    '// Determine if month and day desired
11980 are in string read from file
11981                    '//
11982                    '// Get day and month from known
11983 positions in the read-from-file string
11984                    Dim SubStrMo As String =
11985 myStrRead.Substring(0, 2)
11986                    Dim SubStrYear As String =
11987 myStrRead.Substring(6, 4)
11988                    '//
11989                    '// Compare substrings with desired
11990 Month and Day strings
11991                    Dim intCompSubs1 As Integer = 99
11992                    Dim intCompSubs2 As Integer = 99
11993                    intCompSubs1 =
11994 String.Compare(mySeekMo, SubStrMo)
11995                    intCompSubs2 =
11996 String.Compare(mySeekYr, SubStrYear)
11997                    '//
11998                    '// If both results are "0" i.e. the
11999 same, Add to listbox
12000                    If (intCompSubs1 <> 0 Or intCompSubs2
12001 <> 0) Then
12002                        Continue While
12003                    End If
12004                    If (intCompSubs1 = 0 And intCompSubs2
12005 = 0) Then
12006                        ListBox1.Visible = True
12007                        intItemFound += 1
12008                        ListBox1.Height += 24
12009                        ListBox1.Items.Add(myStrRead)
12010                        ListBox1.Sorted = True
12011                        Continue While
12012                    End If
```

```
12013                    '// End Big If Loop
12014              End If
12015          End While
12016      End Sub
12017      ''
12018      Private Sub btnNextMonth_Click(sender As
12019  System.Object, e As System.EventArgs) Handles
12020  btnNextMonth.Click
12021          intLastLoaded = 0
12022          ListBox1.Height = 24
12023          SetMyCustomFormat()
12024          Dim myDateNextMo As DateTime
12025          Dim myTestDate As DateTime = DateTime.Now
12026          myDateNextMo = myTestDate.AddMonths(1)
12027          '/test code
12028  MessageBox.Show(Convert.ToString(myTestDate),"date
12029  Picker.Text");
12030          mySeekDay = " "
12031          mySeekMo = " "
12032          mySeekYr = " "
12033          mySeekDateFinal = " "
12034          intIdxItemFound = 0
12035          mySeekDay = Convert.ToString(myTestDate.Day)
12036          mySeekMo = Convert.ToString(myDateNextMo.Month)
12037          '//myTestDate.Month)
12038          mySeekYr = Convert.ToString(myTestDate.Year)
12039          '//
12040          Dim intLenMo As Integer = mySeekMo.Length
12041          If (intLenMo = 1) Then
12042              mySeekMo = "0" + mySeekMo
12043          End If
12044          '// Determine if next month is also next Year
12045          '//
12046          If (mySeekMo = "12") Then
12047              mySeekMo = "01"
12048              myTestDate = DateTime.Now.AddYears(1)
12049              mySeekYr =
12050  Convert.ToString(myTestDate.Year)
12051              '//mySeekYr =
12052  Convert.ToString(DateTime.Now.AddYears(1))
12053              mySeekDay = "01"
12054          End If
```

```
12055          Dim intLenDay As Integer = mySeekDay.Length
12056          If (intLenDay = 1) Then
12057              mySeekDay = "0" + mySeekDay
12058          End If
12059          '//
12060          '//
12061          btnHideToDo.Visible = True
12062          ListBox1.Visible = True
12063          Dim myStr As String = " " ' // Note the
12064 spaces in myStr
12065          '// This prevents the code from seeing myStr as
12066          '// empty (null) at the beginning of the
12067 while loop.
12068          '//
12069          '// Declare a StreamReader
12070          Dim mySr As StreamReader
12071          '// Initialze the StreamReader
12072          Dim intStrIdx1 As Integer = 0
12073          Dim intStrIdx2 As Integer = 0
12074          intIdxItemFound = 0
12075          '// Read lines for the file the file, stop
12076 when the end is reached.
12077          myStrRead = "xx"
12078          mySr = New StreamReader("C:\\App Target
12079 Files\\ToDo.txt")
12080          ListBox1.Items.Clear()
12081          intItemFound = 0
12082          While (myStrRead <> "")
12083              myStrRead = mySr.ReadLine()
12084              '// tst for end of file
12085              If (myStrRead = "") Then
12086                  mySr.Close()
12087                  mySr.Dispose()
12088                  Return
12089                  '//intIdxItemFound =
12090 myStrRead.IndexOf(mySeekDateFinal);
12091                  '//
12092              End If
12093              If (myStrRead <> "") Then '// Big IF lOOP
12094                  '// Determine if month and day desired
12095 are in string read from file
12096                  '//
```

```
12097                '// Get day and month from known
12098 positions in the read-from-file string
12099                Dim SubStrMo As String =
12100 myStrRead.Substring(0, 2)
12101                Dim SubStrYear As String =
12102 myStrRead.Substring(6, 4)
12103                Dim SubYear As Integer =
12104 Convert.ToInt32(SubStrYear)
12105                '//
12106                '// Compare substrings with desired
12107 Month and Day strings
12108                Dim intCompSubs1 As Integer
12109                Dim intCompSubs2 As Integer
12110                intCompSubs1 =
12111 String.Compare(mySeekMo, SubStrMo)
12112                intCompSubs2 =
12113 String.Compare(mySeekYr, SubStrYear)
12114                '//
12115                '// If both results are "0" i.e. the
12116 same, Add to listbox
12117                If (intCompSubs1 = 0 And
12118 intCompSubs2 = 0) Then
12119                    ListBox1.Visible = True
12120                    intItemFound += 1
12121                    ListBox1.Height += 24
12122                    ListBox1.Items.Add(myStrRead)
12123                    ListBox1.Sorted = True
12124                End If
12125                Continue While
12126            End If '// End Big If Loop
12127        End While
12128    End Sub '' End next month
12129    '//
12130    Private Sub bntDeleteItem_Click(sender As
12131 System.Object, e As System.EventArgs) Handles
12132 bntDeleteItem.Click
12133        Dim intToDoIdx As Integer =
12134 ListBox1.SelectedIndex
12135        If (intLastLoaded <> 99 Or intToDoIdx = -1)
12136 Then
```

```
12137            MessageBox.Show("To delete an item, click
12138 Load ToDo Items, the click the item to delete, the
12139 click delete", "Delete Attempt")
12140         Return
12141      End If
12142      intToDoIdx = ListBox1.SelectedIndex
12143      strToDelete =
12144 Convert.ToString(ListBox1.SelectedItem)
12145        '// test code MessageBox.Show(strToDelete +"
12146 is at item " +Convert.ToString(intToDoIdx)," To be
12147 deleted;");
12148      ListBox1.Items.RemoveAt(intToDoIdx)
12149      ListBox1.Height = ListBox1.Height-24
12150      '// Delete the file if it exists.
12151      Dim path1 As String = "C:\\App Target
12152 Files\\ToDo.txt"
12153      If (System.IO.File.Exists(path1)) Then
12154          System.IO.File.Delete(path1)
12155          '//test code MessageBox.Show(path1 + "
12156 was deleted", "TempToDoFile deleted ")
12157      End If
12158      '//
12159      Dim ItemCount As Integer =
12160 ListBox1.Items.Count
12161      '//
12162      Dim Y As Integer = 0
12163      '// Read keeper items from listBox2 and
12164 write to file.
12165      While (Y <= ItemCount-1)
12166          ListBox1.SelectedIndex = Y
12167          myStr =
12168 Convert.ToString(ListBox1.SelectedItem)
12169          '// test code MessageBox.Show(myStr,
12170 "Inside write listBox Items kept to file")
12171          If (myStr <> strToDelete) Then
12172              ListBox2.Height += 24
12173              ListBox2.Items.Add(myStr)
12174              '//myWrtTemp.WriteLine(myStr)
12175              Y += 1
12176          End If
12177          If (myStr = strToDelete) Then
```

```
12178                  '//test code MessageBox.Show("Found
12179  string to delete! ","")
12180              Y += 1
12181          End If
12182       End While
12183       myCopyFile()
12184     End Sub ''// ######### End Delete ##########
12185     ''
12186     Public Sub myCopyFile()
12187        ListBox1.Items.Clear()
12188        Dim intItemListBox2 As Integer =
12189  ListBox2.Items.Count
12190        If (File.Exists("C:\\App Target
12191  Files\\ToDo.txt")) Then
12192           File.Delete("C:\\App Target
12193  Files\\ToDo.txt")
12194        End If
12195        Dim myStrToCopy As String = "xxx"
12196        '//
12197        Dim XX As Integer = 0
12198        Dim mySW As StreamWriter = New
12199  StreamWriter("C:\\App Target Files\\ToDo.txt",
12200  True)
12201        While (XX <= intItemListBox2-1)
12202           ListBox2.SelectedIndex = XX
12203           myStrToCopy =
12204  Convert.ToString(ListBox2.SelectedItem)
12205           If (myStrToCopy = "" Or myStrToCopy = "")
12206  Then
12207              mySW.Close()
12208              mySW.Dispose()
12209              Return
12210           End If
12211           If (myStrToCopy <> "" And myStrToCopy <>
12212  "") Then
12213              ListBox1.Items.Add(myStrToCopy)
12214              mySW.WriteLine(myStrToCopy)
12215           End If
12216           XX += 1
12217           If (XX = intItemListBox2) Then
12218              mySW.Close()
12219              mySW.Dispose()
```

```
12220                    ListBox2.Items.Clear()
12221            End If
12222         End While
12223         '// End Copy File
12224      End Sub
12225      '//
12226      Private Sub btnWordSearch_Click(sender As
12227 System.Object, e As System.EventArgs) Handles
12228 btnWordSearch.Click
12229         intIdxItemFound = 0
12230         btnWordSearch.Visible = True
12231         '//
12232         btnHideToDo.Visible = False
12233         ListBox1.Visible = False
12234         ListBox2.Visible = True
12235         ListBox2.Items.Clear()
12236         ListBox2.Height = 24
12237         '//
12238         intItemFound = 0
12239         intIdxItemFound = 0
12240         intIdxItemFound = ListBox1.Items.Count
12241         '// Read lines for the file the file, stop
12242 when the end is reached.
12243         Dim strWordToFind As String =
12244 txtBoxWordSearch.Text
12245         myStrRead = "XX"
12246         '// Note the spaces in myStrRead
12247         '// This prevents the code from seeing myStr as
12248         '// empty (null) at the beginning of the
12249 while loop.
12250         Dim Z As Integer = ListBox1.Items.Count
12251         Dim A As Integer = 0
12252         While (A <= Z-1)
12253            If (A = Z) Then
12254               Return
12255            End If
12256            ListBox1.SelectedIndex = A
12257            myStrRead =
12258 Convert.ToString(ListBox1.SelectedItem)
12259            Dim intCompareIdx As Integer =
12260 myStrRead.IndexOf(strWordToFind)
12261            If (intCompareIdx = -1) Then
```

```
12262                A += 1
12263                Continue While
12264            End If
12265            '//
12266            If (intCompareIdx >= 0) Then
12267                intItemFound += 1
12268                ListBox1.Visible = False
12269                ListBox2.Visible = True
12270                ListBox2.Height += 24
12271                ListBox2.Items.Add(myStrRead)
12272                ListBox2.Sorted = True
12273                A += 1
12274            End If '// End Big If Loop
12275        End While
12276        If (intItemFound = 0) Then
12277            MessageBox.Show("That word was not
12278 found.", "Word Search Results")
12279        End If
12280        txtBoxWordSearch.Text = ""
12281    End Sub '//End Word search
12282    '//
12283    Private Sub btnSaveInfo_Click(sender As
12284 System.Object, e As System.EventArgs) Handles
12285 btnSaveInfo.Click
12286        SetMyCustomFormat()
12287        '// date selected variables declared
12288        mySeekDay = " "
12289        mySeekMo = " "
12290        mySeekYr = " "
12291        mySeekDateFinal = " "
12292        '//Get the Date from the DatePicker
12293        Dim mySaveDate As DateTime =
12294 Convert.ToDateTime(DateTimePicker1.Text)
12295        intIdxItemFound = 0
12296        '//populate selected date variables
12297        mySeekDay = Convert.ToString(mySaveDate.Day)
12298        mySeekMo = Convert.ToString(mySaveDate.Month)
12299        mySeekYr = Convert.ToString(mySaveDate.Year)
12300        '// prefix "0" to single digit days and
12301 month strings
12302        Dim intLenMo As Integer = mySeekMo.Length
12303        If (intLenMo = 1) Then
```

```
12304              mySeekMo = "0" + mySeekMo
12305          End If
12306          Dim intLenDay As Integer = mySeekDay.Length
12307          If (intLenDay = 1) Then
12308              mySeekDay = "0" + mySeekDay
12309          End If
12310          '//Define the date to save string
12311          Dim myDateToSave As String = mySeekMo + "/"
12312 + mySeekDay + "/" + mySeekYr
12313          '//define the string to save
12314          Dim myStringToSave As String = myDateToSave
12315 + " " + txtBoxAddInfo.Text
12316          '// define the streamReader
12317          Dim mySR As StreamReader = New
12318 StreamReader("C:\\App Target
12319 Files\\BlockedDates.txt")
12320          '// Read list of blocked dates
12321          Dim myStrBlockedDate As String = "XX"
12322 '//avoid an empty string to start with
12323          '//
12324          lstBoxBlocked.Items.Clear()
12325          While (myStrBlockedDate <> "")
12326             If (myStrBlockedDate = "") Then
12327                Exit While
12328             End If
12329             myStrBlockedDate = mySR.ReadLine()
12330             '// End when string read is empty
12331             If (myStrBlockedDate <> "") Then
12332                lstBoxBlocked.Items.Add(myStrBlockedDate)
12333             End If
12334          End While
12335          Dim intBlockedDateCount As Integer =
12336 lstBoxBlocked.Items.Count
12337          '//
12338          Dim intFlagBlocked As Integer = 0
12339          Dim intBlockedLoop As Integer = 0
12340          Dim intBlockedDateFound = 0
12341          For intBlockedLoop = 0 To
12342 intBlockedDateCount-1
12343          lstBoxBlocked.SelectedIndex = intBlockedLoop
12344          myStrBlockedDate =
12345 Convert.ToString(lstBoxBlocked.SelectedItem)
```

```
12346            If (myDateToSave = myStrBlockedDate) Then
12347                intBlockedDateFound += 1
12348            End If
12349            Next
12350            If (intBlockedDateFound = 0) Then
12351                '// if Date selected is not matched to a
12352 blocked date save the item
12353                Dim myWrt As StreamWriter = New
12354 StreamWriter("C:\\App Target Files\\ToDo.txt",
12355 True)
12356                myWrt.WriteLine(myStringToSave)
12357                myWrt.Close()
12358                myWrt.Dispose()
12359            End If
12360            '// release streamwriter & File
12361            If (intBlockedDateFound >= 1) Then
12362                '// cannot save to blocked date, return
12363 to user screen
12364                MessageBox.Show("This is a blocked date.
12365 ", " Blocked Date vs Save")
12366                txtBoxAddInfo.Text = ""
12367                Return
12368            End If
12369            '// re-set add info textbox to empty
12370            txtBoxAddInfo.Text = ""
12371            ListBox1.Sorted = True
12372            ListBox1.Visible = True
12373            ''//re-load ToDo Items file
12374            btnLoadToDo.PerformClick()
12375        End Sub '// End SaveInfo
12376        '//
12377        Private Sub btnShowBlockedDates_Click(sender As
12378 System.Object, e As System.EventArgs) Handles
12379 btnShowBlockedDates.Click
12380            lstBoxBlocked.Visible = True
12381            lstBoxBlocked.Items.Clear()
12382            Dim myRdr As StreamReader = New
12383 StreamReader("C:\\App Target
12384 Files\\BlockedDates.txt")
12385            Dim strBlockedDates As String = "XX"
12386            While (strBlockedDates <> "")
12387                strBlockedDates = myRdr.ReadLine()
```

```
12388                    If (strBlockedDates = "") Then
12389                        myRdr.Close()
12390                        myRdr.Dispose()
12391                        Return
12392                    End If
12393                    If (strBlockedDates <> "") Then
12394                        lstBoxBlocked.Items.Add(strBlockedDates)
12395                        lstBoxBlocked.Sorted = True
12396                        btnHideBlockedDates.Visible = True
12397                    End If
12398                End While
12399        End Sub '// end show blocked dates
12400        '//
12401        Private Sub btnHideBlockedDates_Click(sender As
12402 System.Object, e As System.EventArgs) Handles
12403 btnHideBlockedDates.Click
12404            lstBoxBlocked.Items.Clear()
12405            lstBoxBlocked.Visible = False
12406        End Sub
12407        '//
12408        Private Sub btnSaveAndRepeat_Click(sender As
12409 System.Object, e As System.EventArgs) Handles
12410 btnSaveAndRepeat.Click
12411            Dim myStrToSave As String =
12412 txtBoxAddInfo.Text
12413            Dim intCheckedRepeat As Integer = 1
12414            If (radRepeat3Times.Checked) Then
12415                intCheckedRepeat = 3
12416            End If
12417            '//
12418            If (radRepeat6Times.Checked) Then
12419                intCheckedRepeat = 6
12420            End If
12421            '//
12422            If (radRepeat9Times.Checked) Then
12423                intCheckedRepeat = 9
12424            End If
12425            '//
12426            If (radRepeat12Times.Checked) Then
12427                intCheckedRepeat = 12
12428            End If
12429            '//
```

```
12430          If (radRepeat24Times.Checked) Then
12431              intCheckedRepeat = 24
12432          End If
12433          '//
12434          If (radRepeat36Times.Checked) Then
12435              intCheckedRepeat = 36
12436          End If
12437          '//####
12438          DateTimePicker1.CustomFormat = "MM/dd/yyyy"
12439          Dim myDateToSave As DateTime =
12440 DateTimePicker1.Value
12441          '//test code . . .
12442 MessageBox.Show(Convert.ToString(myBaseDate));
12443          '//
12444          '//############# Save to file
12445          '//'
12446          Dim XX As Integer = 1
12447          '// Start of Repeated Save ToDo Items
12448          For XX = 1 To intCheckedRepeat
12449          Dim mySW As StreamWriter = New
12450 StreamWriter("C:\\App Target Files\\ToDo.txt",
12451 True)
12452          '//test code . . .
12453 MessageBox.Show(Convert.ToString(myBaseDate));
12454          mySeekDay = " "
12455          mySeekMo = " "
12456          mySeekYr = " "
12457          '//Get the Date from the DatePicker
12458          intIdxItemFound = 0
12459          '//populate selected date variables
12460          mySeekDay = Convert.ToString(myDateToSave.Day)
12461          mySeekMo = Convert.ToString(myDateToSave.Month)
12462          mySeekYr = Convert.ToString(myDateToSave.Year)
12463          '// prefix "0" to single digit days and
12464 month strings
12465          Dim intLenMo As Integer = mySeekMo.Length
12466          If (intLenMo = 1) Then
12467              mySeekMo = "0" + mySeekMo
12468          End If
12469          Dim intLenDay As Integer = mySeekDay.Length
12470              If (intLenDay = 1) Then
12471              mySeekDay = "0" + mySeekDay
```

```
12472          End If
12473          '//Define the date to save string
12474          Dim myStringDateToSave As String = mySeekMo
12475 + "/" + mySeekDay + "/" + mySeekYr
12476          '//define the string to save
12477          myStringToSave = myStringDateToSave + " " +
12478 txtBoxAddInfo.Text
12479          mySW.WriteLine(myStringToSave)
12480          mySW.Close()
12481          mySW.Dispose()
12482          myDateToSave = myDateToSave.AddMonths(1)
12483          If (mySeekMo = 12) Then
12484             myDateToSave.AddYears(1)
12485             mySeekMo = 1
12486          End If
12487          Next
12488          '// test code . . .
12489 MessageBox.Show(Convert.ToString(myDateToSave));
12490          '//
12491          '//reset radio buttons
12492          radRepeat3Times.Checked = False
12493          radRepeat6Times.Checked = False
12494          radRepeat9Times.Checked = False
12495          radRepeat12Times.Checked = False
12496          radRepeat24Times.Checked = False
12497          radRepeat36Times.Checked = False
12498          ListBox1.Items.Clear()
12499          btnLoadToDo.PerformClick()
12500          txtBoxAddInfo.Text = ""
12501      End Sub '// End of Repeated Months ToDo Item
12502 Save
12503      '//
12504      Private Sub Button1_Click(sender As
12505 System.Object, e As System.EventArgs) Handles
12506 Button1.Click
12507          ListBox2.Visible = False
12508          ListBox2.Items.Clear()
12509      End Sub
12510
12511      Private Sub
12512 ListBox1_SelectedIndexChanged(sender As
```

```
12513 System.Object, e As System.EventArgs) Handles
12514 ListBox1.SelectedIndexChanged
12515       Dim intListBox1Selection As Integer =
12516 ListBox1.SelectedIndex
12517       ListBox1.SelectedIndex =
12518 intListBox1Selection
12519    End Sub
12520 End Class
12521
```

# 12522 Appendix H . . . VB Forms and
# 12523 properties

12524

## 12525 '// Form1 Code

12526

```
12527 Public Class Form1
12528    Dim myIntToPass As Integer = 11
12529    '//
12530    Private Sub btnShowForm2_Click(sender As
12531 System.Object, e As System.EventArgs) Handles
12532 btnShowForm2.Click
12533       '// Dim myForm As Form2 = New Form2
12534       Me.Hide()
12535       Form2.Show()
12536       '//myForm.Show()
12537    End Sub
12538    '//
12539    Private Sub btnGetForm2Property_Click(sender As
12540 System.Object, e As System.EventArgs) Handles
12541 btnGetForm2Property.Click
12542       Dim myForm As Form2 = New Form2()
12543       Dim intMyNum As Integer
12544       If (TextBox1.Text <> "") Then
12545          intMyNum = Convert.ToInt32(TextBox1.Text)
12546          myForm.intMyNumber = intMyNum
12547       End If
12548       If (TextBox1.Text = "") Then
12549          intMyNum = 1
12550          myForm.intMyNumber = intMyNum
12551       End If
```

```
12552        Dim intMultiplied As Integer
12553        intMultiplied = myForm.intMyNumber()
12554        MessageBox.Show(Convert.ToString(intMultiplied))
12555    End Sub
12556    '//
12557    Private Sub btnExit_Click(sender As
12558 System.Object, e As System.EventArgs) Handles
12559 btnExit.Click
12560        Application.Exit()
12561    End Sub
12562 End Class
12563
```

## 12564 '// Form2 code

```
12565
12566 Public Class Form2
12567    '//
12568    Private intToReturn As Integer
12569    ''----------------------------------
12570    Public Property intMyNumber() As Integer
12571      Get
12572         Return intToReturn * 2
12573      End Get
12574      '//
12575      Set(value As Integer)
12576         intToReturn = value
12577      End Set
12578    End Property
12579    '//-------------------------------
12580    '//
12581    Private Sub btnShowForm1_Click(sender As
12582 System.Object, e As System.EventArgs) Handles
12583 btnShowForm1.Click
12584        Dim myForm As Form1 = New Form1()
12585        Me.Hide()
12586        myForm.Show()
12587    End Sub
12588    '//-------------------------------
12589    Private Sub btnMyProperty_Click(sender As
12590 System.Object, e As System.EventArgs) Handles
12591 btnMyProperty.Click
12592        intMyNumber = 88
```

```
12593        Dim myIntTemp As Integer = intMyNumber
12594        MessageBox.Show(Convert.ToString(myIntTemp))
12595      End Sub
12596      '//------------------------------
12597      Private Sub Button1_Click(sender As
12598 System.Object, e As System.EventArgs) Handles
12599 btnExit.Click
12600        Application.Exit()
12601      End Sub
12602 End Class
12603
```

# 12604 Appendix I VS VB Simple Class Proj

```
12605
12606 '// Note: we are using "Public" here to make info
12607 available
12608 '// elsewhere
12609
12610 Public Class AutomobileClass
12611      '//-----------------------------------
12612      '// #################### HorsePower
12613      Private intHorsePower As Integer
12614      ''----------------------------------
12615      Public Property intEngineHP() As Integer
12616        Get
12617            Return intHorsePower
12618        End Get
12619        '//
12620        Set(value As Integer)
12621            intHorsePower = value
12622        End Set
12623      End Property
12624      '//-----------------------------------
12625      '// #################### Car Class
12626      Private strCarClass As String
12627      ''----------------------------------
12628      Public Property strCarType()
12629        Get
12630            Return strCarClass
12631        End Get
12632        '//
12633        Set(value)
```

```
12634                    strCarClass = value
12635              End Set
12636          End Property
12637          '//---------------------------------
12638          '// #################### Car Class
12639          Private decCarPrice As Decimal
12640          ''---------------------------------
12641          Public Property decCarCost() As Decimal
12642              Get
12643                  Return decCarPrice
12644              End Get
12645              '//
12646              Set(value As Decimal)
12647                  decCarPrice = value
12648              End Set
12649          End Property
12650          '// #################### Car Manufacturer
12651          Private strcCarManufacturer As String
12652          ''---------------------------------
12653          Public Property strCarMaker() As String
12654              Get
12655                  Return strcCarManufacturer
12656              End Get
12657              '//
12658              Set(value As String)
12659                  strcCarManufacturer = value
12660              End Set
12661          End Property
12662          '// #################### Car Model
12663          Private strCarModel As String
12664          ''---------------------------------
12665          Public Property strCarModelDesc() As String
12666              Get
12667                  Return strCarModel
12668              End Get
12669              '//
12670              Set(value As String)
12671                  strCarModel = value
12672              End Set
12673          End Property
12674          '// #################### Car Model
12675          Private strCarYear As String
```

```
12676        ''----------------------------------
12677        Public Property strCarYr() As String
12678           Get
12679              Return strCarYear
12680           End Get
12681           '//
12682           Set(value As String)
12683              strCarYear = value
12684           End Set
12685        End Property
12686        '// #################### Car Model
12687        Private strCarColor As String
12688        ''----------------------------------
12689        Public Property strCarPaint() As String
12690           Get
12691              Return strCarColor
12692           End Get
12693           '//
12694           Set(value As String)
12695              strCarColor = value
12696           End Set
12697        End Property
12698     End Class
12699
12700     '// Note: we are using "Public" here to make info
12701     available
12702     '// elsewhere
12703
12704     Public Class Form1
12705     '//
12706     Dim myName as AutomobileClass
12707     '//myName will be used later to demonstrate
12708     '// that we can make a copy of an instantiated
12709     class
12710     '// by just declaring one variable equal to
12711     another variable.
12712     '//
12713        Public Sub btnSave_Click(sender As
12714     System.Object, e As System.EventArgs) Handles
12715     btnSave.Click
12716     '//
```

```vbnet
12717          '// instantiate a working version of
12718 AutomobileClass
12719          Dim myCls As AutomobileClass = New
12720 AutomobileClass()
12721          '//
12722          Dim strMfg As String = txtBoxMfg.Text
12723          myCls.strCarMaker = strMfg
12724          '//
12725          '// Note: the class is expecting a decimal
12726 value.
12727          '//The textBox contents
12728          '// has to be converted into a decimal value
12729          Dim decCost As Decimal = txtBoxPrice.Text
12730          myCls.decCarCost =
12731 Convert.ToDecimal(txtBoxPrice.Text)
12732          '//
12733          Dim myModel As String = txtBoxModel.Text
12734          myCls.strCarModelDesc = myModel
12735          '//
12736          Dim myModelYear As String =
12737 txtBoxModelYr.Text
12738          myCls.strCarYr = myModelYear
12739          '//
12740          Dim intMyEngine As Integer =
12741 txtBoxEngine.Text
12742          myCls.intEngineHP = intMyEngine
12743          '//
12744          Dim myCarColor As String = txtBoxColor.Text
12745          myCls.strCarPaint = myCarColor
12746          '//
12747          Dim myStyle As String = txtBoxAutoStyle.Text
12748          myCls.strCarType = myStyle
12749          '//
12750          myName = myCls
12751          myCls = Nothing
12752      End Sub
12753      '//
12754      Private Sub btnDisplayProperties_Click(sender
12755 As System.Object, e As System.EventArgs) Handles
12756 btnDisplayProperties.Click
12757          lblDisplayProperties.Text = "Make " +
12758 myName.strCarMaker
```

```
12759          '// VBCrLf inserts a carriage return and
12760 newline character
12761          '// in the label's text
12762          lblDisplayProperties.Text =
12763 lblDisplayProperties.Text + vbCrLf + "Model " +
12764 myName.strCarModelDesc
12765          lblDisplayProperties.Text =
12766 lblDisplayProperties.Text + vbCrLf + "Car Class "
12767 + myName.strCarType
12768          lblDisplayProperties.Text =
12769 lblDisplayProperties.Text + vbCrLf + "Year " +
12770 myName.strCarYr
12771          lblDisplayProperties.Text =
12772 lblDisplayProperties.Text + vbCrLf + "Price " +
12773 "$" + Convert.ToString(myName.decCarCost)
12774          lblDisplayProperties.Text =
12775 lblDisplayProperties.Text + vbCrLf + "Color " +
12776 myName.strCarPaint
12777          lblDisplayProperties.Text =
12778 lblDisplayProperties.Text + vbCrLf + "Horse Power
12779 " + Convert.ToString(myName.intEngineHP)
12780          lblDisplayProperties.Visible = True
12781          '//
12782      End Sub
12783      '//
12784      Private Sub btnClearDisplay_Click(sender As
12785 System.Object, e As System.EventArgs) Handles
12786 btnClearDisplay.Click
12787          lblDisplayProperties.Text = ""
12788          lblDisplayProperties.Visible = False
12789          txtBoxMfg.Text = ""
12790          txtBoxModel.Text = ""
12791          txtBoxAutoStyle.Text = ""
12792          txtBoxEngine.Text = ""
12793          txtBoxPrice.Text = ""
12794          txtBoxColor.Text = ""
12795          txtBoxModelYr.Text = ""
12796      End Sub
12797      '//
12798 End Class
12799
```

# 12800 Appendix J VS CS Simple Class Proj

```
12801
12802 using System;
12803 using System.Collections.Generic;
12804 using System.Linq;
12805 using System.Text;
12806 //
12807 namespace VS_CS_Simple_Class_Proj_Feb_2013
12808 {
12809     class AutomobileClass
12810     {
12811         private decimal Price;//Done . . . a check
12812 to insure all
12813         // properties are defined as I code
12814         private int EngHP;// Done
12815         private string Paint;//Done
12816         private string Mfg;//Done
12817         private string Model;//Done
12818         private string Style;//Done
12819         private string Year;//Done
12820         //
12821         public int EngineHorsePower
12822         {
12823             get// start Get
12824             {
12825                 return EngHP;
12826             } // END GET
12827             // start Set
12828             set
12829             {
12830                 if (value >= 0)EngHP = value;
12831             } // End Set
12832         } // End Property Horse Power
12833         //-------------------------------- #1 . . .
12834         //another check I use..details, details!!
12835         // I number properties using comments.
12836         // Nobody knows but me, and now you know too.
12837         public decimal CarCost
12838         {
12839             get// start Get
12840             {
```

```
12841                    return Price;
12842                 } // END GET
12843                 // start Set
12844                 set
12845                 {
12846                    if (value >= 0) Price = value;
12847                 } // End Set
12848              } // End Property CarCost
12849              //------------------------------------- #2
12850              public string CarMaker
12851              {
12852                 get// start Get
12853                 {
12854                    return Mfg;
12855                 } // END GET
12856                 // start Set
12857                 set
12858                 {
12859                    if (value!="") Mfg = value;
12860                    //
12861                 } // End Set
12862              } // End Property CarMaker
12863              //-------------------------------------
12864              public string CarModel
12865              {
12866                 get// start Get
12867                 {
12868                    return Model;
12869                 } // END GET
12870                 // start Set
12871                 set
12872                 {
12873                    if (value!= "") Model = value;
12874                    // Note the absence of variable type
12875 beside "value"
12876                    // VB allows it, C# does not.
12877                 } // End Set
12878              } // End Property CarModel
12879              //------------------------------------- #3
12880              public string CarType
12881              {
12882                 get// start Get
```

```
12883              {
12884                 return Style;
12885              } // END GET
12886              // start Set
12887              set
12888              {
12889                 if (value!= "") Style = value;
12890              } // End Set
12891           } // End Property CarType
12892           //--------------------------------------- #4
12893           public string CarAge
12894           {
12895              get// start Get
12896              {
12897                 return Year;
12898              } // END GET
12899              // start Set
12900              set
12901              {
12902                 if (value!= "") Year = value;
12903              } // End Set
12904           } // End Property CarAge
12905           //--------------------------------------- #5
12906           /* public decimal CarCost
12907           {
12908              get// start Get
12909              {
12910                 return Price;
12911              } // END GET
12912              // start Set
12913              set
12914              {
12915                 if (value >= 0) Price = value;
12916              } // End Set
12917           } // End Property CarCost
12918           //--------------------------------------- #6
12919           public string CarColor
12920           {
12921              get// start Get
12922              {
12923                 return Paint;
12924              } // END GET
```

```
12925              // start Set
12926              set
12927              {
12928                  if (value!="") Paint = value;
12929              } // End Set
12930          } // End Property CarColor
12931          //------------------------------------- #7
12932          //
12933          // All 7 properties defined!!!
12934          //
12935     }//Class
12936 }// namespace
12937 //
12938 //
12939 Event Handlers for Form1
12940 //
12941
12942 using System;
12943 using System.Collections.Generic;
12944 using System.ComponentModel;
12945 using System.Data;
12946 using System.Drawing;
12947 using System.Linq;
12948 using System.Text;
12949 using System.Windows.Forms;
12950
12951 namespace VS_CS_Simple_Class_Proj_Feb_2013
12952 {
12953     public partial class Form1: Form
12954     {
12955         public Form1()
12956         {
12957             InitializeComponent();
12958         }
12959         AutomobileClass myName = new
12960 AutomobileClass();
12961         //
12962         private void btnSave_Click(object sender,
12963 EventArgs e)
12964         {
12965             string myMfg = "";
12966             myMfg = txtBoxMfg.Text;
```

```
12967              string myModel = "";
12968              myModel = txtBoxModel.Text;
12969              string myStyle = "";
12970              myStyle = txtBoxStyle.Text;
12971              string myYear = "";
12972              myYear = txtBoxYr.Text;
12973              int myEngine = 0;
12974              myEngine =
12975 Convert.ToInt32(txtBoxEngine.Text);
12976              string myColor = "";
12977              myColor = txtBoxColor.Text;
12978              Decimal myPrice =
12979 Convert.ToDecimal(txtBoxPrice.Text);
12980              AutomobileClass myCls=new
12981 AutomobileClass();
12982              myCls.CarMaker=myMfg;
12983              myCls.CarModel=myModel;
12984              myCls.CarType=myStyle;
12985              myCls.CarAge=myYear;
12986              myCls.EngineHorsePower=myEngine;
12987              myCls.CarColor=myColor;
12988              myCls.CarCost = myPrice;
12989              myName = myCls;
12990          }
12991
12992          private void btnDisplay_Click_1(object
12993 sender, EventArgs e)
12994          {
12995              lblDisplay.Text = "Make " +
12996 myName.CarMaker;
12997              lblDisplay.Text = lblDisplay.Text +
12998 "\r\n" + "Model " + myName.CarModel;
12999              lblDisplay.Text = lblDisplay.Text +
13000 "\r\n" + "Car Class " + myName.CarType;
13001              lblDisplay.Text = lblDisplay.Text +
13002 "\r\n" + "Year " + myName.CarAge;
13003              lblDisplay.Text = lblDisplay.Text +
13004 "\r\n" + "Price " + "$" +
13005 Convert.ToString(myName.CarCost);
13006              lblDisplay.Text = lblDisplay.Text +
13007 "\r\n" + "Color " + myName.CarColor;
```

```
13008            lblDisplay.Text = lblDisplay.Text +
13009  "\r\n" + "Horse Power " +
13010  Convert.ToString(myName.EngineHorsePower);
13011          //
13012            lblDisplay.Visible = true;
13013        }
13014
13015      private void btnClear_Click(object sender,
13016  EventArgs e)
13017        {
13018            lblDisplay.Text = "";
13019            lblDisplay.Visible = false;
13020            txtBoxColor.Text = "";
13021            txtBoxEngine.Text = "";
13022            txtBoxMfg.Text = "";
13023            txtBoxMfg.Text = "";
13024            txtBoxModel.Text = "";
13025            txtBoxPrice.Text = "";
13026            txtBoxStyle.Text = "";
13027        }
13028     }
13029  }
13030
```

13031 # Appendix K . . . CS Code for Arrays

13032

13033 ## One Dimension Array

```
13034
13035  using System;
13036  using System.Data;
13037  using System.Collections.Generic;
13038  using System.ComponentModel;
13039  using System.Drawing;
13040  using System.Linq;
13041  using System.Text;
13042  using System.Windows.Forms;
13043
13044  namespace VS_CS_Simple_Array
13045  {
13046      public partial class Form1: Form
13047      {
```

```
13048        public Form1()
13049        {
13050            InitializeComponent();
13051        }
13052
13053        private void btnLoadArray_Click(object
13054 sender, EventArgs e)
13055        {
13056            string[] myArray = {"Arthur", "Bill",
13057 "Charles", "David","Edward"};
13058            listBox1.Items.Add(myArray[0]);
13059            listBox1.Items.Add(myArray[1]);
13060            listBox1.Items.Add(myArray[2]);
13061            listBox1.Items.Add(myArray[3]);
13062            listBox1.Items.Add(myArray[4]);
13063        }
13064    }//Partial class
13065 }//Namespace
13066
```

## 13067 Two Dimension Array

```
13068
13069 using System;
13070 using System.Collections.Generic;
13071 using System.ComponentModel;
13072 using System.Data;
13073 using System.Drawing;
13074 using System.Linq;
13075 using System.Text;
13076 using System.Windows.Forms;
13077
13078 namespace VS_CS_Two_Dimension_Array
13079 {
13080    public partial class Form1: Form
13081    {
13082        public Form1()
13083        {
13084            InitializeComponent();
13085        }
13086        //
13087        private void btnLoadArray_Click(object
13088 sender, EventArgs e)
```

```
13089              {
13090                  string[,] myArray;
13091                  myArray= new string[5,2];
13092                  myArray[0, 0] = "Arthur";
13093                  myArray[0, 1] = "Architect";
13094                  myArray[1, 0] = "Bill";
13095                  myArray[1, 1] = "Banker";
13096                  myArray[2, 0] = "Charles";
13097                  myArray[2, 1] = "Chef";
13098                  myArray[3, 0] = "David";
13099                  myArray[3, 1] = "Doctor";
13100                  myArray[4, 0] = "Edward";
13101                  myArray[4, 1] = "Educator";
13102                  // Display Elements in ListBox
13103                  listBox1.Items.Add(myArray[0, 0]);
13104                  listBox1.Items.Add(myArray[0, 1]);
13105                  listBox1.Items.Add(" ");
13106                  listBox1.Items.Add(myArray[1, 0]);
13107                  listBox1.Items.Add(myArray[1, 1]);
13108                  listBox1.Items.Add(" ");
13109                  listBox1.Items.Add(myArray[2, 0]);
13110                  listBox1.Items.Add(myArray[2, 1]);
13111                  listBox1.Items.Add(" ");
13112                  listBox1.Items.Add(myArray[3, 0]);
13113                  listBox1.Items.Add(myArray[3, 1]);
13114                  listBox1.Items.Add(" ");
13115                  listBox1.Items.Add(myArray[4, 0]);
13116                  listBox1.Items.Add(myArray[4, 1]);
13117              }
13118          }
13119  }
13120
```

# 13121 Appendix L . . . C# Struct

```
13122
13123  // Declaring a C# Struct and "fields" within the
13124  struct
13125  struct Date
13126  {
13127      // C# version of a "property" using "fields"
13128      public Date(int mm, int dd, int ccyy) //
13129  accepting parameters as integers
```

```
13130    {
13131        year = ccyy-1900;
13132        month = mm;
13133        day = dd-1;
13134    }
13135    // Declare provate variables
13136    private int year;
13137    private int month;
13138    private int day;
13139 } //
13140 // "Override" tostring method, returns a string to
13141 the calling statement
13142
13143    public override string ToString()
13144    {
13145        return month + "/" + (day + 1) + "/" + (year
13146 + 1900);
13147    }
13148 }
13149
```

13150  Again, I *caution* against copy and paste from the
13151  textbook. Copy and paste from the example file.
13152

## 13153 Appendix M

```
13154
13155 Imports System
13156 Imports System.Array
13157 Imports System.IO
13158 Public Class Structure_Property_form
13159 Public newStruct As New AutomobileStructSpecs
13160 Public myArryLst As ArrayList
13161 Public myObjIdx As Integer = 0
13162 '// Form Load event
13163    Public Sub Structure_Property_form_Load(sender
13164 As System.Object, e As System.EventArgs) Handles
13165 MyBase.Load
13166        myArryLst = New ArrayList
13167        '//
13168    End Sub
13169    '// BtnExit event
```

```
13170      Private Sub btnExit_Click(sender As
13171  System.Object, e As System.EventArgs) Handles
13172  btnExit.Click
13173          Application.Exit()
13174      End Sub
13175      '// btnShowProperty event
13176      Private Sub btnShowProperty_Click(sender As
13177  System.Object, e As System.EventArgs)
13178          lblOwnership.Text = newStruct.CarOwner
13179          '//lblOwnership.Text = newStruct.CarOwner
13180      End Sub '// End btnDisplay
13181      '//
13182      '// btnSaveToFile
13183      Private Sub btnSaveToFile_Click(sender As
13184  System.Object, e As System.EventArgs) Handles
13185  btnSaveToFile.Click
13186          '//
13187          Dim myMfg As String = ""
13188          myMfg = txtBoxMfg.Text '//                    #1
13189          newStruct.CarMaker = myMfg
13190          '//
13191          Dim myAutoModel As String = ""
13192          myAutoModel = txtBoxModel.Text
13193          newStruct.CarModel = myAutoModel '//        #2
13194          '//
13195          Dim myAutoStyle As String = ""
13196          myAutoStyle = txtBoxStyle.Text
13197          newStruct.CarStyle = myAutoStyle '//        #3
13198          '//
13199          Dim myAutoEngine As String = ""
13200          myAutoEngine = txtBoxEngine.Text() '//      #4
13201          newStruct.CarEngine = myAutoEngine
13202          '//
13203          Dim myAutoColor As String = ""
13204          myAutoColor = txtBoxColor.Text() '//        #5
13205          newStruct.CarColor = myAutoColor
13206          '//
13207          Dim myAutoOwner As String = ""
13208          myAutoOwner = txtBoxOwner.Text() '//        #6
13209          newStruct.CarOwner = txtBoxOwner.Text
13210          '//
13211          Dim myAutoFinancer As String = ""
```

```
13212          myAutoFinancer = txtBoxFinancer.Text() '// #7
13213          newStruct.Financing = myAutoFinancer
13214          '//
13215          Dim myAutoCost As String = ""
13216          myAutoCost = txtBoxCost.Text() '//          #8
13217          newStruct.CarPrice = myAutoCost
13218          '//
13219          '// Create StreanWriter
13220          Dim myWrt As StreamWriter
13221          myWrt = New StreamWriter("C:\\App Target
13222          Files\\AutomobileStructSpecs.txt", True)
13223          '//
13224          '// Write info to file for new record
13225          '//
13226          myWrt.WriteLine(myMfg) '//               #1 Make
13227  sure I don't miss one
13228          myWrt.WriteLine(myAutoModel) '//         #2
13229          myWrt.WriteLine(myAutoStyle) '//         #3
13230          myWrt.WriteLine(myAutoColor) '//         #4
13231          myWrt.WriteLine(myAutoEngine) '//        #5
13232          myWrt.WriteLine(myAutoOwner) '//         #6
13233          myWrt.WriteLine(myAutoFinancer) '//      #7
13234          myWrt.WriteLine(myAutoCost) '//          #8 Last
13235  line to
13236          '// write to file
13237          '//
13238          '// . . . Release resources and file
13239          myWrt.Close()
13240          myWrt.Dispose()
13241          '//
13242      End Sub '// End btnSaveToFile event
13243      '//
13244      Private Sub btnDisplay_Click(sender As
13245  System.Object, e As System.EventArgs) Handles
13246  btnDisplay.Click
13247          Dim myRdr As StreamReader
13248          myRdr = New StreamReader("C:\\App Target
13249  Files \\AutomobileStructSpecs.txt")
13250          '//
13251          '// Read the file in and set the struct
13252  properties
13253          '//
```

```
13254            Dim myStrFromFile As String = " . . ."
13255            Dim intRecordCount As Integer = 0
13256            ''
13257            While myStrFromFile <> "" '// Start file
13258 reading
13259                '//
13260                Dim myCarBuilder As String = "" '//
13261 property #1
13262                myCarBuilder = myRdr.ReadLine() '// I
13263 know CarBuilder is first, that's how we wrote to
13264 the file
13265                '// Check for end of file
13266                If (myCarBuilder = "" Or myCarBuilder =
13267 Nothing) Then
13268                    myRdr.Close()
13269                    myRdr.Dispose()
13270                    Exit Sub
13271                End If
13272                '//
13273                '// Assign string "myCarBuilder" to
13274 newStruct."CarMaker" property of struct
13275                newStruct.CarMaker = myCarBuilder
13276                '//
13277                '//CarBuilder is first Line read from
13278 file for each record
13279                '// We know we read in 8 lines for each
13280 record nd assign each one
13281                '// to the correct Struct property
13282                '//
13283                Dim myAutoMod As String = "" '// property #2
13284                myAutoMod = myRdr.ReadLine()
13285                newStruct.CarModel = myAutoMod
13286                '//
13287                Dim myAutoStyle As String = "" '// property #3
13288                myAutoStyle = myRdr.ReadLine()
13289                newStruct.CarStyle = myAutoStyle
13290                '//
13291                Dim myAutoColor As String = "" '// property #4
13292                myAutoColor = myRdr.ReadLine()
13293                newStruct.CarColor = myAutoColor
13294                '//
13295                Dim myCarHP As String = "" '// property #5
```

```
13296            myCarHP = myRdr.ReadLine()
13297            newStruct.CarEngine = myCarHP
13298            '//
13299            Dim myAutoOwner As String = "" '//property #6
13300            myAutoOwner = myRdr.ReadLine()
13301            newStruct.CarOwner = myAutoOwner
13302            '//
13303            Dim myLoan As String = "" '// property #7
13304            myLoan = myRdr.ReadLine() '
13305            newStruct.Financing = myLoan
13306            '//
13307            Dim myAmt As String = "" '// property #8
13308            myAmt = myRdr.ReadLine()
13309            newStruct.CarPrice = myAmt
13310            '//
13311            '// completed reading in 1 record from file
13312            Dim myListing As String = "" '// Created
13313 right here, not read in.
13314            '// concatenate a string to display in
13315 our listBox from strings we read from file.
13316            myListing = myCarBuilder & " " &
13317 myAutoMod & " " & myAutoOwner
13318            '//
13319            '// increment the Record from file
13320 counter "intRecordCount"
13321            intRecordCount = intRecordCount + 1
13322            '// Add object to ArrayList
13323            myArryLst.Add(newStruct)
13324            '//
13325            ListBox1.Items.Add(myListing)
13326        End While '// End "While" . . . Stop file
13327 reading While loop after all records have been
13328 read.
13329        '// The reading actually stopped a little
13330 earlier whe we tried to read in another string and
13331 got ""
13332        '// as the contents of the string.
13333    End Sub '// end btnDisplay event handler
13334    '// At this point the screen with a populated
13335 listBox becomes visible to the user.
13336    '//
```

```
13337     '// This next occurs when user selects an item
13338  in the listBox.
13339     Private Sub
13340  ListBox1_SelectedIndexChanged(sender As
13341  System.Object, e As System.EventArgs) Handles
13342  ListBox1.SelectedIndexChanged
13343        '// HERE IS THE HEART of our program . . . .
13344  getting the index for the item the user selected
13345        '// from the listBox display. Each time we
13346  read in a record (8 lines from file) we created a
13347  string to display
13348        '// in our listBox -AND- we added an object
13349  (newStruct) to our ArryLst. Since the addition to
13350  the listBox
13351        '//and ArryLst occur at the sametime . . .
13352  they both are assigned the same numerical index.
13353        '//
13354        '// If the user selects Item 2 (or whatever)
13355  in the list box, I know I can use the index of 2
13356  to
13357        '// access the correct object in the
13358  ArrayList. Remember, indexes start with "0" and
13359  add one to "0"
13360        '// for the second item added etc, etc
13361        '//
13362        '// Get the correct object fromthe ArrayList
13363        myObjIdx = ListBox1.SelectedIndex
13364        newStruct = myArryLst.Item(myObjIdx)
13365        '//
13366        '// Use the property content from the Struct
13367  (newStruct) properties
13368        '// to populate the text property of the
13369  textBoxes
13370        txtBoxMfg.Text = newStruct.CarMaker '// # 1
13371        txtBoxModel.Text = newStruct.CarModel '// # 2
13372        txtBoxColor.Text = newStruct.CarColor '// # 3
13373        txtBoxEngine.Text = newStruct.CarEngine '// # 4
13374        txtBoxOwner.Text = newStruct.CarOwner '// # 5
13375        txtBoxFinancer.Text = newStruct.Financing '// # 6
13376        txtBoxCost.Text = newStruct.CarPrice '// # 7
13377        txtBoxStyle.Text = newStruct.CarStyle '// # 8
13378        '//
```

```
13379      End Sub '// End btnDisplay Click event
13380      '//
13381      '// Clear the textBoxes and listBox to add a
13382 bew record.
13383      Private Sub btnClear_Click(sender As
13384 System.Object, e As System.EventArgs) Handles
13385 btnClear.Click
13386          txtBoxColor.Text = ""
13387          txtBoxCost.Text = ""
13388          txtBoxEngine.Text = ""
13389          txtBoxFinancer.Text = ""
13390          txtBoxMfg.Text = ""
13391          txtBoxModel.Text = ""
13392          txtBoxStyle.Text = ""
13393          txtBoxOwner.Text = ""
13394          ListBox1.Items.Clear()
13395      End Sub '// end btnClear click event
13396 End Class '// end of class for this form.
13397
```

13398 # Appendix N VB Code VS VB Structs
13399 # with File IO
13400

13401 ## The Struct definition
13402

```
13403 Public Structure AutomobileStructSpecs
13404 '//
13405    Private Mfg As String '// # 1
13406    Private Model As String '// 2
13407    Private Style As String '// 3
13408    Private EngHP As String '//# 4
13409    Private CarPaint As String '// # 5
13410    Private Banker As String '//# 6
13411    Private Ownership As String '// # 7
13412    Private CarCost As String '//# 8
13413    '//
13414    Public Property CarMaker() As String '//
13415 Property #1 CarMaker
13416        Get
13417            Return Mfg
```

```
13418          End Get
13419          '//
13420          Set(ByVal value As String)
13421             Mfg = value
13422          End Set
13423          '//
13424       End Property '// . . . End Property #1 CarMaker
13425       '//
13426       Public Property CarModel() As String '//
13427  Property #2 CarModel
13428          Get
13429             Return Model
13430          End Get
13431          '//
13432          Set(ByVal value As String)
13433             Model = value
13434          End Set
13435          '//
13436       End Property '// . . . End Property #2 CarModel
13437       '//
13438       Public Property CarStyle() As String '//
13439  Property #3 CarStyle
13440          Get
13441             Return Style
13442          End Get
13443          '//
13444          Set(ByVal value As String)
13445             Style = value
13446          End Set
13447       '//
13448       End Property '// . . .End Property #3 CarStyle
13449       '//
13450       Public Property CarEngine() As String '//
13451  Property #4 CarEngine
13452          Get
13453             Return EngHP
13454          End Get
13455          '//
13456          Set(ByVal value As String)
13457             EngHP = value
13458          End Set
13459          '//
```

```
13460     End Property '// . . . End Property #4 CarEngine
13461     '//
13462     '//
13463     Public Property CarColor() As String '//
13464 Property #5 CarColor
13465         Get
13466             Return CarPaint
13467         End Get
13468         '//
13469         Set(ByVal value As String)
13470             CarPaint = value
13471         End Set
13472         '//
13473     End Property '// . . . End Property #5 CarColor
13474     '//
13475     Public Property CarOwner() As String '//
13476 Property #6 CarOwner
13477         Get
13478             Return Ownership
13479         End Get
13480         '//
13481         Set(ByVal value As String)
13482             Ownership = value
13483         End Set
13484         '//
13485     End Property '// . . . End Property #6 CarOwner
13486     '//
13487     Public Property Financing() As String '// . . .
13488 Property #7 Financing
13489         Get
13490             Return Banker
13491         End Get
13492         Set(ByVal value As String)
13493             Banker = value
13494         End Set
13495     End Property '// . . . Property #7 Financing
13496     Public Property CarPrice() As String '//
13497 Property #8 CarPrice
13498         Get
13499             Return CarCost
13500         End Get
13501         Set(value As String)
```

```
13502              CarCost = value
13503          End Set
13504      End Property '// . . . End Property #8 CarPrice
13505      '//
13506 End Structure
13507
```

# 13508 The form and event handlers

```
13509
13510 Imports System
13511 Imports System.Array
13512 Imports System.IO
13513 Imports System.IO.DirectoryNotFoundException
13514 Public Class Structure_Property_form
13515     Public newStruct As New AutomobileStructSpecs
13516     Public myArryLst As ArrayList
13517     Public myObjIdx As Integer = 0
13518     Public intIdxSelected As Integer
13519     Public intSelectedEditIdx As Integer
13520     '// Form Load event
13521     Public Sub Structure_Property_form_Load(sender
13522 As System.Object, e As System.EventArgs) Handles
13523 MyBase.Load
13524         myArryLst = New ArrayList
13525         '//
13526     End Sub
13527     '// BtnExit event
13528     Private Sub btnExit_Click(sender As
13529 System.Object, e As System.EventArgs) Handles
13530 btnExit.Click
13531         Application.Exit()
13532     End Sub
13533     '// btnShowProperty event
13534     Private Sub btnShowProperty_Click(sender As
13535 System.Object, e As System.EventArgs)
13536         lblOwnership.Text = newStruct.CarOwner
13537         '//lblOwnership.Text = newStruct.CarOwner
13538     End Sub '// End btnDisplay
13539     '//
13540     '// btnSaveToFile
```

```
13541      Private Sub btnSaveToFile_Click(sender As
13542 System.Object, e As System.EventArgs) Handles
13543 btnSaveToFile.Click
13544        '//
13545        Dim myMfg As String = "" '// #1 Mfg
13546        myMfg = txtBoxMfg.Text
13547        newStruct.CarMaker = myMfg
13548        '//
13549        Dim myAutoModel As String = "" '// #2 Model
13550        myAutoModel = txtBoxModel.Text
13551        newStruct.CarModel = myAutoModel
13552        '//
13553        Dim myAutoStyle As String = "" '// #3 Style
13554        myAutoStyle = txtBoxStyle.Text
13555        newStruct.CarStyle = myAutoStyle
13556        '//
13557        Dim myAutoEngine As String = "" '// #4 Engine
13558        myAutoEngine = txtBoxEngine.Text()
13559        newStruct.CarEngine = myAutoEngine
13560        '//
13561        Dim myAutoColor As String = "" '// #5 Color
13562        myAutoColor = txtBoxColor.Text()
13563        newStruct.CarColor = myAutoColor
13564        '//
13565        Dim myAutoOwner As String = "" '// #6 Owner
13566        myAutoOwner = txtBoxOwner.Text()
13567        newStruct.CarOwner = txtBoxOwner.Text
13568        '//
13569        Dim myAutoFinancer As String = "" '//#7 Financer
13570        myAutoFinancer = txtBoxFinancer.Text()
13571        newStruct.Financing = myAutoFinancer
13572        '//
13573        Dim myAutoCost As String = ""
13574        myAutoCost = txtBoxCost.Text() '// #8 Cost
13575        newStruct.CarPrice = myAutoCost
13576        '//
13577        '// Create StreamWriter
13578        Dim myWrt As StreamWriter
13579        myWrt = New StreamWriter("C:\\App Target
13580 Files\\AutomobileStructSpecs.txt", True)
13581        '//
13582        '// Write info to file for new record
```

```
13583        '//
13584        myWrt.WriteLine(myMfg) '//          #1 mfg
13585        myWrt.WriteLine(myAutoModel) '//    #2 model
13586        myWrt.WriteLine(myAutoStyle) '//    #3 Style
13587        myWrt.WriteLine(myAutoEngine) '// #4 Engine
13588        myWrt.WriteLine(myAutoColor) '//    #5 Color
13589        myWrt.WriteLine(myAutoOwner) '//    #6 Owner
13590        myWrt.WriteLine(myAutoFinancer) '// #7 Financer
13591        myWrt.WriteLine(myAutoCost) '//     #8 Cost
13592        '//
13593        '// ------------- Release resources and file
13594        myWrt.Close()
13595        myWrt.Dispose()
13596        '//
13597     End Sub '// ----------- End btnSaveToFile event
13598        '//
13599     Private Sub btnDisplay_Click(sender As
13600 System.Object, e As System.EventArgs) Handles
13601 btnDisplay.Click
13602        ListBox1.Items.Clear()
13603        myArryLst.Clear()
13604        Dim myRdr As StreamReader
13605        myRdr = New StreamReader("C:\\App Target
13606 Files \\AutomobileStructSpecs.txt")
13607        '//
13608        '// Read the file in and set the struct
13609 properties
13610        '//
13611        Dim myStrFromFile As String = " . . ."
13612        Dim intRecordCount As Integer = 0
13613        ''
13614        While myStrFromFile <> "" '// Start file
13615 reading
13616           '//
13617           '// Assign strings i.e. "myCarBuilder" to
13618 newStruct."CarMaker" property of struct
13619           '// I know CarBuilder is first becuase
13620 that's how we wrote info to the file
13621           '// So, we read and assign each string to
13622 the correct Struct property
13623           '//
```

```
13624              Dim myCarBuilder As String = "" '//
13625  property #1
13626              myCarBuilder = myRdr.ReadLine()
13627              '// Check for end of file
13628              If (myCarBuilder = "" Or myCarBuilder =
13629  Nothing) Then
13630                  myRdr.Close()
13631                  myRdr.Dispose()
13632                  Exit While
13633                  ElseIf (myCarBuilder <> "" And
13634  myCarBuilder <> Nothing) Then '// ElseIF gives the
13635  code an alternative action to execute
13636                  newStruct.CarMaker = myCarBuilder
13637              End If
13638              '//
13639              Dim myAutoMod As String = "" '// property #2
13640              myAutoMod = myRdr.ReadLine()
13641              newStruct.CarModel = myAutoMod
13642              '//
13643              Dim myAutoStyle As String = "" '// property #3
13644              myAutoStyle = myRdr.ReadLine()
13645              newStruct.CarStyle = myAutoStyle
13646              '//
13647              Dim myAutoColor As String = "" '// property #4
13648              myAutoColor = myRdr.ReadLine()
13649              newStruct.CarColor = myAutoColor
13650              '//
13651              Dim myCarHP As String = "" '// property #5
13652              myCarHP = myRdr.ReadLine()
13653              newStruct.CarEngine = myCarHP
13654              '//
13655              Dim myAutoOwner As String = "" '//property #6
13656              myAutoOwner = myRdr.ReadLine()
13657              newStruct.CarOwner = myAutoOwner
13658              '//
13659              Dim myLoan As String = "" '// property #7
13660              myLoan = myRdr.ReadLine() '
13661              newStruct.Financing = myLoan
13662              '//
13663              Dim myAmt As String = "" '// property #8
13664              myAmt = myRdr.ReadLine()
13665              newStruct.CarPrice = myAmt
```

```
13666          '//
13667          '// To this point, we completed reading
13668 in 1 record from file
13669          '// Create a listing string to show in
13670 the list box.
13671          '// A concatenated a string to display in
13672 our listBox from strings we read from file.
13673          Dim myListing As String = myCarBuilder &
13674 " " & myAutoMod & " " & myAutoStyle & " " &
13675 myAutoOwner
13676          '// increment the Record from file
13677 counter "intRecordCount"
13678          intRecordCount = intRecordCount + 1
13679          '// Add object to ArrayList
13680          myArryLst.Add(newStruct)
13681          '// Show the listing in the listBox
13682          ListBox1.Items.Add(myListing)
13683      End While '// End "While" . . . Stop file
13684 reading While loop after all records have been
13685 read.
13686      '// The reading actually stopped a little
13687 earlier when we tried to read in another string
13688 and got "" (empty)
13689      '// or "nothing" as the contents of the
13690 string.
13691      myRdr.Close()
13692      myRdr.Dispose()
13693      '// At this point the screen with a
13694 populated listBox becomes visible to the user.
13695   End Sub '// end btnDisplay event handler
13696   '//
13697   Private Sub ListBox1_SelectedIndexChanged
13698 (sender As System.Object, e As System.EventArgs)
13699 Handles ListBox1.SelectedIndexChanged
13700      '// This event occurs when user selects
13701 (Clicks on) an item in the listBox.
13702      '// Note: We are NOT readubg from a file
13703 here, we are using properties of our selected
13704 Object
13705      '// form the ArrayList.
13706      '//
```

```
13707         '// HERE IS THE HEART BEAT of our
13708  program . . . . getting the index for the item the
13709  user selected
13710         '// from the listBox display. Each time we
13711  read in a record (8 lines from file) we created a
13712  string to display
13713         '// in our listBox -AND- we added an object
13714  (newStruct) to our ArryLst. Since the addition to
13715  the listBox
13716         '//and ArryLst occur at the sametime . . .
13717  they both are assigned the same numerical index.
13718         '//
13719         '// If the user selects Item 2 (or whatever)
13720  in the list box, I know I can use the index of 2
13721  (or whatever) to
13722         '// access the correct object in the
13723  ArrayList. Remember, indexes start with "0" and
13724  add one to "0"
13725         '// for the second item added etc, etc
13726         '//
13727         '// Get the correct object fromthe ArrayList
13728         Dim myObjCount As Integer = myArryLst.Count
13729         myObjIdx = ListBox1.SelectedIndex
13730         If (myObjIdx = -1 Or myObjIdx > myObjCount-1)
13731  Then
13732             Return '// means exit this event handler
13733  block of code
13734         End If
13735         '// Set the newStruct object to our selected
13736  ArrayList object
13737         newStruct = myArryLst.Item(myObjIdx)
13738         '//
13739         '// Use the property content from the Struct
13740  (newStruct) properties
13741         '// to populate the text property of the
13742  textBoxes
13743         txtBoxMfg.Text = newStruct.CarMaker '// # 1
13744         txtBoxModel.Text = newStruct.CarModel '// # 2
13745         txtBoxStyle.Text = newStruct.CarStyle '// # 3
13746         txtBoxEngine.Text = newStruct.CarEngine '// # 4
13747         txtBoxColor.Text = newStruct.CarColor '// # 5
13748         txtBoxOwner.Text = newStruct.CarOwner '// # 6
```

```
13749        txtBoxFinancer.Text = newStruct.Financing '// # 7
13750        txtBoxCost.Text = newStruct.CarPrice '// # 8
13751        '//
13752     End Sub '// End btnDisplay Click event
13753     '//
13754     '// Clear the "textBoxes" and "listBox" to add
13755 a new record to file.
13756     Private Sub btnClear_Click(sender As
13757 System.Object, e As System.EventArgs) Handles
13758 btnClear.Click
13759        txtBoxMfg.Text = ""
13760        txtBoxModel.Text = ""
13761        txtBoxStyle.Text = ""
13762        txtBoxEngine.Text = ""
13763        txtBoxColor.Text = ""
13764        txtBoxCost.Text = ""
13765        txtBoxFinancer.Text = ""
13766        txtBoxOwner.Text = ""
13767        ListBox1.Items.Clear()
13768     End Sub '// end btnClear click event
13769     '// Delete a "selected" record
13770     Private Sub btnDeleteSelectedRecord_Click
13771 (sender As System.Object, e As System.EventArgs)
13772 Handles btnDeleteSelectedRecord.Click
13773        intIdxSelected = ListBox1.SelectedIndex
13774        If (intIdxSelected = -1) Then
13775           MessageBox.Show("No record selected to
13776 delete. Click a record and then '' Delete ''",
13777 "Delete attempt failed")
13778           Return '// exits this event handler
13779        End If
13780        '//
13781        '// Now to purge the file of the old
13782 record . . .
13783        '//
13784        '// We are going to read Delete the Selected
13785 Item from the listBox1 and remove that object from
13786 the ArrayList.
13787        '//
13788        '// Next, we are going to delete to the OLD
13789 AutomobileStructSpecs.txt file.
13790        '//
```

```
13791          '// Finally, we will retrieve the properties
13792 of the remaining Objects in the Array list and
13793          '// Write them to a "New"
13794 AutomobileSructSpecs.txt file.
13795          '//
13796          '// THIS is where knowing-the-order of items
13797 being read from or written to file is crucial!!!
13798          '// It is another instance and example of
13799 the "IMPORTANCE" of "INDEX" numbers.
13800          '//
13801          '// First we know the index of the item
13802 selected, it needs to be "RemovedAt" that index
13803          '// in both the listBox1 and the ArrayList.
13804          '//
13805          ListBox1.SelectedIndex = intIdxSelected '//
13806 Assures that we have the right item selected.
13807          Dim strMyStrMfg As String =
13808 ListBox1.SelectedItem
13809          '*// Using MessageBox to get User input
13810 Example . . .
13811          '*// Specify the buttons to be shown in the
13812 MessageBox . . . verify "Delete" or "Cancel"
13813 Delete
13814          If MessageBox.Show(strMyStrMfg & " is
13815 located at index " & Convert.ToString
13816 (intIdxSelected) & "." & " Click OK to remove this
13817 item. Click Cancel to keep this item ", _
13818          " 'DELETE' verification ",
13819 MessageBoxButtons.OKCancel, _
13820          MessageBoxIcon.Information,
13821 MessageBoxDefaultButton.Button1) _
13822          = Windows.Forms.DialogResult.OK Then
13823          '// IF . . . the user clicked "OK"
13824 proceed to delete the record.
13825          '// Proceed by clearing the txtBoxes and
13826 removing the item from the ArrayList
13827          ListBox1.Items.RemoveAt(intIdxSelected)
13828          myArryLst.RemoveAt(intIdxSelected)
13829          '//
13830          txtBoxMfg.Text = "" '//          #1
13831          txtBoxModel.Text = "" '//        #2
13832          txtBoxStyle.Text = "" '//        #3
```

```
13833              txtBoxEngine.Text = "" '//     #4
13834              txtBoxColor.Text = "" '//      #5
13835              txtBoxFinancer.Text = "" '//   #6
13836              txtBoxOwner.Text = "" '//      #7
13837              txtBoxCost.Text = "" '//       #8
13838              ReCreateFile()
13839              Else
13840              Exit Sub '// IF . . . the user clicked
13841 "Cancel" abort the Delete operation!!!!
13842         End If '// End If
13843     End Sub '// End btnDeleteSelectedRecord Click
13844     '//
13845     Private Sub ListBox1_DoubleClick(sender As
13846 System.Object, e As System.EventArgs) Handles
13847 ListBox1.DoubleClick
13848         Return
13849     End Sub
13850     '//
13851     Public Sub ReCreateFile()
13852         '//Remember this sub was called from the
13853 btnDeleteSelectedRecord_Click event
13854         '// A this point the targeted items has been
13855 removed frm the ArrayList and the listBox1
13856         '// All that remains are recors we want to
13857 retain . . .
13858         Dim myFileTest As Boolean = False '//
13859 Boolean is a "Logocal variable", True means
13860 Condition tested for existed.
13861         '// CK file, delete old file if it exists
13862         myFileTest = My.Computer.FileSystem.FileExists
13863 ("C:\\App Target Files\\AutomobileStructSpecs.txt")
13864         '// ("C:\\ App Target
13865 Files\\AutomobileStructSpecs.txt")
13866         '// This is a good way to compare two
13867 strings . . . ..
13868         '//place one below the other in a comment
13869         '//
13870         '// CK file, delete old file if it exists
13871         If (myFileTest = True) Then
13872             My.Computer.FileSystem.DeleteFile ("C:\\App
13873 Target Files\\AutomobileStructSpecs.txt")
13874         End If
```

```
13875          '// Create info we need to re-write the
13876 AutomobileStructSpecs.txt file.
13877          Dim ArrayListItemCount As Integer =
13878 myArryLst.Count−1
13879          '// ArrayListItemCountItemCount says how
13880 many objects in the ArrayList (0 to whatever) the
13881 count was -1
13882          '// to get properties from and write them to
13883 file
13884          Dim myObj As Object
13885          Dim XX As Integer = 0
13886          For Each myObj In myArryLst
13887          '//
13888          newStruct = myArryLst.Item(XX)
13889          '//
13890          Dim myStrDEl1 As String = newStruct.CarMaker
13891 '// # 1
13892          Dim myStrDEl2 As String = newStruct.CarModel
13893 '// # 2
13894          Dim myStrDEl3 As String = newStruct.CarStyle
13895 '// #3
13896          Dim myStrDEl4 As String = newStruct.CarEngine
13897 '// #4
13898          Dim myStrDEl5 As String = newStruct.CarColor
13899 '// #5
13900          Dim myStrDEl6 As String = newStruct.CarOwner
13901 '// # 6
13902          Dim myStrDEl7 As String = newStruct.Financing
13903 '// #7
13904          Dim myStrDEl8 As String = newStruct.CarPrice
13905 '// #8
13906          '// re-create (Write) the file
13907 "AutomobileStructSpecs.txt"
13908          Dim myWrt As StreamWriter = New
13909 StreamWriter("C:\\App Target
13910 Files\\AutomobileStructSpecs.txt", True)
13911          '// Remember "true" here means create a file
13912 if it doesn't exist, append it if it does.
13913          myWrt.WriteLine(myStrDEl1) '// #1
13914          myWrt.WriteLine(myStrDEl2) '// #2
13915          myWrt.WriteLine(myStrDEl3) '// #3
13916          myWrt.WriteLine(myStrDEl4) '// #4
```

```
13917        myWrt.WriteLine(myStrDEl5) '// #5
13918        myWrt.WriteLine(myStrDEl6) '// #6
13919        myWrt.WriteLine(myStrDEl7) '// #7
13920        myWrt.WriteLine(myStrDEl8) '// #8
13921        '// One record written to file.
13922        '// Release the system resources and the file
13923        myWrt.Close()
13924        myWrt.Dispose()
13925        '// Increment our object index number,
13926 "Foreach" doesn't do this for us automatically.
13927        XX = XX + 1
13928        Next '// End point of 1st Foreach
13929 "object" . . . . Go on to next Struct object in
13930 ArrayList.
13931    End Sub '// End Sub Re-createFile
13932    '//
13933    Public Sub btnEdit_Click(sender As
13934 System.Object, e As System.EventArgs) Handles
13935 btnEdit.Click
13936        intSelectedEditIdx = ListBox1.SelectedIndex
13937        If (intSelectedEditIdx = -1) Then
13938 MessageBox.Show("You must first select a listing
13939 to EDIT", "NO ITEM SELECTED!! ")
13940        '// Re-set backcolors of controls
13941        lblMfg.BackColor = Color.Cyan
13942        txtBoxMfg.BackColor = Color.Cyan '//      #1
13943        lblModel.BackColor = Color.Cyan
13944        txtBoxModel.BackColor = Color.Cyan '//     #2
13945        lblStyle.BackColor = Color.Cyan
13946        txtBoxStyle.BackColor = Color.Cyan '//     #3
13947        lblEngine.BackColor = Color.Cyan
13948        txtBoxEngine.BackColor = Color.Cyan '//    #4
13949        lblEngine.BackColor = Color.Cyan
13950        txtBoxColor.BackColor = Color.Cyan '//     #5
13951        lblColor.BackColor = Color.Cyan
13952        txtBoxFinancer.BackColor = Color.Cyan '// #6
13953        lblFinancier.BackColor = Color.Cyan
13954        txtBoxOwner.BackColor = Color.Cyan '//     #7
13955        lblOwnership.BackColor = Color.Cyan
13956        txtBoxCost.BackColor = Color.Cyan '//      #8
13957        lblCost.BackColor = Color.Cyan
13958        '//
```

```
13959        ListBox1.BackColor = Color.Cyan
13960        btnSaveEdits.Visible = True
13961        MessageBox.Show("To makes CHANGES—RE-TYPE
13962 the information in the desired TEXTBOX(s) then
13963 CLICK—SAVE EDITS ", "Edit Instruction")
13964        '//
13965        newStruct =
13966 myArryLst.Item(intSelectedEditIdx)
13967        '//
13968        Dim strEditMfg As String =
13969 newStruct.CarMaker '// #1
13970        txtBoxMfg.Text = strEditMfg
13971        txtBoxMfg.ForeColor = Color.Red
13972        Dim strEditMod As String =
13973 newStruct.CarModel '// #2
13974        txtBoxModel.Text = strEditMod
13975        txtBoxModel.ForeColor = Color.Red
13976        Dim strEditStyle As String =
13977 newStruct.CarStyle '// #3
13978        txtBoxStyle.Text = strEditStyle
13979        txtBoxStyle.ForeColor = Color.Red
13980        Dim strEditEng As String =
13981 newStruct.CarEngine '// #4
13982        txtBoxEngine.Text = strEditEng
13983        txtBoxEngine.ForeColor = Color.Red
13984        Dim strEditColor As String =
13985 newStruct.CarColor '// #5
13986        txtBoxColor.Text = strEditColor
13987        txtBoxColor.ForeColor = Color.Red
13988        Dim strEditBanker As String =
13989 newStruct.Financing '// #6
13990        txtBoxFinancer.Text = strEditBanker
13991        txtBoxFinancer.ForeColor = Color.Red
13992        Dim strEditOwner As String =
13993 newStruct.CarOwner '// #7
13994        txtBoxOwner.Text = strEditOwner
13995        txtBoxOwner.ForeColor = Color.Red
13996        Dim strEditCost As String =
13997 newStruct.CarPrice '// #8
13998        txtBoxCost.Text = strEditCost
13999        txtBoxCost.ForeColor = Color.Red
14000        '//
```

```
14001    End Sub '// End btnEdit_Click
14002    '//
14003    Public Sub btnSaveEdits_Click(sender As
14004 System.Object, e As System.EventArgs) Handles
14005 btnSaveEdits.Click
14006        Dim strChangedMfg = txtBoxMfg.Text '// #1
14007        txtBoxMfg.ForeColor = Color.MistyRose
14008        '//
14009        Dim strChangedMod As String =
14010 txtBoxModel.Text '// #2
14011        txtBoxModel.ForeColor = Color.MistyRose
14012        '//
14013        Dim strChangedStyle As String =
14014 txtBoxStyle.Text '// #3
14015        txtBoxStyle.ForeColor = Color.MistyRose
14016        '//
14017        Dim strChangedEng As String =
14018 txtBoxEngine.Text '// #4
14019        txtBoxEngine.ForeColor = Color.MistyRose
14020        '//
14021        Dim strChangedColor As String =
14022 txtBoxColor.Text '// #5
14023        txtBoxColor.ForeColor = Color.MistyRose
14024        '//
14025        Dim strChangedBanker As String =
14026 txtBoxFinancer.Text '// #6
14027        txtBoxFinancer.ForeColor = Color.MistyRose
14028        '//
14029        Dim strChangedOwner As String =
14030 txtBoxOwner.Text '// #7
14031        txtBoxOwner.ForeColor = Color.MistyRose
14032        '//
14033        Dim strChangedCost As String =
14034 txtBoxCost.Text '// #8
14035        txtBoxCost.ForeColor = Color.MistyRose
14036        '//
14037        '// Delete old Object from ArrayList and
14038 listing in ListBox1
14039        myArryLst.RemoveAt(intSelectedEditIdx)
14040        ListBox1.Items.RemoveAt(intSelectedEditIdx)
14041        '//
14042        '// Re-Assign values to newStruct
```

```
14043        '//
14044        Dim myMfg As String = "" '// #1 Mfg
14045        myMfg = txtBoxMfg.Text
14046        newStruct.CarMaker = myMfg
14047        '//
14048        Dim myAutoModel As String = "" '// #2 Model
14049        myAutoModel = txtBoxModel.Text
14050        newStruct.CarModel = myAutoModel
14051        '//
14052        Dim myAutoStyle As String = "" '// #3 Style
14053        myAutoStyle = txtBoxStyle.Text
14054        newStruct.CarStyle = myAutoStyle
14055        '//
14056        Dim myAutoEngine As String = "" '// #4 Engine
14057        myAutoEngine = txtBoxEngine.Text()
14058        newStruct.CarEngine = myAutoEngine
14059        '//
14060        Dim myAutoColor As String = "" '// #5 Color
14061        myAutoColor = txtBoxColor.Text()
14062        newStruct.CarColor = myAutoColor
14063        '//
14064        Dim myAutoOwner As String = "" '// #6 Owner
14065        myAutoOwner = txtBoxOwner.Text()
14066        newStruct.CarOwner = txtBoxOwner.Text
14067        '//
14068        Dim myAutoFinancer As String = "" '//#7 Financer
14069        myAutoFinancer = txtBoxFinancer.Text()
14070        newStruct.Financing = myAutoFinancer
14071        '//
14072        Dim myAutoCost As String = ""
14073        myAutoCost = txtBoxCost.Text() '// #8 Cost
14074        newStruct.CarPrice = myAutoCost
14075        '// Add newStruct to myArryLst . . . with
14076 edited information
14077        myArryLst.Add(newStruct)
14078        '// Call Sub CreateEditedFile to erase old
14079 info and save the new info
14080        CreateEditedFile()
14081    End Sub '// End Save Edits
14082    '//
14083    Public Sub CreateEditedFile()
```

```
14084        '//Remember this sub was called from the
14085 btnSaveEdits_Click event
14086        '// At this point the targeted item has been
14087 removed from the ArrayList and listBox1
14088        '//
14089        '// A new object has been added to myArryLst
14090 containing updated info
14091        '// All that remain are records we want to
14092 keep . . .
14093        '// This code writes those items to file.
14094        '//
14095        '// CK file, delete old file if it exists
14096        Dim myFileTest As Boolean = False '//
14097 Boolean is a "Logocal variable", True means
14098 Condition tested for existed.
14099        myFileTest = My.Computer.FileSystem.FileExists
14100 ("C:\\App Target Files\\AutomobileStructSpecs.txt")
14101        '// ("C:\\ App Target
14102 Files\\AutomobileStructSpecs.txt")
14103        '// This is a good way to compare two
14104 strings when coding errors are hard to find in
14105 long strings . . . ..
14106        '// place one below the other in a comment.
14107 BUT,at Times, there are "invisible" errors in
14108 strings.
14109        '// When typing, you might hit a "control"
14110 character, that you cannot see displayed.
14111        '// If a code block fails and you see no
14112 error in the strings, delete the string and copy
14113        '// it from a place where it does function
14114 correctly -or- as a last resort, re-type the
14115        '// entire string "including" surrounding
14116 parenthese and quotation marks.
14117        '//
14118        '// BELIEVE ME IT HAPPENS!!!
14119        '//
14120        '// CK file, delete old file if it exists
14121        If (myFileTest = True) Then
14122            My.Computer.FileSystem.DeleteFile ("C:\\App
14123 Target Files\\AutomobileStructSpecs.txt")
14124        End If
```

```
14125         '// Create info we need to re-write the
14126 AutomobileStructSpecs.txt file.
14127         Dim ArrayListItemCount As Integer =
14128 myArryLst.Count—1
14129         '// ArrayListItemCountItemCount says how
14130 many objects in the ArrayList (0 to whatever) the
14131 count was -1
14132         '// to get properties from and write them to
14133 file
14134         '//
14135         '// Remember, The old object was deleted,
14136 the new info object added to the myArryLst
14137         Dim myObj As Object
14138         Dim XX As Integer = 0
14139         '// . . .For Each Loop
14140         For Each myObj In myArryLst
14141         '//
14142         newStruct = myArryLst.Item(XX)
14143         '//
14144         Dim myStrEdited1 As String =
14145 newStruct.CarMaker '// # 1
14146         Dim myStrEdited2 As String =
14147 newStruct.CarModel '// # 2
14148         Dim myStrEdited3 As String =
14149 newStruct.CarStyle '// #3
14150         Dim myStrEdited4 As String =
14151 newStruct.CarEngine '// #4
14152         Dim myStrEdited5 As String =
14153 newStruct.CarColor '// #5
14154         Dim myStrEdited6 As String =
14155 newStruct.CarOwner '// # 6
14156         Dim myStrEdited7 As String =
14157 newStruct.Financing '// #7
14158         Dim myStrEdited8 As String =
14159 newStruct.CarPrice '// #8
14160         '// re-create (Write) the file
14161 "AutomobileStructSpecs.txt"
14162         Dim myWrt As StreamWriter = New
14163 StreamWriter("C:\\App Target
14164 Files\\AutomobileStructSpecs.txt", True)
14165         '// Remember "true" here means create a file
14166 if it doesn't exist, append it if it does.
```

```
14167        myWrt.WriteLine(myStrEdited1) '// #1
14168        myWrt.WriteLine(myStrEdited2) '// #2
14169        myWrt.WriteLine(myStrEdited3) '// #3
14170        myWrt.WriteLine(myStrEdited4) '// #4
14171        myWrt.WriteLine(myStrEdited5) '// #5
14172        myWrt.WriteLine(myStrEdited6) '// #6
14173        myWrt.WriteLine(myStrEdited7) '// #7
14174        myWrt.WriteLine(myStrEdited8) '// #8
14175        '// One record written to file.
14176        '// Release the system resources and the file
14177        myWrt.Close()
14178        myWrt.Dispose()
14179        '// Increment our object index number,
14180  "Foreach" doesn't do this for us automatically.
14181        XX = XX + 1
14182        Next '// End point of 1st Foreach
14183  "object" . . . . Go on to next Struct object in
14184  ArrayList.
14185      End Sub
14186      '//
14187  End Class '// end of class for this form.
14188
```

## 14189 Appendix O

```
14190
14191  using System;
14192  using System.Collections.Generic;
14193  using System.Linq;
14194  using System.Text;
14195
14196  namespace VS_CS_Struct_with_File_IO
14197  {// ----------------------------Start Namespace
14198  // Example how to call from within form code block
14199  // clsmyCls myObj1 = new clsmyCls();
14200  //
14201  // -------------- Start class AutomobileStructSpec
14202  class AutomobileStructSpecs
14203      {
14204          class myClsAutoInfo
14205          {
14206              private String CarMfg = "";
14207              public String myCarMfg
```

```
14208                // --- start property CarMfg --------- #1
14209                {
14210                   get // -------------- start Get CarMfg
14211                   {
14212                      return CarMfg;
14213                   } // ----------------- END GET CarMfg
14214                   // ----------------- start Set CarMfg
14215                   set
14216                   {
14217                      if (value!= "")
14218                      CarMfg = value;
14219                   } // ----------------- End Set CarMfg
14220                } // --- End CarMfgproperty CarMfg --- #1
14221                //
14222
14223                private String myCarMod;
14224                //
14225                public String myCarModel
14226                {
14227                   get // -------------------- start Get
14228                   {
14229                      return myCarMod;
14230                   } // ---------------------- END GET
14231                   // start Set
14232                   set
14233                   {
14234                      if(value!= "") myCarMod=value;
14235                   } // --------------- End Set CarModel
14236                   //
14237                } // - End CarModel property CarModel #2
14238                //
14239                private String CarStyle;
14240                // Start CarStyle property CarStyle -- #3
14241                public String myCarStyle
14242                {
14243                   get // -------------------- start Get
14244                   {
14245                      return CarStyle;
14246                   } // ---------------------- END GET
14247                   // start Set
14248                   set
14249                   {
```

```
14250                    if (value!= "") CarStyle = value;
14251                } // --------------- End Set CarModel
14252                //
14253            } // - End CarStyle property CarStyle #3
14254            //
14255            //
14256            private String CarEng;
14257            // Start CarEng property CarEng------- #4
14258            public String myCarEng
14259            {
14260                get // -------------------- start Get
14261                {
14262                    return CarEng;
14263                } // ------------------------ END GET
14264                // start Set
14265                set
14266                {
14267                    if (value!= "") CarEng = value;
14268                } // --------------- End Set CarModel
14269                //
14270            } // - End CarStyle property CarStyle #4
14271            //
14272            private String CarColor = "";
14273            public String myCarColor
14274            // ------- start property CarColor --- #5
14275            {
14276                get // ------------ start Get CarColor
14277                {
14278                    return CarColor;
14279                } // --------------- END GET CarColor
14280                //
14281                set
14282                {
14283                    if (value!= "")
14284                    CarColor = value;
14285                } // --------------- End Set CarColor
14286            } // ------------- End CarColor ----- #5
14287            //
14288
14289            private String CarFinancer;
14290            public String myCarFinanceModel
14291            {
```

```
14292                    get // -------------------- start Get
14293                    {
14294                       return CarFinancer;
14295                    } // ----------------------- END GET
14296                    // start Set
14297                    set
14298                    {
14299                       if (value!= "") CarFinancer =
14300  value;
14301                    } // ------------ End Set CarFinancer
14302                    //
14303                } // End CarModel property CarFinancer #6
14304                //
14305                private String CarOwner;
14306                // -------- Start property CarOwner -- #7
14307                public String myCarOwner
14308                {
14309                    get // -------------------- start Get
14310                    {
14311                       return CarOwner;
14312                    } // ----------------------- END GET
14313                    // start Set
14314                    set
14315                    {
14316                       if (value!= "") CarOwner = value;
14317                    } // --------------- End Set CarOwner
14318                    //
14319                } // – End CarStyle property CarOwner #7
14320                //
14321                private String CarCost;
14322                // ---- Start CarEng property CarEng-- #8
14323          public String myCarCost
14324                {
14325                    get // -------------------- start Get
14326                    {
14327                       return CarCost;
14328                    } // ----------------------- END GET
14329                    // start Set
14330                    set
14331                    {
14332                       if (value!= "") CarCost = value;
14333                    } // ---------------- End Set CarCost
```

```
14334              //
14335          } // - End CarStyle property CarCost - #8
14336        }// End myClsAutoInfo
14337     } // End class AutomobileStructSpecs
14338 }// ---------------------------- End Namespace
14339
```

# 14340 **Appendix P**

```
14341
14342 //
14343 // ---------------- Beginning of libraries for
14344 this class and namespace ----------------
14345 using System;
14346 using System.Collections;
14347 using System.IO;
14348 using System.Collections.Generic;
14349 using System.ComponentModel;
14350 using System.Data;
14351 using System.Drawing;
14352 using System.Linq;
14353 using System.Text;
14354 using System.Windows;
14355 using System.Windows.Forms;
14356 // ----- Beginning of Namespace -----
14357 //
14358 namespace VS_CS_Struct_with_File_IO
14359 {// ----- Curly backets OK for this Method
14360     public partial class frmVSCSStructwithFileIO:
14361 Form // ----- Begin Partial -----
14362     {// --------- Curly backets OK for this Method
14363         // If declared before init is public/Global
14364 variable
14365         public int myObjIdx;
14366         public int intIdxSelected;
14367         public int intCountOfRecords;
14368         public int StartObject;
14369         public int intSelectedIdx=999; // For use in
14370 btnDelete_Click
14371         public int YY = 999;// For use in
14372 btnDelete_Click, passed to ReCreateFile(YY)
14373         public int XX = 999;// For use in
14374 btnDelete_Click, passed to ReCreateFile(XX)
```

```
14375          public int XYZEdit = 999;// For use in
14376 btnDelete_Click, passed to ReCreateFile(XX)
14377          public int intSelectedEditIdx;
14378          public ArrayList myArrylst = new
14379 ArrayList(40);
14380          //
14381          //Initialize the form
14382          //
14383          public frmVSCSStructwithFileIO() // -----
14384 Init the form -----
14385            {
14386                InitializeComponent();
14387            }
14388
14389          // Defining AutoStruct Structure
14390          public struct AutoStruct // Start Struct
14391 AutoStruct
14392            {
14393            // ##################################
14394            // declare the fields #1) CarMaker
14395            public string CarMfg;
14396            public string CarBuilder;
14397            // define a constructor
14398            public string CarMaker(string
14399 myCarBuilder)
14400              {
14401                CarBuilder = myCarBuilder;
14402                return CarBuilder;
14403              } // End #1) CarMaker
14404            // ##################################
14405
14406            public string CarMod; // Start #2)
14407 CarMod
14408            public string CarModel;
14409            // define a constructor
14410            public string CarMods(string CarsMod)
14411              {
14412                CarModel = CarsMod;
14413                return CarModel;
14414              } // // End #2) CarMod
14415            // ##################################
14416            // Start Style
```

```
14417              public string CarsStyle; // Start #3)
14418 CarStyle
14419              public string myCarStyle;
14420              // define a constructor
14421              public string CarStyles(string
14422 myCarStyleInPut)
14423                 {
14424                    myCarStyle = myCarStyleInPut;
14425                    return myCarStyle;
14426                 } // // End Style #3 CarStyle
14427              // ##################################
14428              public string CarsEngine; // Start #4)
14429 CarEngine
14430              public string myCarEng;
14431              // define a constructor
14432              public string myCarsEngine(string
14433 myCarHP)
14434                 {
14435                    myCarEng = myCarHP;
14436                    return myCarEng;
14437                 } // // End Engine #4 CarEngine
14438              // ##################################
14439              public string CarsColor; // Start #5)
14440 CarColor
14441              public string myCarsColor;
14442              // define a constructor
14443              //
14444              public string myCarsColors(string
14445 Paint)
14446                 {
14447                    myCarsColor = Paint;
14448                    return myCarsColor;
14449                 } // // End Engine #5) CarColor
14450              // ##################################
14451              public string CarsFinancer; // Start
14452 #6) CarFinancer
14453              public string myCarsBanker;
14454              public string CarsLien;
14455              // define a constructor
14456              public string myCarsFinancer(string
14457 Finance)
14458                 {
```

```
14459                    CarsLien = Finance;
14460                    CarsFinancer = Finance;
14461                    myCarsBanker = Finance;
14462                    return CarsLien;
14463                } // // End Financer #6) CarFinancer
14464                // ################################
14465                public string myCarOwner;
14466                public string CarOwner; // Start Owner
14467 #7) CarOwner
14468                public string myCarRealOwner;
14469                // define a constructor
14470                public string CarsRealOwner(string
14471 myCarOwner)
14472                {
14473                    myCarOwner = myCarOwner;
14474                    myCarRealOwner = myCarOwner;
14475                    return myCarRealOwner;
14476                } // // End Owner #7) CarOwner
14477                // ################################
14478                public string CarCost; // Start #8)
14479 CarsCost
14480                public string myCarPrice;
14481                // define a constructor
14482                public string CarsCost(string Cost)
14483                {
14484                    CarCost = Cost;
14485                    return myCarPrice;
14486                } // // End CarsCost #8) CarsCost
14487                // ################################
14488            }// End -------------------Struct
14489 AutoStruct
14490            // End Definition AutoStruct Structure
14491 Curly Brackets ---- OK to Here!!
14492            private void btnExit_Click(object sender,
14493 EventArgs e)
14494            {
14495                Application.Exit();
14496            } // -----Curly brackets ------ OK to
14497 Here!!
14498            // ################# Start Display
14499 records
```

```
14500            public void btnDisplay_Click(object
14501 sender, EventArgs e)
14502            {
14503                listBox1.Items.Clear();
14504                myArrylst.Clear();
14505                AutoStruct newStruct = new
14506 AutoStruct();
14507                StreamReader myRdr;
14508                myRdr = new StreamReader("C:\\App
14509 Target Files \\AutomobileStructSpecs.txt");
14510                //Define String variables and Read the
14511 file in and set the struct properties
14512                string myStrFromFileMaker = ". . ."; // #1
14513                string myStrFromFileMod = ". . .";// #2
14514                string myStrFromFileStyle = ". . .";// #3
14515                string myStrFromFileEng = ". . .";// #4
14516                string myStrFromFileColor = ". . .";// #5
14517                string myStrFromFileFinance =
14518 ". . .";// #6
14519                string myStrFromFileOwner = ". . .";// #7
14520                string myStrFromFileCost = ". . .";// #8
14521                //
14522                string myStrFromFile = ". . .";//
14523 String read in from file and count records read in.
14524                while (myStrFromFile!= null &&
14525 myStrFromFile!= null)// Start file reading
14526                {
14527                    /*
14528                    // Clearing strings because
14529 starting to read new record of 8 items
14530                    // -------------------------------
14531                    myStrFromFileMaker = ". . ."; // #1
14532                    myStrFromFileMod = ". . .";// #2
14533                    myStrFromFileStyle = ". . .";// #3
14534                    myStrFromFileEng = ". . .";// #4
14535                    myStrFromFileColor = ". . .";// #5
14536                    myStrFromFileFinance = ". . .";// #6
14537                    myStrFromFileOwner = ". . .";// #7
14538                    myStrFromFileCost = ". . .";// #8
14539                    */
14540                    //
```

```
14541                     intCountOfRecords = 0; // keep
14542 records read in.
14543                     //
14544                     // Read the first string of the
14545 first -or- next record from file "Every string" --
14546 -- read will
14547                     // be tested in case partial
14548 records are found Assign strings i.e.
14549 "myCarBuilder" etc to
14550                     // newStruct."CarMaker" property of
14551 struct I know the Manufacturer is first because
14552 that's
14553                     // the order in which we wrote info
14554 to the file. So, we read and assign each string to
14555 the correct
14556                     // Struct property
14557                     //
14558                     myStrFromFileMaker =
14559 myRdr.ReadLine();// #)1
14560                     //MessageBox.Show("#1-Line 160 Got
14561 1 Line Mfg " + myStrFromFileMaker,"btnDisplay_
14562 Click");
14563                     if (myStrFromFileMaker == "" ||
14564 myStrFromFileMaker==null)
14565                     {
14566                         intCountOfRecords =
14567 myArrylst.Count;
14568                         lblDisplayedRecords.Text = "";
14569                         lblDisplayedRecords.Text =
14570 "There are "+Convert.ToString(intCountOfRecords)+"
14571 records";
14572                         myRdr.Close();
14573                         myRdr.Dispose();
14574                         return;
14575                     }
14576                     if (myStrFromFileMaker!= null &&
14577 myStrFromFileMaker!= null)// #)1
14578                     {
14579
14580     newStruct.CarMaker(myStrFromFileMaker);
14581                     }
```

```
14582                    // If the first string is good,
14583  there are 7 more for this record
14584                    // unless it is a faulty partial
14585  record.
14586                    {
14587                    // -----------------------Start #2
14588                    myStrFromFileMod =
14589  myRdr.ReadLine();// #)2
14590                    if (myStrFromFileMod == "" ||
14591  myStrFromFileMod == null)
14592                        {
14593                            myRdr.Close();
14594                            myRdr.Dispose();
14595                            MessageBox.Show(" Line 185 . . .
14596  Partial record found in file, aborted display!",
14597  "Partial record found!");
14598                            return;
14599                        }
14600                    if (myStrFromFileMod!= null &&
14601  myStrFromFileMod!= "")
14602                        {
14603                            newStruct.CarMods
14604  (myStrFromFileMod);
14605                        }
14606                    // ---------------------- Start #3
14607                    myStrFromFileStyle =
14608  myRdr.ReadLine();// #)3
14609                    if (myStrFromFileStyle == "" ||
14610  myStrFromFileStyle == null)
14611                        {
14612                            myRdr.Close();
14613                            myRdr.Dispose();
14614                            MessageBox.Show("Line 185 . . .
14615  Partial record found in file, aborted display!",
14616  "Partial record found!");
14617                            return;
14618                        }
14619                    if (myStrFromFileStyle!= "" &&
14620  myStrFromFileStyle!= null)
14621                        {
14622                            newStruct.CarStyles
14623  (myStrFromFileStyle);
```

```
14624                         //MessageBox.Show("Line
14625 206 . . . Partial record found in file, aborted
14626 display!", "Partial record found!");
14627                     }
14628                     // ---------------------- Start#4
14629                     myStrFromFileEng =
14630 myRdr.ReadLine();// #)4
14631                     if (myStrFromFileEng == "" ||
14632 myStrFromFileEng == null)
14633                         {
14634                         myRdr.Close();
14635                         myRdr.Dispose();
14636                         MessageBox.Show("Line 214 . . .
14637 Partial record found in file, aborted display!",
14638 "Partial record found!");
14639                         return;
14640                         }
14641                     if (myStrFromFileEng!= "" &&
14642 myStrFromFileEng!= null)
14643                         {
14644                         newStruct.myCarsEngine
14645 (myStrFromFileEng);
14646                         }
14647                     //---------------------- Start #5
14648                     myStrFromFileColor =
14649 myRdr.ReadLine();// #)5
14650                     if (myStrFromFileColor == "" ||
14651 myStrFromFileColor==null)
14652                         {
14653                         myRdr.Close();
14654                         myRdr.Dispose();
14655                         MessageBox.Show("Line 228 . . .
14656 Partial record found in file, aborted display!",
14657 "Partial record found!");
14658                         return;
14659                         }
14660                     if (myStrFromFileColor!= "" &&
14661 myStrFromFileColor!= null)
14662                         {
14663                         newStruct.myCarsColors
14664 (myStrFromFileColor);
14665                         }
```

```
14666                    // #### // --- Start #6 // Reversed
14667 with Banker
14668                    myStrFromFileFinance =
14669 myRdr.ReadLine();// #)6
14670                    if (myStrFromFileFinance == "" ||
14671 myStrFromFileFinance == null)
14672                    {
14673                        myRdr.Close();
14674                        myRdr.Dispose();
14675                        MessageBox.Show("Line 242 . . .
14676 Partial record found in file, aborted display!",
14677 "Partial record found!");
14678                        return;
14679                    }
14680                    if (myStrFromFileFinance!= "" &&
14681 myStrFromFileFinance!= null)
14682                    {
14683                        newStruct.myCarsFinancer
14684 (myStrFromFileFinance);
14685                    }
14686                    // --------------------- Start #7
14687                    string myStrFromFileCarOwner =
14688 myRdr.ReadLine();// #)7
14689                    newStruct.CarsRealOwner
14690 (myStrFromFileCarOwner);
14691                    if (myStrFromFileCarOwner == "" ||
14692 myStrFromFileCarOwner == null)
14693                    {
14694                        myRdr.Close();
14695                        myRdr.Dispose();
14696                        MessageBox.Show("Line 257 . . .
14697 Partial record found in file, aborted display!",
14698 "Partial record found!");
14699                        return;
14700                    }
14701                    if (myStrFromFileCarOwner!= "" &&
14702 myStrFromFileCarOwner!= null)
14703                    {
14704                        newStruct.CarsRealOwner
14705 (myStrFromFileCarOwner);
14706                    }
```

```
14707                    myStrFromFileCost =
14708 myRdr.ReadLine();// #)8
14709                    if (myStrFromFileCost == "" ||
14710 myStrFromFileCost == null)
14711                    {
14712                        myRdr.Close();
14713                        myRdr.Dispose();
14714                        MessageBox.Show("Line 270 . . .
14715 Partial record found in file, aborted display!",
14716 "Partial record found!");
14717                        return;
14718                    }
14719                    if (myStrFromFileCost!= "" &&
14720 myStrFromFileCost!= null)
14721                    {
14722                        newStruct.CarsCost
14723 (myStrFromFileCost);
14724                        intCountOfRecords += 1;
14725                        lblDisplayedRecords.Text = "";
14726                        lblDisplayedRecords.Text =
14727 Convert.ToString(intCountOfRecords);
14728                    }
14729                    // --- 8 lines --- 1 Record Read in
14730 complete
14731                    // --- Create Listing to Add to
14732 listBox1 ---
14733                    string myListing = "";
14734                    myListing = myStrFromFileMaker + "
14735 " + myStrFromFileMod + " " + myStrFromFileStyle +
14736 " " + myStrFromFileOwner;
14737                        listBox1.Items.Add(myListing);
14738                        /* ----- Add to myArrylst ----- */
14739                        intSelectedIdx =
14740 listBox1.SelectedIndex;
14741                        myArrylst.Add(newStruct);
14742                        /*-- Item added to listBox and
14743 Array-- */
14744                } // . . .Matching up with "if!= "",!=
14745 null"
14746            } // . . .—Ends While Loop - Starts Loop
14747 again-
14748        } // . . . End of btnDisplay_ Click ----- //
```

```
14749      //
14750      private void btnDelete_Click(object sender,
14751 EventArgs e)
14752      {
14753      // Get the properties we need to identify
14754 the correct Lines to delete from File
14755      // Advise user if no item selected
14756      intSelectedIdx = listBox1.SelectedIndex;
14757      YY = intSelectedIdx; // ----- "Passed" as an
14758 integer to ReCreateFile
14759      if (intSelectedIdx == -1)
14760      {
14761          MessageBox.Show("No item selected to
14762 delete, Select an item the click delete . . .","No
14763 item selected advisor");
14764      }
14765      //
14766      // ----- Now know "which item" was
14767 selected from the listBox1 ---- to be deleted
14768      // If item selected, proceed to get the
14769 properties needed
14770      Object myObj;
14771      myObj = new Object();
14772      AutoStruct newStruct = new AutoStruct();
14773      myObj = myArrylst[intSelectedIdx];
14774      // ----- Now know "which item"
14775 "Struct/Object" ----- converted into "newStruct"
14776      newStruct =
14777 (AutoStruct)Convert.ChangeType (myObj,
14778 typeof(AutoStruct));
14779      // ----- Confirm decision before deleting
14780 ***
14781      string strMyStrMfg =
14782 listBox1.SelectedItem.ToString();
14783      if (MessageBox.Show(strMyStrMfg + " is
14784 located at index " + Convert.ToString
14785 (intSelectedIdx) + "." + " Click OK to remove this
14786 item. Click Cancel to keep this item ", " 'DELETE'
14787 verification ", MessageBoxButtons.OKCancel,
14788 MessageBoxIcon.Information,
14789 MessageBoxDefaultButton.Button1) ==
14790 DialogResult.OK);
```

```
14791              {
14792                  // IF . . . user clicked "OK" delete
14793  record.
14794                  // Clear txtBoxes Remove item
14795  ArrayList
14796                  // --- Use "textBox.text" properties!!!!!
14797                  //
14798                  string txtBoxMfgInfo=txtBoxMfg.Text; // #1
14799                  string txtBoxModelInfo =
14800  txtBoxModel.Text; // #2
14801                  string txtBoxStyleInfo =
14802  txtBoxModel.Text; // #3
14803                  string txtBoxEngineInfo =
14804  txtBoxEngine.Text; // #4
14805                  string txtBoxColorInfo =
14806  txtBoxColor.Text; // #5
14807                  string txtBoxFinancerInfo =
14808  txtBoxFinancer.Text; // #6
14809                  string txtBoxOwnerInfo =
14810  txtBoxOwner.Text; // #7
14811                  string txtBoxCostInfo =
14812  txtBoxCost.Text; // #8
14813                  // Blank the textBoxes --- Blank the
14814  textBoxes --- Blank the textBoxes --- Blank the
14815  textBoxes
14816                  txtBoxMfg.Text = "";// #1---
14817  Blank the textBoxe
14818                  txtBoxModel.Text = "";// #2---
14819  Blank the textBoxe
14820                  txtBoxStyle.Text = ""; // #3---
14821  Blank the textBoxe
14822                  txtBoxEngine.Text = ""; // #4---
14823  Blank the textBoxe
14824                  txtBoxColor.Text = ""; // #5---
14825  Blank the textBoxe
14826                  txtBoxFinancer.Text = "";// #6---
14827  Blank the textBoxe
14828                  txtBoxOwner.Text = ""; // #7---
14829  Blank the textBoxe
14830                  txtBoxCost.Text = ""; // #8---
14831  Blank the textBoxe
14832                  //
```

```
14833                  // --- Pass to ReCreateFile(with
14834 strings)
14835                  //
14836                  // ----- textBoxes blanked but -----
14837 Object NOT Removed from myArraylst or listBox1
14838 YET!!
14839                  //
14840                  // ---- Strings go to ReCreate file
14841 function
14842                  // ---- | #1 | #2 | #3 |#4 | #5 | #6 | #7 |#8
14843                  // strings go here-v v v v v v v
14844                  // Integer here |
14845                  // v
14846                  listBox1.Items.RemoveAt
14847 (intSelectedIdx);
14848                  myArrylst.RemoveAt(intSelectedIdx);
14849                  ReCreateFile();
14850                  listBox1.SelectedIndex = 0;
14851             } // --- End if clicked OK Delete
14852 messageBox button
14853         } // ---- End btnDeleteSelectedRecord Click
14854         //
14855         // Works with btnDelete file to remove a
14856 record from file
14857         //
14858         public void ReCreateFile()
14859         {// ------ OK
14860         //
14861             int intmySelectedIdx = 0;
14862             //
14863             // The myArrylst has only the record
14864 objects we want to keep listed. "BUT" this did "NOT"
14865             // actually "DELETE" those properties of
14866 the deleted "Object" saved in the permanent hard
14867 drive file.
14868             // We do that by getting rid of the old
14869 file and creating a "NEW" file "without" the
14870 listing and Object
14871             // that was part of listBox1 and
14872 myArrylst!!!!!!!!!!!!
14873             //
14874             int intArrayCount = myArrylst.Count-1;
```

```
14875              //
14876              // DELETE the OLD
14877 AutomobileStructSpecs.txt file "IF" it "EXISTS"
14878              //
14879              Boolean myTest1 = File.Exists("C:\\App
14880 Target Files\\AutomobileStructSpecs.txt");
14881              if(myTest1==true)
14882              {
14883                  File.Delete("C:\\App Target
14884 Files\\AutomobileStructSpecs.txt");
14885                  MessageBox.Show(" The old file was
14886 deleted ");
14887              }
14888              //
14889              int StartObj = 0; // Begin with object
14890 indexed as "0" and
14891              // ----- continue to the (myArrylst count
14892 -1), remember . . .
14893              // ----- the "Count" is an actual number
14894 of the objects,
14895              // ----- "BUT" numbering starts with zero
14896              //
14897              // ###!!!! Double Check the File NAME
14898 ###!!!!
14899              StreamWriter myWrt = new
14900 StreamWriter("C:\\App Target
14901 Files\\AutomobileStructSpecs.txt",true);
14902              // REMEMBER "true" means "Append" it if
14903 it exists, create it if it does "NOT" exist!!!
14904              //
14905              // Start writing to new or appended file
14906 beginning with Object zero in the myArrylst
14907              // "End" at the object count minus "-1"
14908 one, because of zero based counting.
14909              int ObjectSavedCount = 0;
14910              MessageBox.Show("I am now ready to Begin
14911 saving . . . " +
14912 Convert.ToString(intArrayCount),"Array count to
14913 save");
14914              // Used as starting point in "While"
14915 below
14916              int intXYZ =0;
```

```
14917              // While Loop does the actual writing to
14918  file
14919              while(intXYZ <= intArrayCount-1)
14920              {
14921                  // Test for exceeding the limit of
14922  (intArrayCount-1)
14923                  if (intXYZ >= intArrayCount)
14924  {myWrt.Close(); myWrt.Dispose(); return;}
14925                  // Ceate an instance of the object in
14926  myarrylst, then convertinto a "Struct"
14927                  Object myObj;
14928                  myObj = new Object();
14929                  myObj = myArrylst[intXYZ];
14930                  AutoStruct newStruct = new
14931  AutoStruct();
14932                  newStruct = (AutoStruct)Convert.ChangeType
14933  (myObj, typeof(AutoStruct));
14934                  newStruct = (AutoStruct)Convert.ChangeType
14935  (myObj, typeof(AutoStruct));
14936                  //
14937                  // Retrieve a set of record properties
14938  from "EACH OBJECT in myArrylst
14939                  //
14940                  string myNewStrCarMaker =
14941  newStruct.CarBuilder; // #1)
14942                  string myNewStrCarMod =
14943  newStruct.CarModel; // #2)
14944                  string myNewStrCarStyle =
14945  newStruct.myCarStyle; // #3)
14946                  string myNewStrCarEng =
14947  newStruct.myCarEng;// #4)
14948                  string myNewStrCarColor =
14949  newStruct.myCarsColor;// #5)
14950                  string myNewStrCarFinancer =
14951  newStruct.myCarsBanker;// #6)
14952                  string myNewStrCarOwner =
14953  newStruct.myCarRealOwner; //#7)
14954                  string myNewStrCarCost =
14955  newStruct.CarCost;// #8)
14956                  //
14957                  // ------ write to a new file. -------
```

```
14958                    myWrt.WriteLine(myNewStrCarMaker); //
14959 #1) If you don't number it's easy to leave one off
14960                    myWrt.WriteLine(myNewStrCarMod); //---
14961 #2)
14962                    myWrt.WriteLine(myNewStrCarStyle); //-
14963 #3)
14964                    myWrt.WriteLine(myNewStrCarEng); //---
14965 #4)
14966                    myWrt.WriteLine(myNewStrCarColor); //-
14967 #5)
14968                    myWrt.WriteLine(myNewStrCarFinancer);//-
14969 #6)
14970                    myWrt.WriteLine(myNewStrCarOwner);//--
14971 #7)
14972                    myWrt.WriteLine(myNewStrCarCost);//---
14973 #8)
14974                    // One record written to file.
14975                    //
14976                    intSelectedIdx += 1; // Increment
14977 counter for the next Object/Record
14978                    intXYZ = intXYZ + 1; // Yeah, I could
14979 have typed "intXYZ += 1;". same thing.
14980                    ObjectSavedCount += 1; /// Count the
14981 good records/Objects saved to file
14982               } // -----End For While ----- OK!!!!
14983          // This is here because the is a learning
14984 exercise . . . seeing is believing
14985               //
14986          // After the for Loop ends all desirable
14987 records "Object" properties have been
14988          // written to temporary file so, as a
14989 learner, tell yourself when the job is done!!!
14990               //
14991          MessageBox.Show("I have saved . . . " +
14992 Convert.ToString(ObjectSavedCount)+" Objects to
14993 file ", "Array count to save");
14994          // Now you saw the results of your work.
14995          // By the way, this is an excellent aid
14996 to trouble shooting code.          '
14997          lblDisplayedRecords.Text = "";
14998          lblDisplayedRecords.Text = "There are " +
14999 Convert.ToString(intCountOfRecords) + " records.";
```

```
15000          //
15001          myWrt.Close();
15002          myWrt.Dispose();
15003          //
15004      }// ----- End ReCreateFile ---- Works with
15005 btnDelete_click event ---- OK!!!
15006      //
15007      public void listBox1_SelectedIndexChanged
15008 (object sender, EventArgs e)
15009      {// OK!!!!
15010          XX = listBox1.SelectedIndex;
15011          // MessageBox.Show(myStrSender);
15012          // To populate the textBoxes e need a
15013 Struct instantiate the has the properties
15014          // we want to display for the particular
15015 item chosen by the user.
15016          intSelectedIdx = listBox1.SelectedIndex;
15017          if (intSelectedIdx == -1) {intSelectedIdx
15018 = 0;}
15019          int intArrayCount = 0;
15020          intArrayCount = myArrylst.Count; //
15021 ###!!! Coming up Zero
15022          /*---------------------------------------*/
15023          Object myObj; // cannnot create a struct
15024 directly from the ArrayList.
15025          // ----- This is the first Struct in this
15026 event handler block.
15027          // It does not know what has been created
15028 or used before so we nedd to define it.
15029          //
15030          myObj = new Object();
15031          //
15032          // The 2nd step
15033          // "Object is the base calss" . . .
15034 cannot go directly from Object to Struct
15035          // must take an itmediate step.
15036          AutoStruct newStruct = new AutoStruct();
15037          myObj = myArrylst[intSelectedIdx];
15038          newStruct = (AutoStruct)Convert.ChangeType
15039 (myObj, typeof(AutoStruct));
15040          //
```

```
15041            // Take the properties from the Struct we
15042 created
15043            string myNewStrCarMaker =
15044 newStruct.CarBuilder; // #1)
15045            string myNewStrCarMod =
15046 newStruct.CarModel; // #2)
15047            string myNewStrCarStyle =
15048 newStruct.myCarStyle; // #3)
15049            string myNewStrCarEng =
15050 newStruct.myCarEng;// #4)
15051            string myNewStrCarColor =
15052 newStruct.myCarsColor;// #5)
15053            string myNewStrCarFinancer =
15054 newStruct.CarsLien;// #6)
15055            string myNewStrCarOwner =
15056 newStruct.myCarRealOwner;// #7)
15057            string myNewStrCarCost =
15058 newStruct.CarCost;// #8)
15059            // Put the strings of properties in the
15060 textBoxes
15061            txtBoxMfg.Text = myNewStrCarMaker; ////
15062 ItWorks!!!!-------------------------------- #1)
15063            txtBoxModel.Text = myNewStrCarMod;// --
15064 #2)
15065            txtBoxStyle.Text = myNewStrCarStyle;// --
15066 #3)
15067            txtBoxEngine.Text = myNewStrCarEng;// ---
15068 #4)
15069            txtBoxColor.Text = myNewStrCarColor;// --
15070 #5)
15071            txtBoxFinancer.Text = myNewStrCarFinancer;//
15072 #6)
15073            txtBoxOwner.Text = myNewStrCarOwner;// --
15074 #7)
15075            txtBoxCost.Text = myNewStrCarCost;// ----
15076 #8)
15077            //
15078        } // End SectedIndexChanged OK!!!!
15079        //
15080        private void btnEdit_Click(object sender,
15081 EventArgs e)
15082        {// ------------------------------ OK!!!!
```

```
15083              intSelectedEditIdx =
15084 listBox1.SelectedIndex;
15085              if (intSelectedEditIdx == -1)
15086              {MessageBox.Show("You must first select a
15087 listing to EDIT", "NO ITEM SELECTED!! ");}
15088              // Re-set backcolors of controls
15089              lblMfg.BackColor = Color.Cyan;
15090              txtBoxMfg.BackColor = Color.Cyan; //    #1
15091              lblModel.BackColor = Color.Cyan;
15092              txtBoxModel.BackColor = Color.Cyan; // #2
15093              lblStyle.BackColor = Color.Cyan;
15094              txtBoxStyle.BackColor = Color.Cyan; // #3
15095              lblEngine.BackColor = Color.Cyan;
15096              txtBoxEngine.BackColor = Color.Cyan; // #4
15097              lblEngine.BackColor = Color.Cyan;
15098              txtBoxColor.BackColor = Color.Cyan; // #5
15099              lblColor.BackColor = Color.Cyan;
15100              txtBoxFinancer.BackColor = Color.Cyan; // #6
15101              lblFinancer.BackColor = Color.Cyan;
15102              txtBoxOwner.BackColor = Color.Cyan; // #7
15103              lblFinancer.BackColor = Color.Cyan;
15104              txtBoxCost.BackColor = Color.Cyan; //    #8
15105              lblCost.BackColor = Color.Cyan;
15106              //
15107              listBox1.BackColor = Color.Cyan;
15108              btnSaveMyEdits.Visible = true;
15109              MessageBox.Show("To makes CHANGES—RE-TYPE
15110 the information in the desired TEXTBOX(s) then
15111 CLICK—SAVE EDITS ", "Edit Instruction");
15112              //
15113              Object myObj = new Object();
15114              AutoStruct newStruct = new AutoStruct();
15115              myObj=myArrylst[intSelectedEditIdx];
15116              newStruct = (AutoStruct)Convert.ChangeType
15117 (myObj, typeof(AutoStruct));
15118              myObj = myArrylst[intSelectedEditIdx];
15119              //
15120              string strEditMfg = newStruct.CarBuilder;
15121 // ---------- #1)
15122              txtBoxMfg.Text = strEditMfg;
15123              txtBoxMfg.ForeColor = Color.Red;
```

```
15124          string strEditMod = newStruct.CarModel;
15125  // -----------#2)
15126          txtBoxModel.Text = strEditMod;
15127          txtBoxModel.ForeColor = Color.Red;
15128          string strEditStyle =
15129  newStruct.myCarStyle; // ------------ #3)
15130          txtBoxStyle.Text = strEditStyle;
15131          txtBoxStyle.ForeColor = Color.Red;
15132          string strEditEng = newStruct.myCarEng;//
15133  ------------- #4)
15134          txtBoxEngine.Text = strEditEng;
15135          txtBoxEngine.ForeColor = Color.Red;
15136          string strEditColor =
15137  newStruct.myCarsColor;// --------- #5)
15138          txtBoxColor.Text = strEditColor;
15139          txtBoxColor.ForeColor = Color.Red;
15140          string strEditBanker =
15141  newStruct.CarsLien;//------------- #6)
15142          txtBoxFinancer.Text = strEditBanker;
15143          txtBoxFinancer.ForeColor = Color.Red;
15144          string strEditOwner =
15145  newStruct.myCarRealOwner; // ----- #7)
15146          txtBoxOwner.Text = strEditOwner;
15147          txtBoxOwner.ForeColor = Color.Red;
15148          string strEditCost =
15149  newStruct.CarCost;// ------------- #8)
15150          txtBoxCost.Text = strEditCost;
15151          txtBoxCost.ForeColor = Color.Red;
15152          //
15153      } // End btnEdit_Click OK!!!
15154      //
15155      private void btnClear_Click(object sender,
15156  EventArgs e)// Line 699
15157      {
15158          txtBoxMfg.Text = "";
15159          txtBoxModel.Text = "";
15160          txtBoxStyle.Text = "";
15161          txtBoxEngine.Text = "";
15162          txtBoxColor.Text = "";
15163          txtBoxCost.Text = "";
15164          txtBoxFinancer.Text = "";
15165          txtBoxOwner.Text = "";
```

```
15166              listBox1.Items.Clear();
15167          }
15168          //
15169          private void btnSaveRecord_Click(object
15170 sender, EventArgs e)
15171          {
15172              AutoStruct newStruct = new AutoStruct();
15173              //
15174              string myMfg = "";// #1 Mfg
15175              myMfg = txtBoxMfg.Text;
15176              newStruct.CarBuilder = myMfg;
15177              //
15178              string myAutoModel = "";// #2 Model
15179              myAutoModel = txtBoxModel.Text;
15180              newStruct.CarModel = myAutoModel;
15181              //
15182              string myAutoStyle = "";// #3 Style
15183              myAutoStyle = txtBoxStyle.Text;
15184              newStruct.myCarStyle = myAutoStyle;
15185              //
15186              string myAutoEngine = ""; // #4 Engine
15187              myAutoEngine = txtBoxEngine.Text;
15188              newStruct.myCarEng = myAutoEngine;
15189              //
15190              string myAutoColor = ""; // #5 Color
15191              myAutoColor = txtBoxColor.Text;
15192              newStruct.myCarsColor = myAutoColor;
15193              //
15194              string myAutoOwner = "";// #6 Owner
15195              myAutoOwner = txtBoxOwner.Text;
15196              newStruct.myCarRealOwner = txtBoxOwner.Text;
15197              //
15198              string myAutoFinancer = ""; //#7 Financer
15199              myAutoFinancer = txtBoxFinancer.Text;
15200              newStruct.myCarsBanker = myAutoFinancer;
15201              //
15202              string myAutoCost = "";
15203              myAutoCost = txtBoxCost.Text; // #8 Cost
15204              newStruct.myCarPrice = myAutoCost;
15205              //
15206              // Calls WriteToFile to do the actual
15207 save to file function
```

```
15208              //
15209              myWriteToFile(myMfg, myAutoModel,
15210 myAutoStyle, myAutoEngine, myAutoColor,
15211 myAutoOwner, myAutoFinancer, myAutoCost);
15212              //
15213              // Add listing to listBox1 and myArrylst
15214              //
15215              string myListing = "";
15216              myListing = myMfg + " " + myAutoModel + "
15217 " + myAutoStyle;
15218              listBox1.Items.Add(myListing);
15219              myArrylst.Add(newStruct);
15220              //
15221              intCountOfRecords = myArrylst.Count;
15222              lblDisplayedRecords.Text = "There are "+
15223 Convert.ToString(intCountOfRecords)+" records";
15224          } /// End Save record --------------- Works
15225 with btnSave_click calls WriteToFile OK!!!
15226          //
15227          //WriteToFile works with btnSave_Click Event
15228          //
15229          void myWriteToFile(string myMfgIn, string
15230 myAutoModIn, string myAutoStyleIn, string
15231 myAutoEngineIn, string myAutoColorIn, string
15232 myAutoOwnerIn, string myAutoFinancerIn, string
15233 myAutoCostIn)
15234          {// -------------------------- OK . . .!!!
15235              StreamWriter myWrt = new StreamWriter
15236 ("C:\\App Target Files\\AutomobileStructSpecs.txt",
15237 true); //
15238              //
15239              // Write info to file for new record
15240              //
15241              string myMfg = myMfgIn;
15242              myWrt.WriteLine(myMfg);// #1 mfg
15243              //
15244              string myAutoModel = myAutoModIn;
15245              myWrt.WriteLine(myAutoModel);// #2 model
15246
15247              string myAutoStyle = myAutoStyleIn;
15248              myWrt.WriteLine(myAutoStyle);// #3 Style
15249              //
```

```
15250              string myAutoEngine = myAutoEngineIn;
15251              myWrt.WriteLine(myAutoEngine);// #4 Engine
15252              //
15253              string myAutoColor = myAutoColorIn; // #5
15254 Color
15255              myWrt.WriteLine(myAutoColor);
15256              //
15257              string myAutoOwner = myAutoOwnerIn;
15258              myWrt.WriteLine(myAutoOwner);// #6 Owner
15259              //
15260              string myAutoFinancer = myAutoFinancerIn;
15261 // #7 Financer
15262              myWrt.WriteLine(myAutoFinancer);
15263              //
15264              string myAutoCost = myAutoCostIn;// #8
15265 Cost
15266              myWrt.WriteLine(myAutoCost);
15267              //
15268              // ALL 8 Itetms for new record written to
15269 file
15270              // ----------- Release resources and file
15271          myWrt.Close();
15272          myWrt.Dispose();
15273      } // End WriteToFile WORKS WTH btnSave_Click
15274 Event . . . . OK!!!
15275      //
15276      //
15277      //
15278      private void btnClearForNew_Click(object
15279 sender, EventArgs e)
15280      {
15281          txtBoxMfg.Text = "";
15282          txtBoxModel.Text = "";
15283          txtBoxStyle.Text = "";
15284          txtBoxEngine.Text = "";
15285          txtBoxColor.Text = "";
15286          txtBoxFinancer.Text = "";
15287          txtBoxOwner.Text = "";
15288          txtBoxCost.Text = "";
15289      }
15290      public void btnSaveMyEdits_Click(object
15291 sender, EventArgs e)
```

```
15292            {
15293                // -- "Define" the selected item index --
15294                //
15295                intSelectedIdx = listBox1.SelectedIndex;
15296                // Set variable to SelectedIdx "Easier to
15297 type"
15298                XYZEdit = intSelectedIdx;
15299                // Create an instance of an Object
15300                Object myObj;
15301                myObj = new Object();
15302                // Convert Object myObj into an instance
15303 of the AutoStruct Struct
15304                AutoStruct newStruct = new AutoStruct();
15305                myObj = myArrylst[XYZEdit];// Get an
15306 AutoStruct object from the myArrylst
15307                newStruct =
15308 (AutoStruct)Convert.ChangeType(myObj,
15309 typeof(AutoStruct));
15310                //
15311                // -----Now we know "which item"
15312 "Struct/Object" ----- converted into "newStruct"
15313                // ----- Start "setting the properties"
15314 of that "Object" to the Edited values
15315                string myMfg = "";// #1 Mfg
15316                myMfg = txtBoxMfg.Text;
15317                newStruct.CarMaker(myMfg);
15318                //newStruct.myCarMfg = myMfg;
15319                //
15320                string myAutoModel = "";// #2 Model
15321                myAutoModel = txtBoxModel.Text;
15322                newStruct.CarMods(myAutoModel);
15323                //newStruct.myCarModel = myAutoModel;
15324                //
15325                string myAutoStyle = "";// #3 Style
15326                myAutoStyle = txtBoxStyle.Text;
15327                newStruct.CarStyles(myAutoStyle);
15328                //newStruct.myCarStyle = myAutoStyle;
15329                //
15330                string myAutoEngine = ""; // #4 Engine
15331                myAutoEngine = txtBoxEngine.Text;
15332                newStruct.myCarsEngine(myAutoEngine);
15333                //newStruct.myCarEng = myAutoEngine;
```

```
15334            //
15335            string myAutoColor = ""; // #5 Color
15336            myAutoColor = txtBoxColor.Text;
15337            newStruct.myCarsColors(myAutoColor);
15338            //newStruct.myCarColor = myAutoColor;
15339            //
15340            string myAutoFinancer = ""; //#6 Financer
15341            myAutoFinancer = txtBoxFinancer.Text;
15342            newStruct.myCarsFinancer(myAutoFinancer);
15343            //newStruct.myCarFinanceModel = myAutoFinancer;
15344            //
15345            string myAutoOwner = "";// #7 Owner
15346            myAutoOwner = txtBoxOwner.Text;
15347            newStruct.CarsRealOwner(myAutoOwner);
15348            //newStruct.myCarOwner = txtBoxOwner.Text;
15349            //
15350            string myAutoCost = "";
15351            myAutoCost = txtBoxCost.Text; // #8 Cost
15352            newStruct.CarsCost(myAutoCost);
15353            //
15354            // ----- Ended setting the properties of
15355 that Object to the Edited values
15356            //
15357            // The file still has to be updated . . .
15358 that's next DELETE "Old" file
15359            // Delete the
15360 OldAutomobileStructSpecs.txt file "IF" it exists
15361            //Boolean myTest1;
15362            //myTest1 = File.Exists("C:\\App Target
15363 Files\\AutomobileStructSpecs.txt");
15364            //if (myTest1 == true) {File.Delete
15365 ("C:\\App Target Files\\AutomobileStructSpecs.txt");}
15366            // Deleted the old file if it existed
15367            //Delete the Old "AutoTemp.txt
15368 file" . . . "IF" it exists
15369            //Boolean myTest2;
15370            //myTest2 = File.Exists("C:\\App Target
15371 Files\\AutoTemp.txt");
15372            //if (myTest2 == true) {File.Delete
15373 ("C:\\App Target Files\\AutoTemp.txt");}
15374            //Deleted the Old "AutoTemp.txt
15375 file" . . . "IF" it existed
```

```
15376          //
15377          // Write Edited "info" from Objects
15378 properties to file
15379          // for Edited record to file by calling
15380 SEPERATE METHOD
15381          //
15382          int intmyArryCount = myArrylst.Count -1;
15383          // Use XYZ as a counter to write to file
15384 "Object properties"
15385          //XYZEdit = 0;
15386          // --------- Iterate myArrylist Objects,
15387 get properties and call WriteEdits() ----------
15388          // while (XYZEdit <= intmyArryCount-1)
15389          // {
15390          // if (XYZEdit >= intmyArryCount)
15391          // {
15392          // break;
15393          //}
15394          // Re-Define Sruct Objects on each pass
15395 through while Loop
15396          //Object myObj2 = new Object();
15397          // Convert Object myObj into an instance
15398 of the AutoStruct Struct
15399          //AutoStruct newStruct2 = new
15400 AutoStruct();
15401          //myObj2 = myArrylst[XYZEdit];// Get an
15402 AutoStruct object from the myArrylst
15403          //newStruct2 =
15404 (AutoStruct)Convert.ChangeType(myObj2,
15405 typeof(AutoStruct));
15406          //XYZEdit += 1;
15407          // //StreamWriter myWrt = new
15408 StreamWriter("C:\\App Target
15409 Files\\AutomobileStructSpecs.txt", true);
15410          ///*** newStruct =
15411 (AutoStruct)Convert.ChangeType
15412          // --------- Call method to write to file
15413          // --------- Repeat until all Object
15414 properties are written to file
15415          // --------- Release resources and file
15416          /* */
```

```
15417            //newStruct = (AutoStruct)Convert.ChangeType
15418 (myObj, typeof(AutoStruct));
15419          //
15420          /* */
15421          WriteEdits(myMfg, myAutoModel, myAutoStyle,
15422 myAutoEngine, myAutoColor, myAutoFinancer,
15423 myAutoOwner, myAutoCost);
15424
15425          MessageBox.Show("Edits were written to
15426 file", "btnSaveEdits Saved");
15427          myArrylst.RemoveAt(XYZEdit);
15428          listBox1.Items.RemoveAt(XYZEdit);
15429        }// --- End btnSaveMyEdits_Click --- Curly
15430 backets OK for this Method
15431          //
15432          /* ----------- WriteEdits method -------- */
15433        public void WriteEdits(string myMfgIn,string
15434 myAutoModelIn,string myAutoStyleIn,string
15435 myAutoEngineIn,string myAutoColorIn,string
15436 myAutoFinancerIn,string myAutoOwnerIn,string
15437 myAutoCostsIn)
15438      {
15439          StreamWriter myWrt = new StreamWriter
15440 ("C:\\App Target Files\\AutomobileStructSpecs.txt",
15441 true);
15442          //
15443          //XYZEdit = XYZIn;
15444          //
15445          string myMfg = myMfgIn;
15446          string myAutoModel = myAutoModelIn;
15447          string myAutoStyle = myAutoStyleIn;
15448          string myAutoEngine = myAutoEngineIn;
15449          string myAutoColor = myAutoColorIn;
15450          string myAutoFinancer = myAutoFinancerIn;
15451          string myAutoOwner = myAutoOwnerIn;
15452          string myAutoCosts = myAutoCostsIn;
15453          // Start writing lines for 1 record to file
15454          myWrt.WriteLine(myMfg);// #1 mfg
15455          myWrt.WriteLine(myAutoModel);// #2 model
15456          myWrt.WriteLine(myAutoStyle);// #3 Style
15457          myWrt.WriteLine(myAutoEngine);// #4
15458 Engine
```

```
15459                 myWrt.WriteLine(myAutoColor);// #5 Color
15460                 myWrt.WriteLine(myAutoFinancer);// #6
15461 Financer
15462                 myWrt.WriteLine(myAutoOwner);// #7 Owner
15463                 myWrt.WriteLine(myAutoCosts);// #8 Cost
15464                 // --------- End writing lines for 1
15465 record to file
15466                 //
15467                 // ----------- Release resources and file
15468                 myWrt.Close();
15469                 myWrt.Dispose();
15470             }
15471
15472         private void txtBoxModel_TextChanged(object
15473 sender, EventArgs e)
15474             {
15475
15476             }
15477
15478         private void lblModel_Click(object sender,
15479 EventArgs e)
15480             {
15481
15482             }
15483
15484         private void lblStyle_Click(object sender,
15485 EventArgs e)
15486             {
15487
15488             }
15489
15490         private void lblEngine_Click(object sender,
15491 EventArgs e)
15492             {
15493
15494             }
15495
15496         private void lblColor_Click(object sender,
15497 EventArgs e)
15498             {
15499
15500             }
```

```
15501
15502        private void lblFinancer_Click(object
15503 sender, EventArgs e)
15504        {
15505
15506        }
15507
15508        private void lblOwner_Click(object sender,
15509 EventArgs e)
15510        {
15511
15512        }
15513
15514        private void lblCost_Click(object sender,
15515 EventArgs e)
15516        {
15517
15518        }
15519
15520        private void txtBoxMfg_TextChanged(object
15521 sender, EventArgs e)
15522        {
15523
15524        }
15525
15526        private void lblMfg_Click(object sender,
15527 EventArgs e)
15528        {
15529
15530        }
15531
15532        private void txtBoxStyle_TextChanged(object
15533 sender, EventArgs e)
15534        {
15535
15536        }
15537
15538        private void txtBoxEngine_TextChanged(object
15539 sender, EventArgs e)
15540        {
15541
15542        }
```

```
15543
15544        private void txtBoxColor_TextChanged(object
15545 sender, EventArgs e)
15546        {
15547
15548        }
15549
15550        private void
15551 txtBoxFinancer_TextChanged(object sender,
15552 EventArgs e)
15553        {
15554
15555        }
15556
15557        private void txtBoxOwner_TextChanged(object
15558 sender, EventArgs e)
15559        {
15560
15561        }
15562
15563        private void txtBoxCost_TextChanged(object
15564 sender, EventArgs e)
15565        {
15566
15567        } // End writing one record to
15568 file . .   . . .. End WriteEdits
15569     } // --- End of Partial // --- Curly backets OK
15570 for this Method
15571 }// #### ------- Curly brackets for this set OK!!!
15572
```

15573 # Appendix Q MessageBox Results . . .
15574 # Confirm Delete

```
15575
15576 string myStrCoName = "";
15577     myStrCoName = txtBoxCompanyName.Text;
15578     string myStrCoID = "";
15579     myStrCoID =
15580 txtBoxCustomerID.Text;//Convert.ToString(dataGridV
15581 iew1[1, myRowIdx].Value);
```

```
15582      DialogResult result =
15583  MessageBox.Show(myStrCoName +" . . . " + myStrCoID
15584  + " Delete this record?", "Delete confirmation",
15585      MessageBoxButtons.OKCancel);
15586      switch (result)
15587      {
15588         case DialogResult.OK:
15589         {
15590            this.Text = "[OK]";
15591            break;
15592         }
15593         case DialogResult.Cancel:
15594         {
15595            this.Text = "[Cancel]";
15596            return;
15597         }
15598      }
```